365 DAYS OF PIKES PEAK The Journey

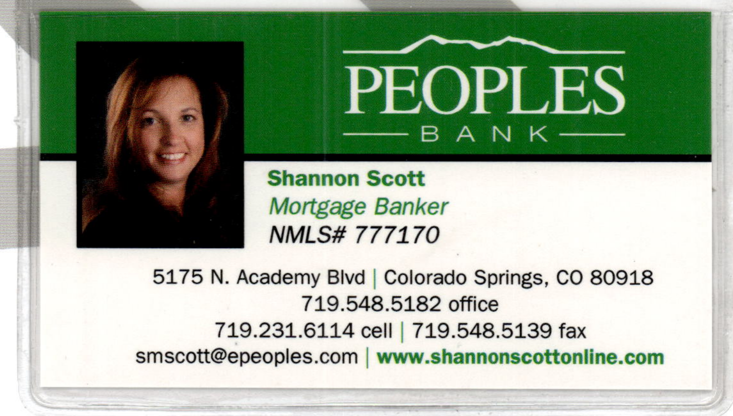

First Edition

Softcover First Edition

Copyright Page

The Pikes Peak Guy
P.O. Box 7070
Woodland Park, CO 80863
www.MyPeak365.com

Images available as gallery Prints. Please contact the author for details

ISBN 10: 0-9849655-4-8

ISBN 13: 978-0-9849655-4-0

Library of Congress Control Number 2012930363

Edited by Andrea Furniss

Published by The Pikes Peak Guy Press
Woodland Park, Colorado

Designed in the USA

Printed and Bound in China through
Bolton Associates, Inc. San Rafeal, CA USA

365 DAYS OF PIKES PEAK *The Journey*

Photography by

THE PIKES PEAK *Guy*

PIKES PEAK GUY PRESS
WOODLAND PARK, COLORADO

Introduction

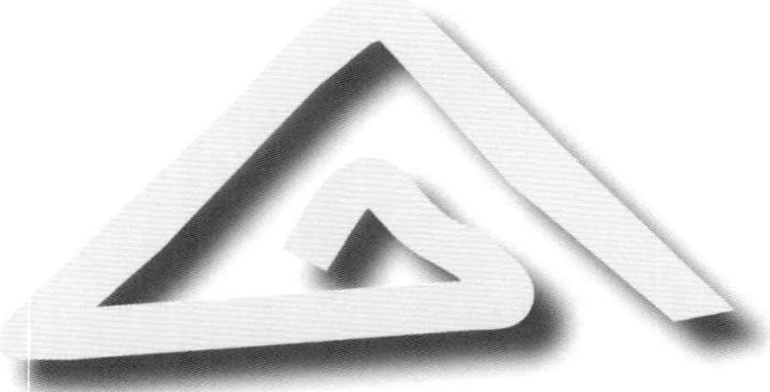

I remember the first time I told someone that I was working on this book and his response was, "I have always thought about doing that one day – that is my idea exclamation!!" I say I remember the "first time", because it wasn't the last. As I shared my project throughout the year, I was overwhelmed by the reaction of everyone I spoke to about it, and knew from the minute I began this endeavor it was a project that people have been waiting for. This mountain has captivated the imagination of the community that lives in its shadow, and the nation that calls it "America's Mountain." The same beauty that inspired Katharine Lee Bates to write the words "… Purple mountains majesty above the fruited plains..." inspires those of us that live near it to want to capture that beauty in photographs when we can, and share them with the world. And so I did. I spent an entire year taking a unique picture of Pikes Peak each day, with this book being the culmination of that effort.

I could have never anticipated the way this project touched people and impacted their lives, and how that would motivate me each day. Thousands of people from all over the world viewed these images millions of times throughout the course of the project and shared their own stories about Pikes Peak along the way. Some were stories of inspiration, some more stories of lost, but what was interesting to me was how this mountain binds us as a community. At the same time, Pikes Peak isn't just my mountain, it's America's Mountain. And according to the official Pikes Peak Highway website, is the most visited mountain in the country.

As a photographer, I thought I looked at the Peak more than others, but once I started displaying my photographs of Pikes Peak, I learned that I wasn't the only one who felt a special connection to the this mountain. Each time I would publish one of my photographs of the Peak, people would share how these images touched them. Just after a gallery show, these conversations had me thinking about the early concepts of this project and by coincidence friend asked me what was next on my photographic agenda. I shared my ideas about taking a unique picture of Pikes Peak every day for an entire year and he said, "you have to do this project!" Several conversations later, and tons of encouragement to just get out there and do it, I decided to take on the challenge. This project took place from June 1, 2010 to May 31, 2011 and I had no idea what was in store for me over the year…

The challenges – My sole mission early on in the project was to capture the most beautiful moment the Peak had offered each and every day in a photograph. The concept sounds simple enough, but there were numerous challenges that came along with a project like this, some obvious, some not so transparent. Also, publishing this project out to the web and social media in real time each day, while asking for input and suggestions, added an entirely unexpected (but very positive) element to the project.

The truth was I had no idea what I was in for when I started this project. I had no idea how big an effort it would really be, how much time it would take, or even come close to understanding how hard it would be to balance this project with real life. My idea of what it would take was completely unrealistic, but once I began the project I quickly had to find a way to balance it all and make sure I found a way to enjoy every minute. This project was full of challenges and I had to learn to adapt quickly early on.

I think my biggest challenge was trying to be in the right place at the right time to catch a beautiful shot every single day for an entire year while shooting 365 unique pictures of the same subject. The not so obvious challenges were the "life factors." No matter how much you plan, you can't plan for the unexpected surprises life throws at you. I could make a laundry list of all the unexpected things that popped over the course of the year, but I will summarize by saying that it was everything from wrecking my truck in a blizzard to personal illness and everything else in between.

I did several interviews with local media as the project went on and I was often asked about these unexpected moments during the project. One interviewer asked me to finish the sentence, "I will never forget the day…" I paused for a minute and started to complete this sentence. "I will never forget the first day I took over 100 amazing photographs and spent 6 hours trying to narrow them down to pick just one as the Picture of the Day, and in the process I had totally forgotten my appointment to register my son for school that day!" Then I said, "No, no, no, I will never forget the day I was stalked by a bear deep in the forest and…" Interrupting myself, I stopped mid-sentence and said, "NO! It was the day I slid down a snow bank and got stuck on the mountain in the middle of winter… but then there was the day I found myself standing shirtless in the middle of a blinding spring blizzard! Oh, and then there was the one day when a buck threatened me with his antlers and wouldn't let me walk back to my truck!" Needless to say, this "life factor" had an extraordinary impact on the project, and taught me that if I can do this, I can do anything!

By writing about my journey each day and publishing that out to the web and social media (Facebook, Twitter and my Blog), the project became a community effort. I had no intention of including these writings in the book, but as the project went on, the stories about how I got my shot seemed to become just as interesting to the followers as the shot itself. Thus they became a big part of the book. I have to warn you though, I am not a writer and I have included my stories in spite of my lack of ability.

Social media gave me the ability to gather a tribe of like-minded people and get them involved in the process from the beginning. At the same time they were able to share this project with their friends and family as well, and share their Peak. I honestly believe that this social media factor was the most powerful and influential element in this project. The growth of the fan base, the feedback and comments, and the words of encouragement kept me striving for improvement each day. I knew there were thousands of people out there each and every day that were waiting for their daily photo of the Peak, and I was not going to let them down.

Your journey throughout the book and the year – As you go through this book looking at the photos and reading the stories, keep in mind that my goal was to photograph the best moment each day had to offer and capture the drama and the clouds or brilliant colors of the sky. Some days were more dramatic than others, but each day was beautiful in its own way I hope I captured that.

In this softcover version of the book, I was limited by space so I couldn't include the writings from each day or a full size photo from each day, so I focused on each week. I chose my personal favorite from each week as the primary photo and included my journal from that day. The other six images of the week are above and below my journal.

I believe I live in one of the most beautiful places in the world, and Pikes Peak is the center of the that beauty. Being able to capture that beauty in photographs over the course of an entire year was a challenge, but it was tremendously fun and a real life adventure.

I am just an ordinary guy who hoped to create something extraordinary by capturing the beauty of Pikes Peak in photographs every single day for a year and sharing that with the world. Thanks for coming along on my journey through 365 days of Pikes Peak.

~The Pikes Peak Guy

Chapter 1

Summer

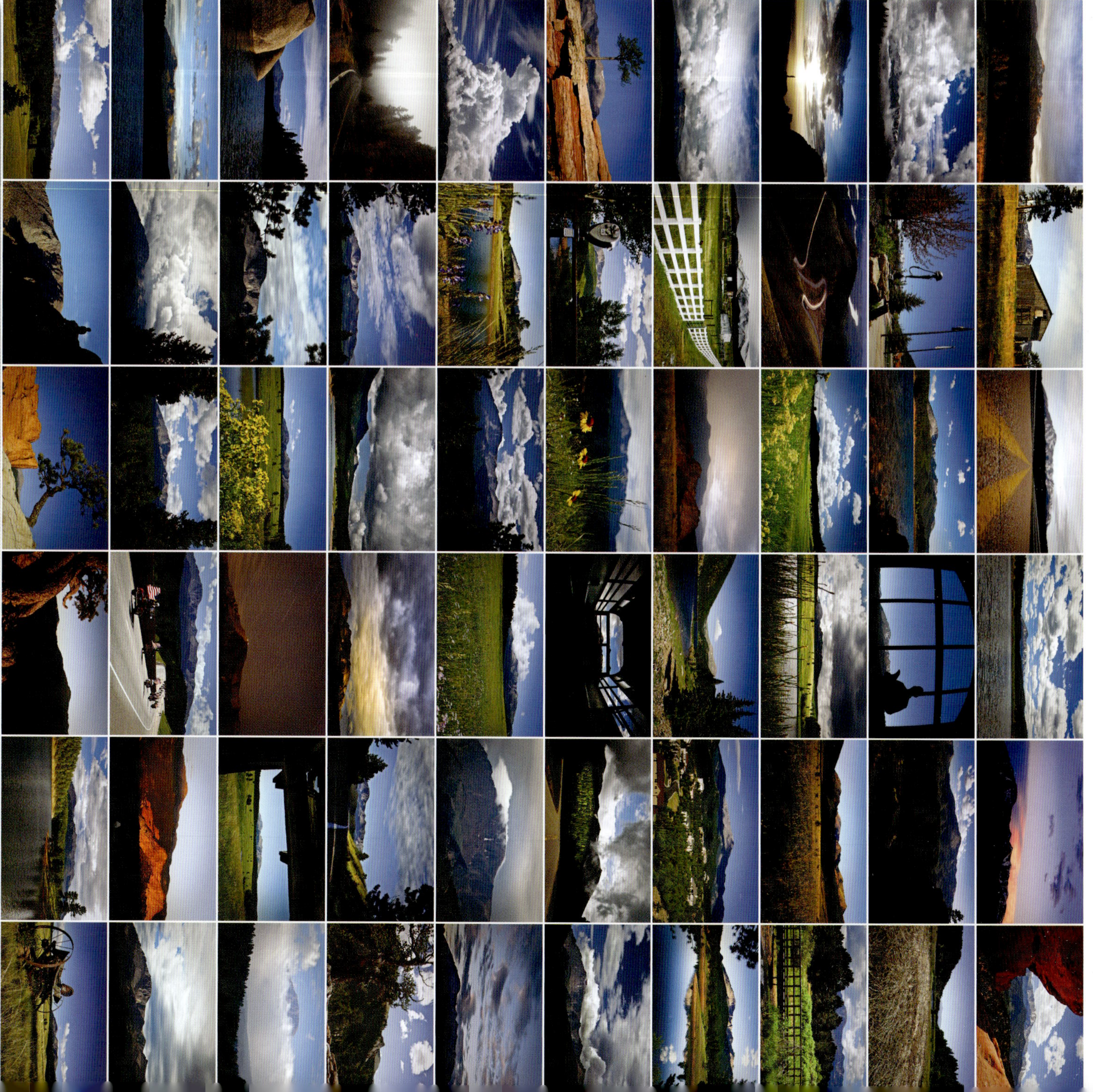

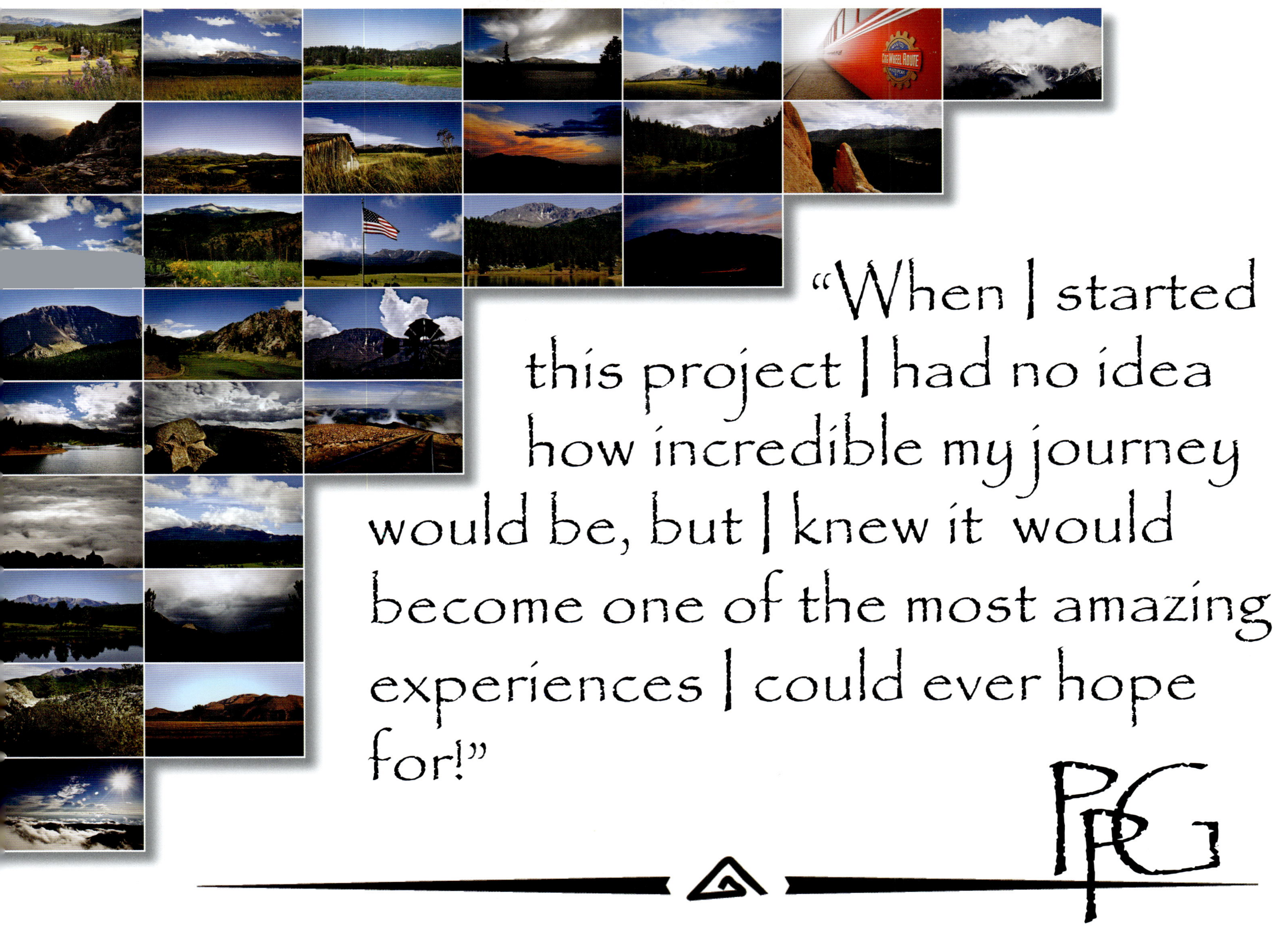
"When I started this project I had no idea how incredible my journey would be, but I knew it would become one of the most amazing experiences I could ever hope for!"
PPG

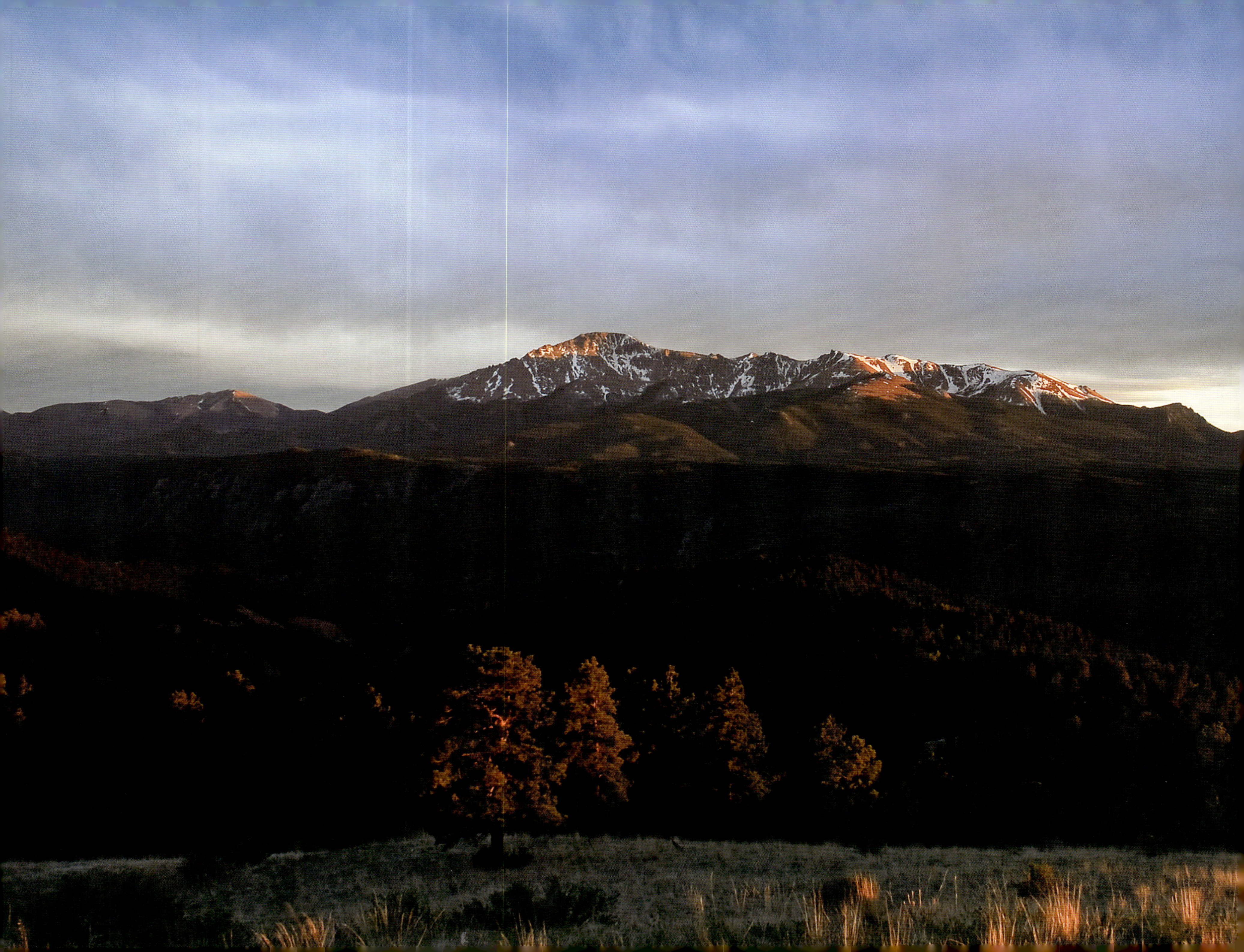

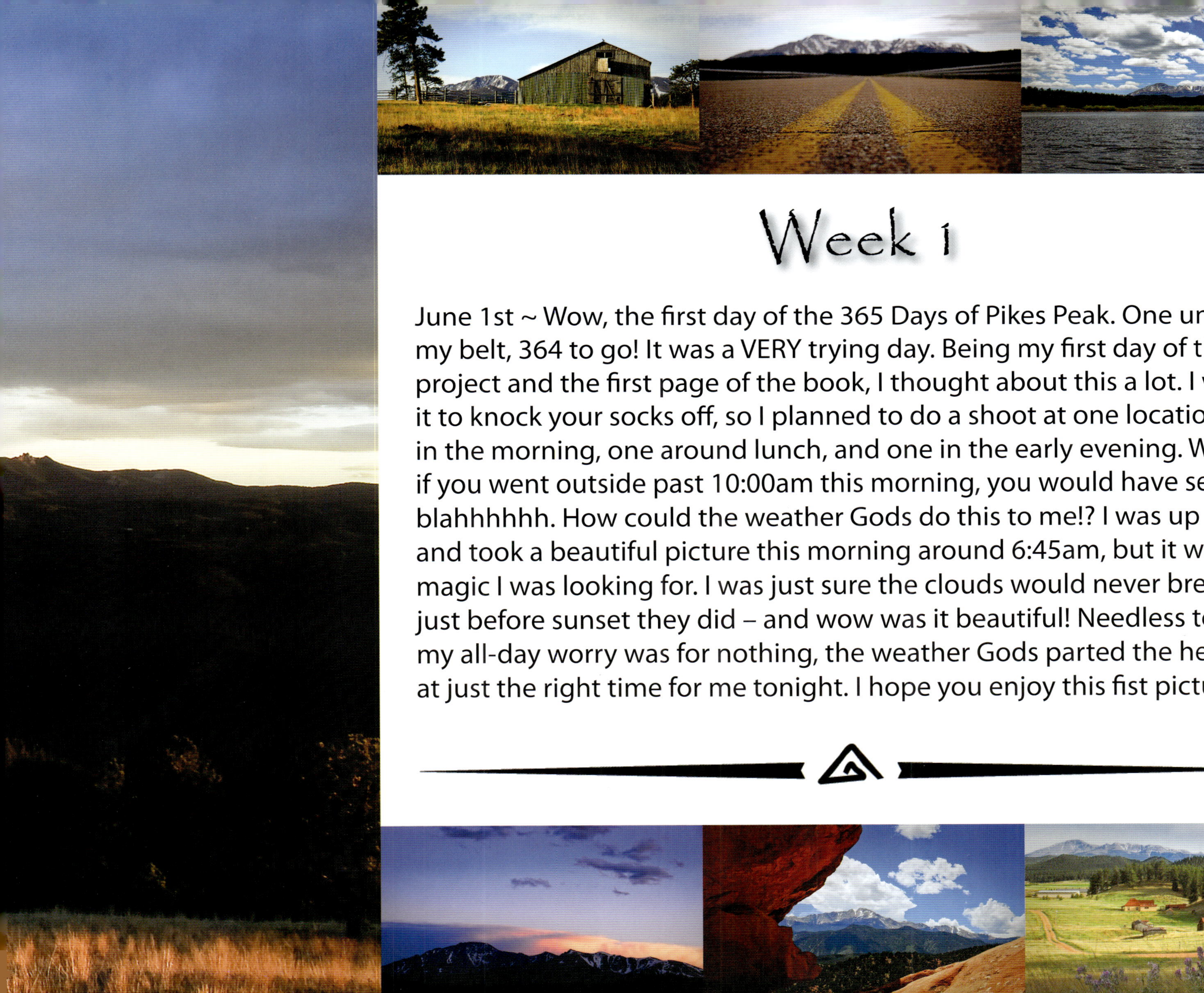

Week 1

June 1st ~ Wow, the first day of the 365 Days of Pikes Peak. One under my belt, 364 to go! It was a VERY trying day. Being my first day of the project and the first page of the book, I thought about this a lot. I wanted it to knock your socks off, so I planned to do a shoot at one location in the morning, one around lunch, and one in the early evening. Well, if you went outside past 10:00am this morning, you would have seen blahhhhhh. How could the weather Gods do this to me!? I was up early and took a beautiful picture this morning around 6:45am, but it wasn't the magic I was looking for. I was just sure the clouds would never break, then just before sunset they did – and wow was it beautiful! Needless to say, my all-day worry was for nothing, the weather Gods parted the heavens at just the right time for me tonight. I hope you enjoy this fist picture!

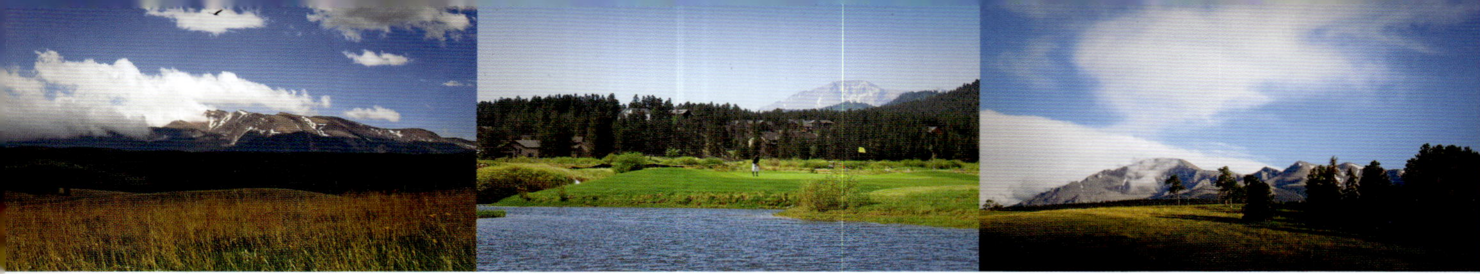

Week 2

June 10th ~ I got set up early this evening to get a completely different shot than this. I was actually hoping to get a sunny shot with blue skies, green trees and glassy water- well, you can see that didn't work out at all. I got there around 6:00pm, because I was afraid the clouds would set in and the sun would be gone. Sure enough the wind kicked up and it started to rain a little, so I sat on a rock and listened to my iPod and waited it out, hoping to at least end up with a sunset photo. Just as the rain stopped, the sun dropped below the clouds and (no joke on this one) Here Comes the Sun from the Beatles White album started to play on my iPod… As the storm clouds parted and the sun came out, there was no doubt in my mind that this was the one ~ and the song made it that much more memorable!

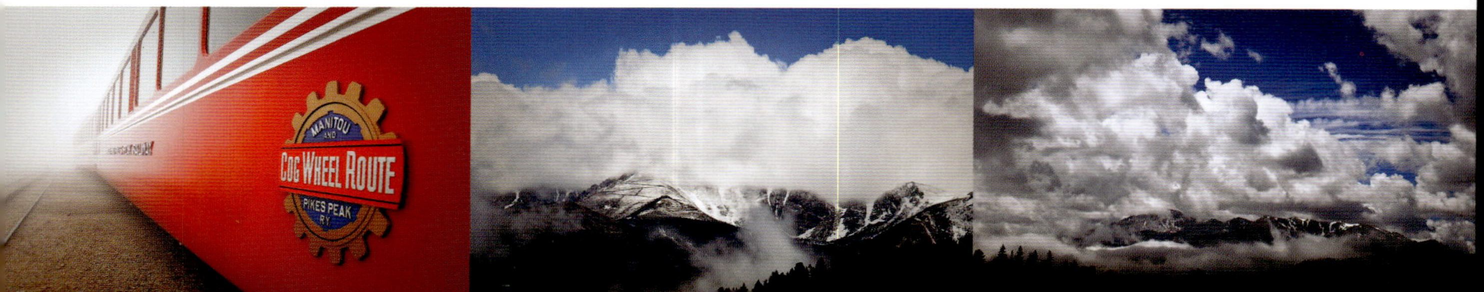

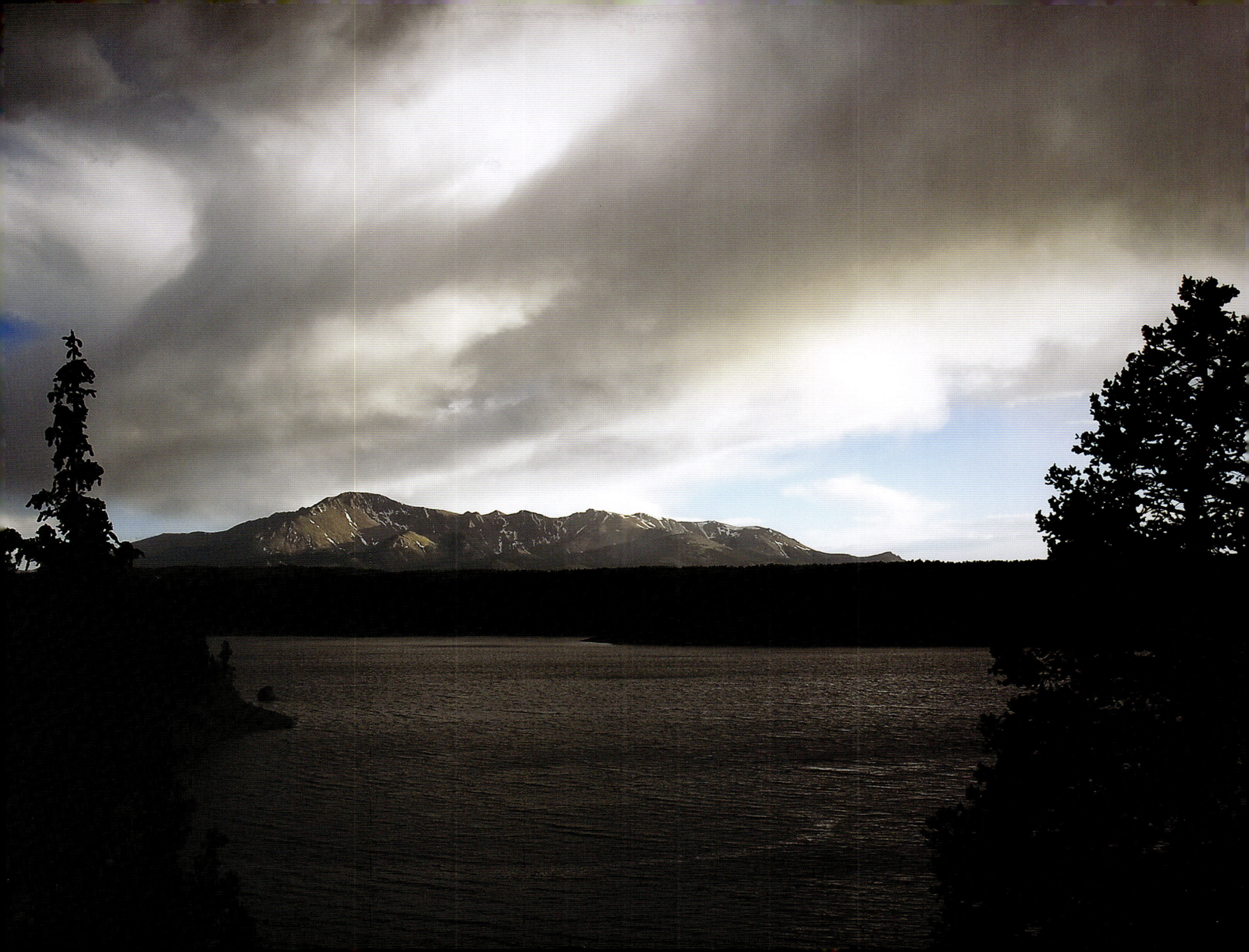

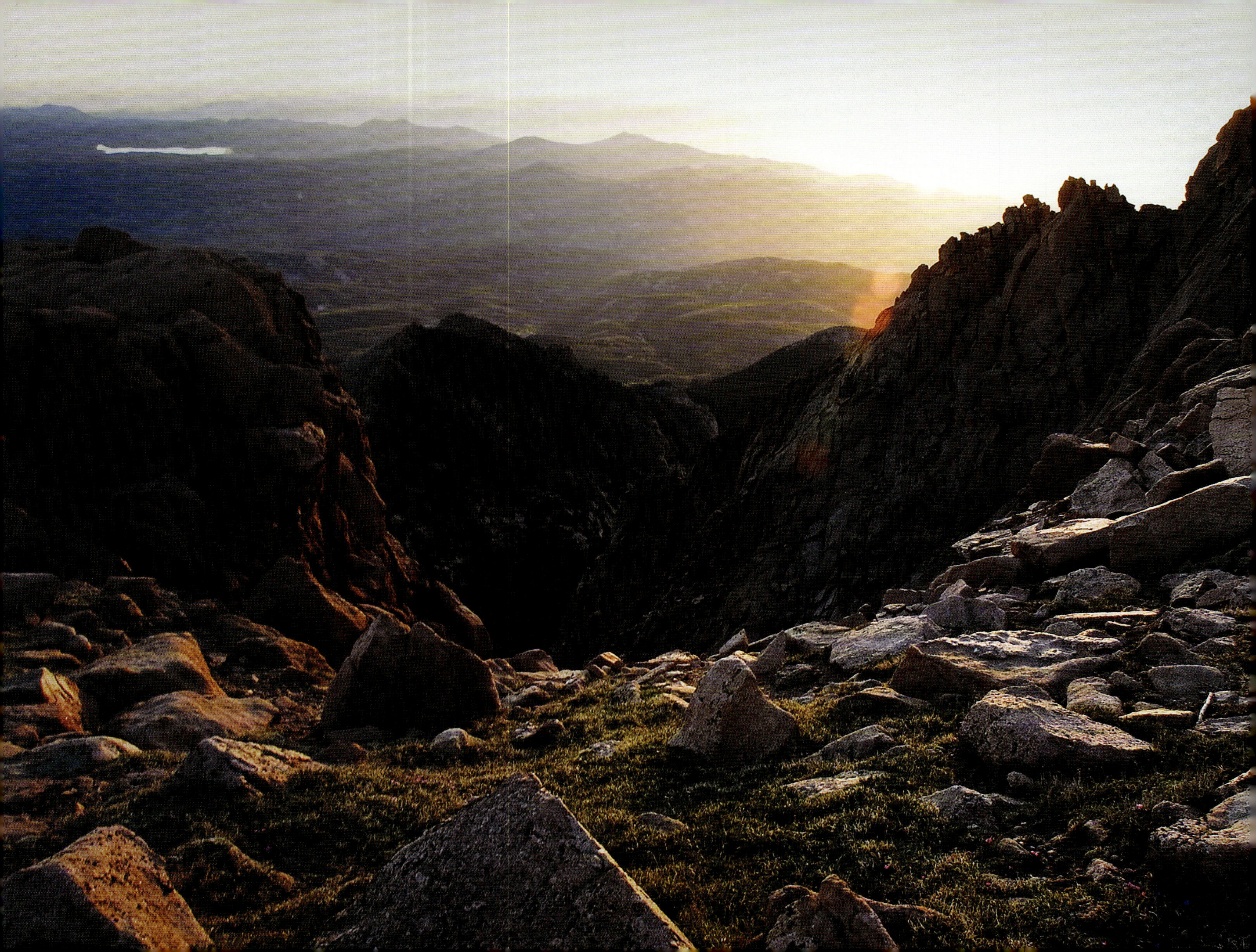

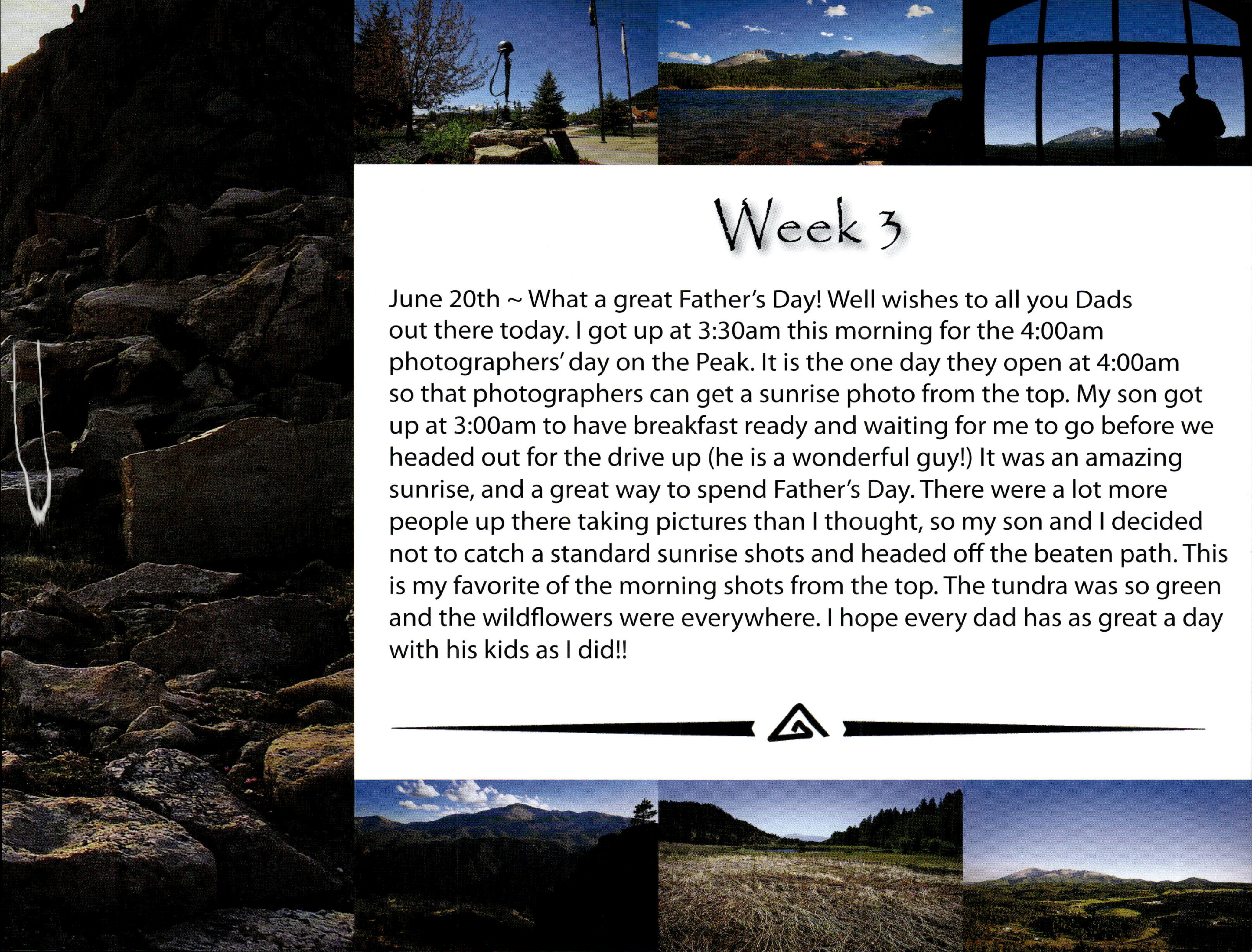

Week 3

June 20th ~ What a great Father's Day! Well wishes to all you Dads out there today. I got up at 3:30am this morning for the 4:00am photographers' day on the Peak. It is the one day they open at 4:00am so that photographers can get a sunrise photo from the top. My son got up at 3:00am to have breakfast ready and waiting for me to go before we headed out for the drive up (he is a wonderful guy!) It was an amazing sunrise, and a great way to spend Father's Day. There were a lot more people up there taking pictures than I thought, so my son and I decided not to catch a standard sunrise shots and headed off the beaten path. This is my favorite of the morning shots from the top. The tundra was so green and the wildflowers were everywhere. I hope every dad has as great a day with his kids as I did!!

Week 4

June 27th ~ Today I was at the 88th Annual Pikes Peak International Hill Climb to get my Picture of the Day and to enjoy the race. This was my very first time at the Hill Climb and I got there before dawn to get my choice of spots. It was about 5:00am when I got to the top, parked, and got my camera gear out – and I started shooting immediately. I started with the full moon, then the sunrise… everything of interest prior to the actual start of the race. I knew I was going to be getting plenty of pictures of race cars that day (along with the few hundred others photographing the race today…) but I was worried race cars just weren't my style and may not work with the book. Once the sun came up, I decided to get a long exposure, early light shot of this twisting stretch of road just below Devil's Playground. I realized that the large number of cars streaming up the road so early in the morning would only happen on race day… and this kind of shot was just my style!

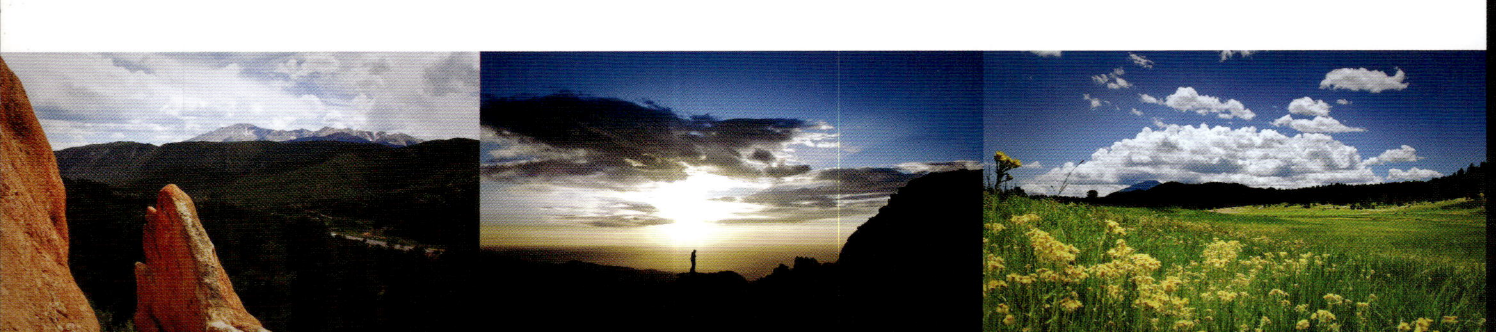

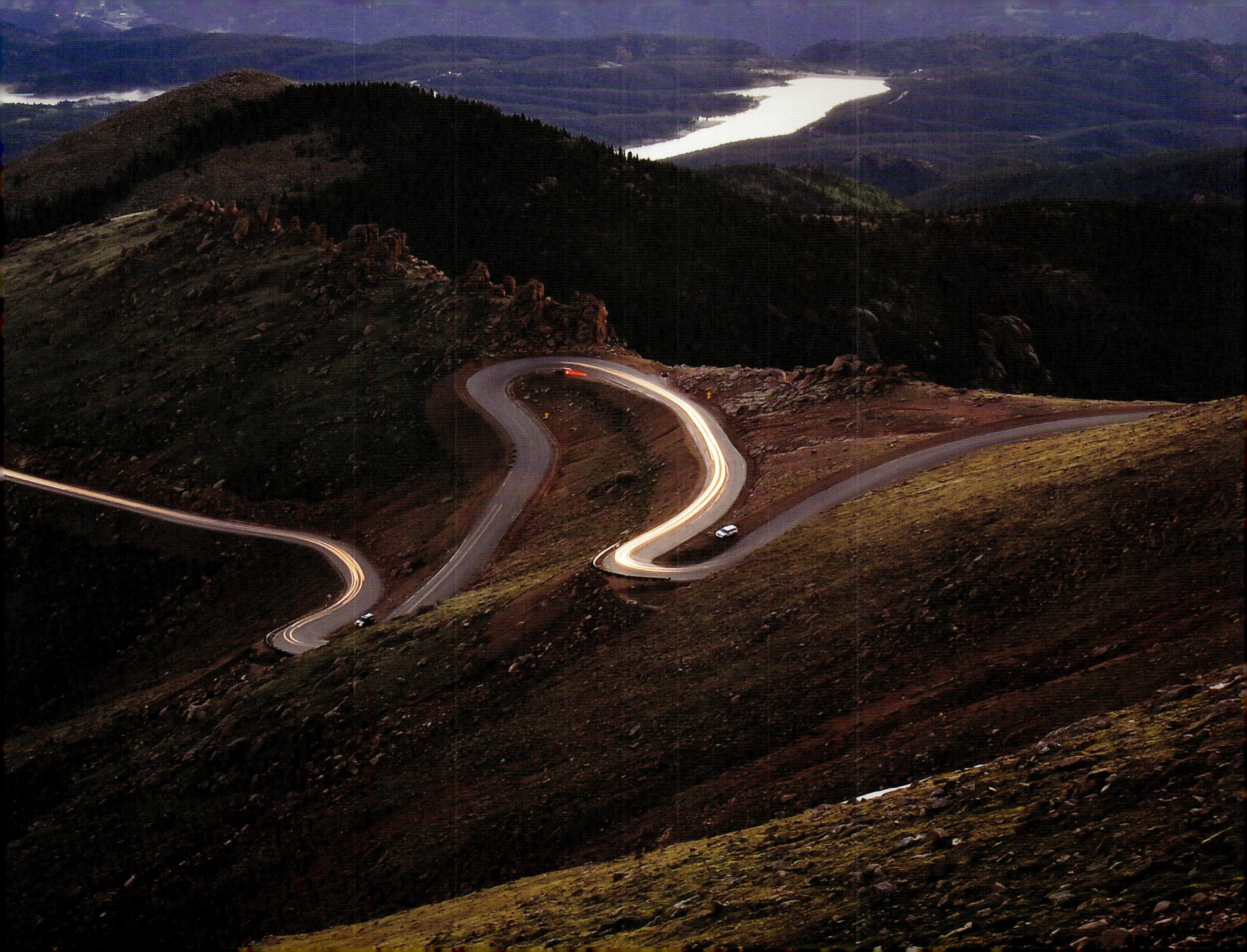

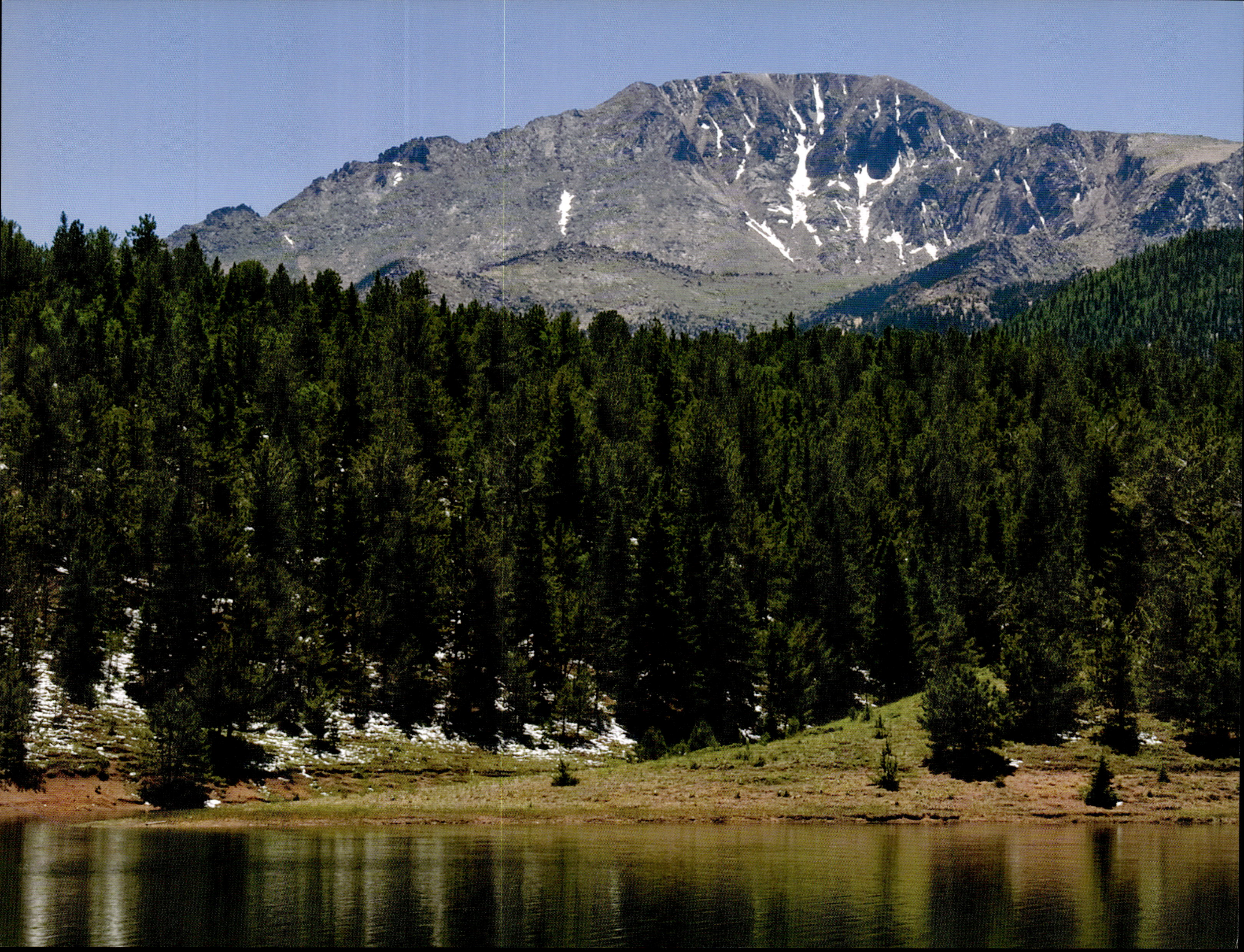

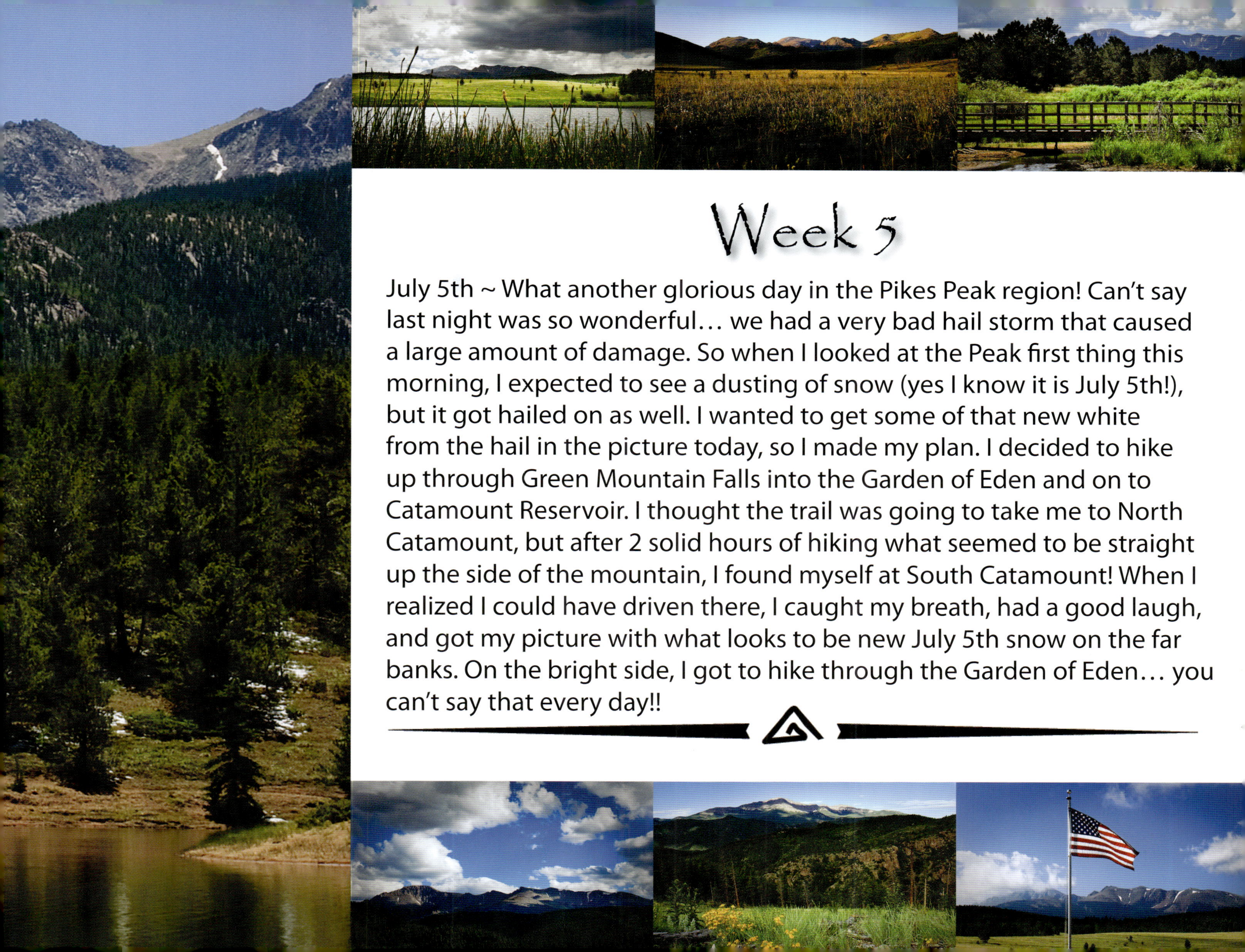

Week 5

July 5th ~ What another glorious day in the Pikes Peak region! Can't say last night was so wonderful… we had a very bad hail storm that caused a large amount of damage. So when I looked at the Peak first thing this morning, I expected to see a dusting of snow (yes I know it is July 5th!), but it got hailed on as well. I wanted to get some of that new white from the hail in the picture today, so I made my plan. I decided to hike up through Green Mountain Falls into the Garden of Eden and on to Catamount Reservoir. I thought the trail was going to take me to North Catamount, but after 2 solid hours of hiking what seemed to be straight up the side of the mountain, I found myself at South Catamount! When I realized I could have driven there, I caught my breath, had a good laugh, and got my picture with what looks to be new July 5th snow on the far banks. On the bright side, I got to hike through the Garden of Eden… you can't say that every day!!

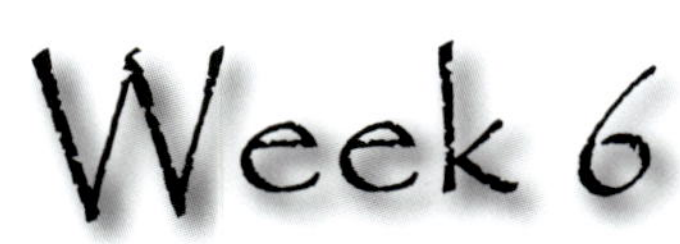

July 12th ~ I couldn't help myself… I know I have published a lot of pictures of the Peak with water in the foreground so far, but look at this! How could I resist making this the picture of the day? I took pictures from every angle today - from Monument, from the Springs, from Divide, from Woodland Park and finally I ended up on the Pikes Peak Highway. I was on my way to check out the statue of Big Foot outside the Crystal Reservoir Gift Shop to see if it would make a good picture. I decided to hike around for a while and see if there were any interesting views, and of course there were. But I had taken so many pictures today, I decided to head back to the truck when I looked over my shoulder and saw this. All I can say is Wow!

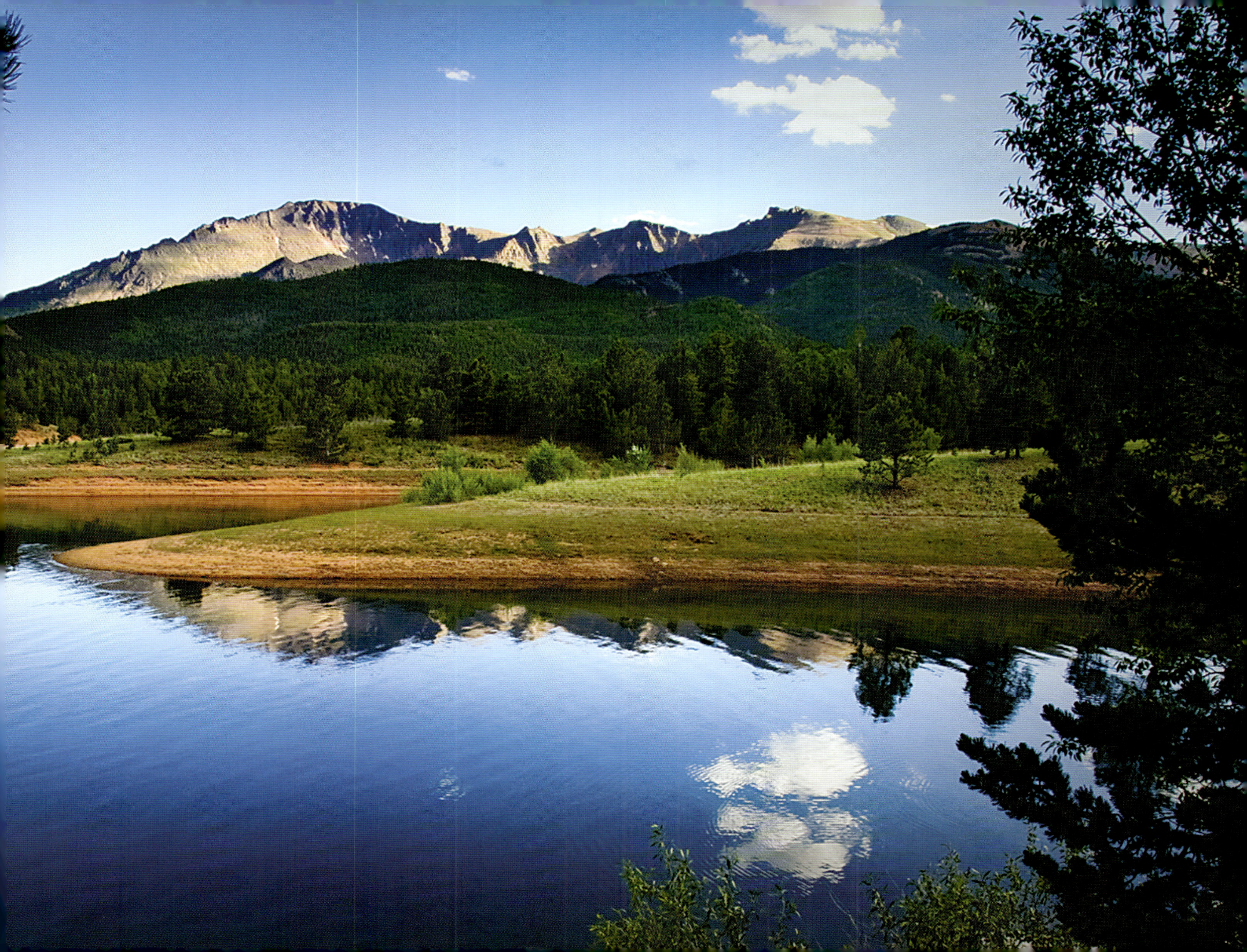

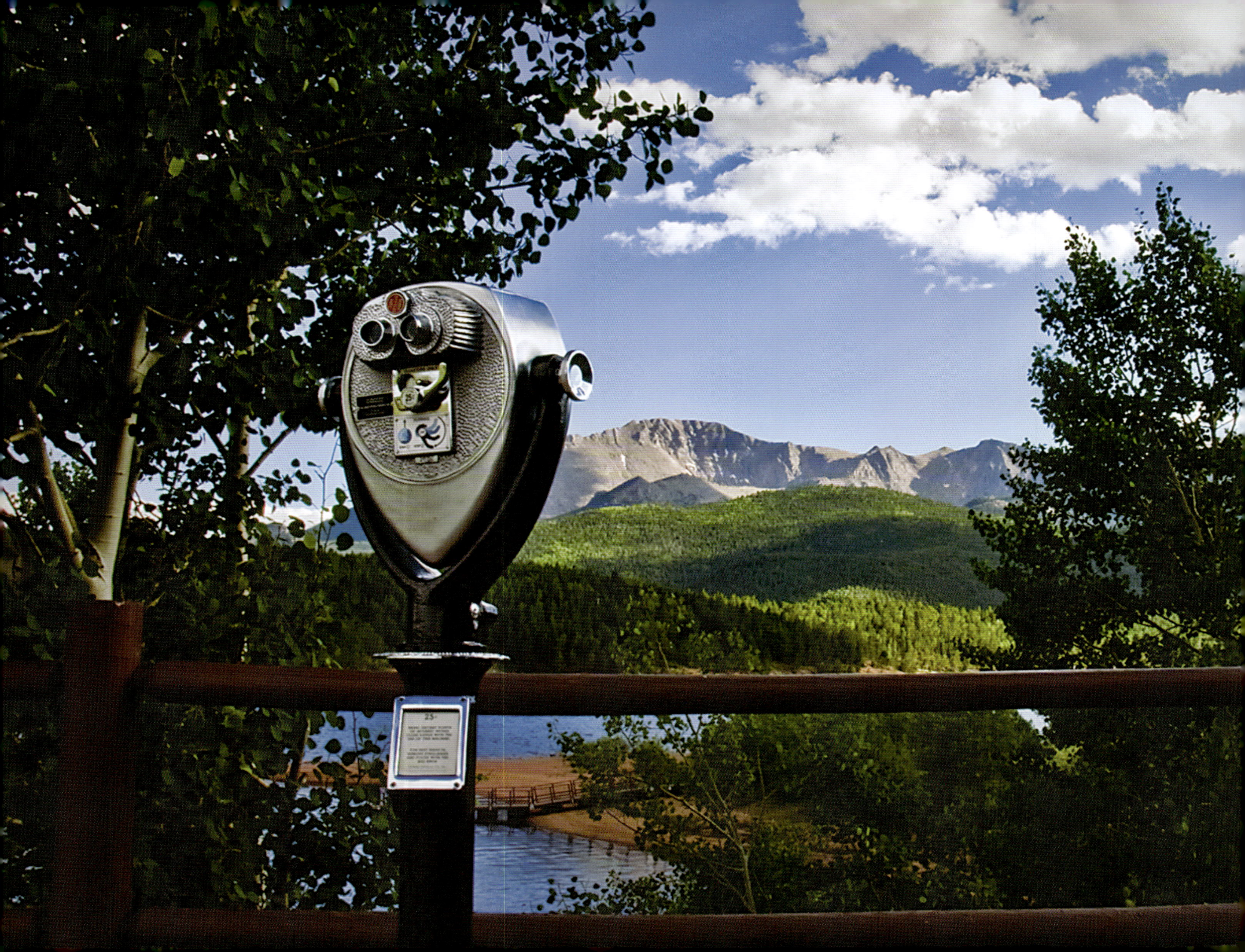

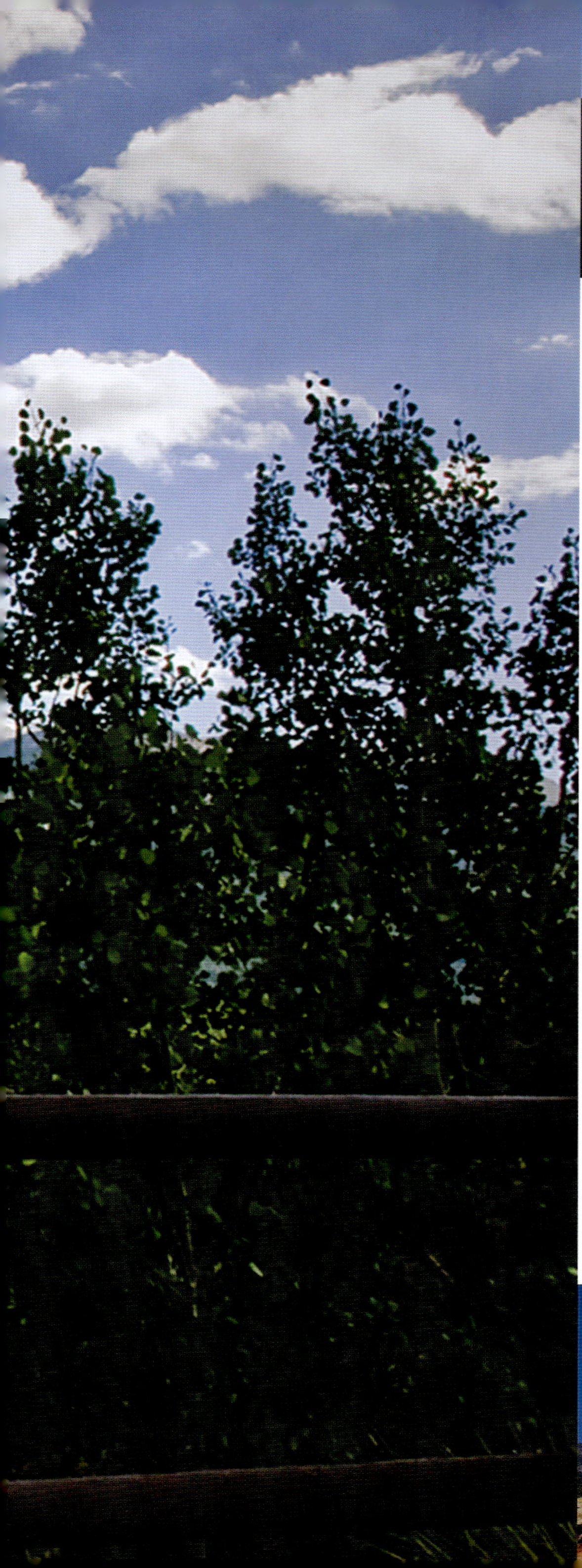

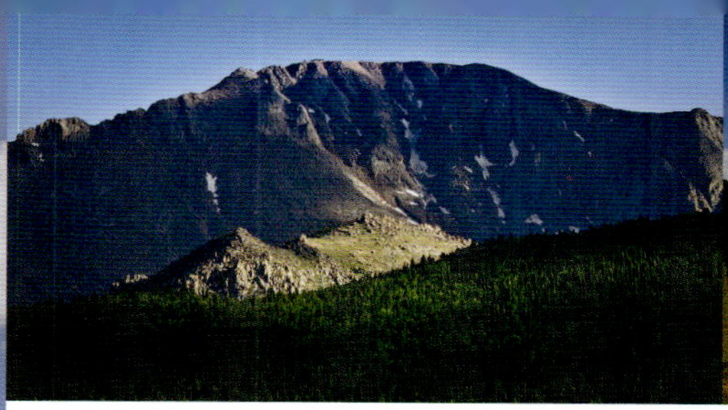

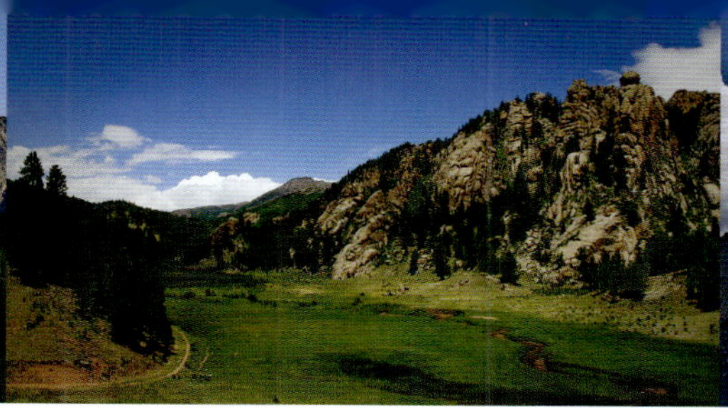

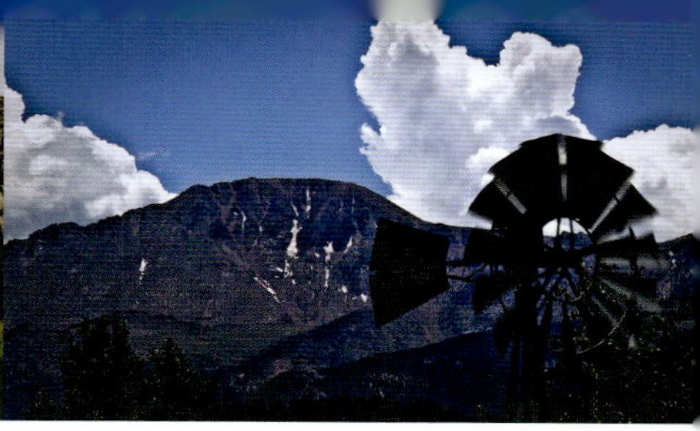

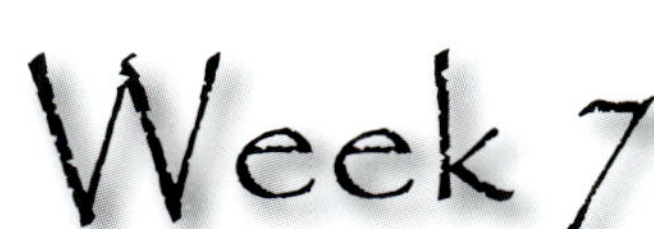

July 17th ~ It is interesting where inspiration can come from on this project. In my journal from the day prior, I wrote about how there was a guy taking a picture of me… taking a picture of the Peak. He figured that anyone lugging that much camera gear around had to have a good shot in mind. This made me think back to this coin operated binocular that I saw one day while up on the Peak at the Crystal Reservoir Gift Shop. I set out today to capture the view that this giant view-finder looking contraption was set up to view… (that is a mouthful!) and so today's picture is inspired by yesterday's photo shoot – a view of the view.

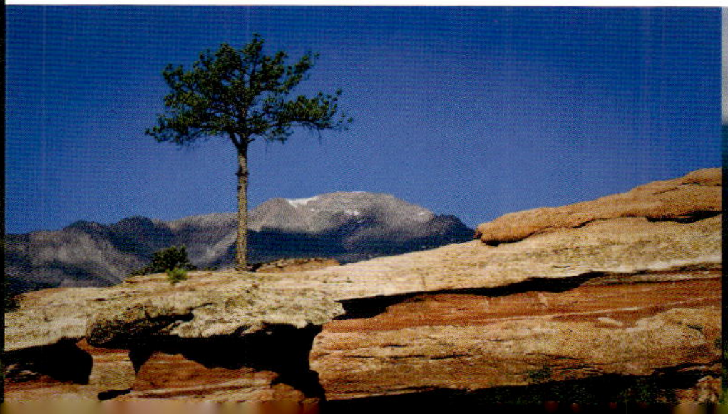

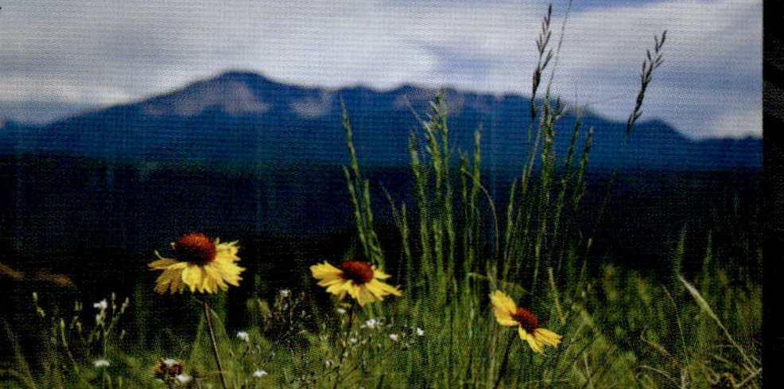

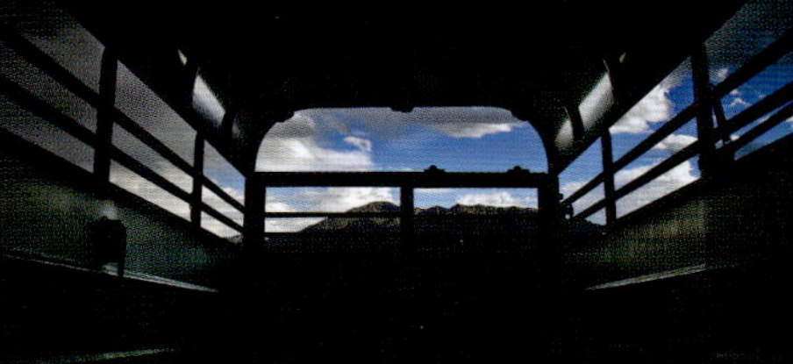

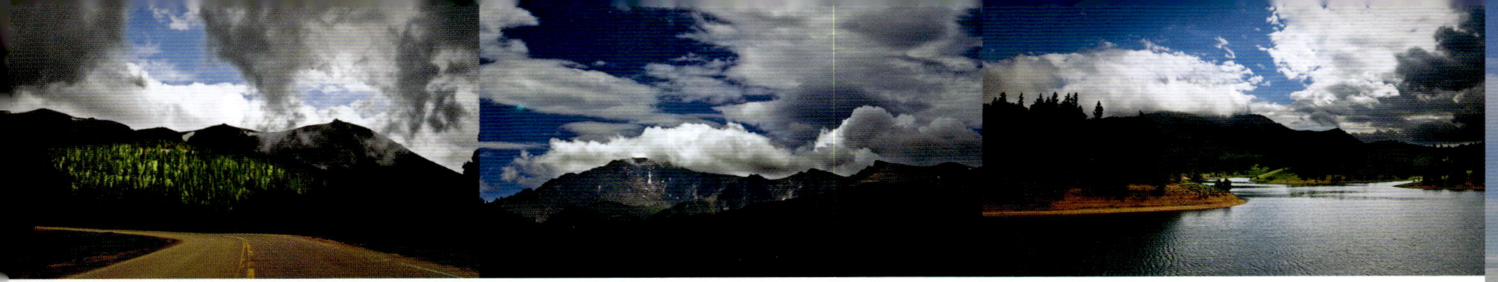

Week 8

July 24th ~ Throughout this project I have had many firsts, and today was another! After 10 years of living here, today I rode the Pikes Peak Cog Railway for the very first time. The Cog Railway was one of the first companies to sponsor this project with free rides to the top, but I hadn't had a chance to go take advantage of this arrangement until today. I really wasn't sure what to expect, but I can honestly say that I can't believe it took me this long to do that! It was a great ride, with unbelievable scenery along the way and a view you can only get riding the rail. When I saw the clouds coming in like this, I headed down the tracks on foot to get this shot… I just had to go after it, no matter how hard the hike back up was!

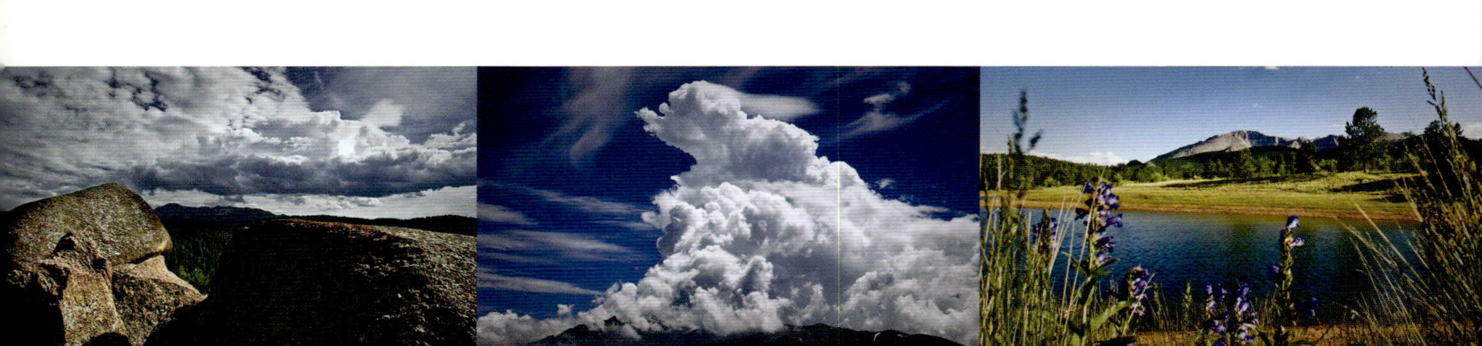

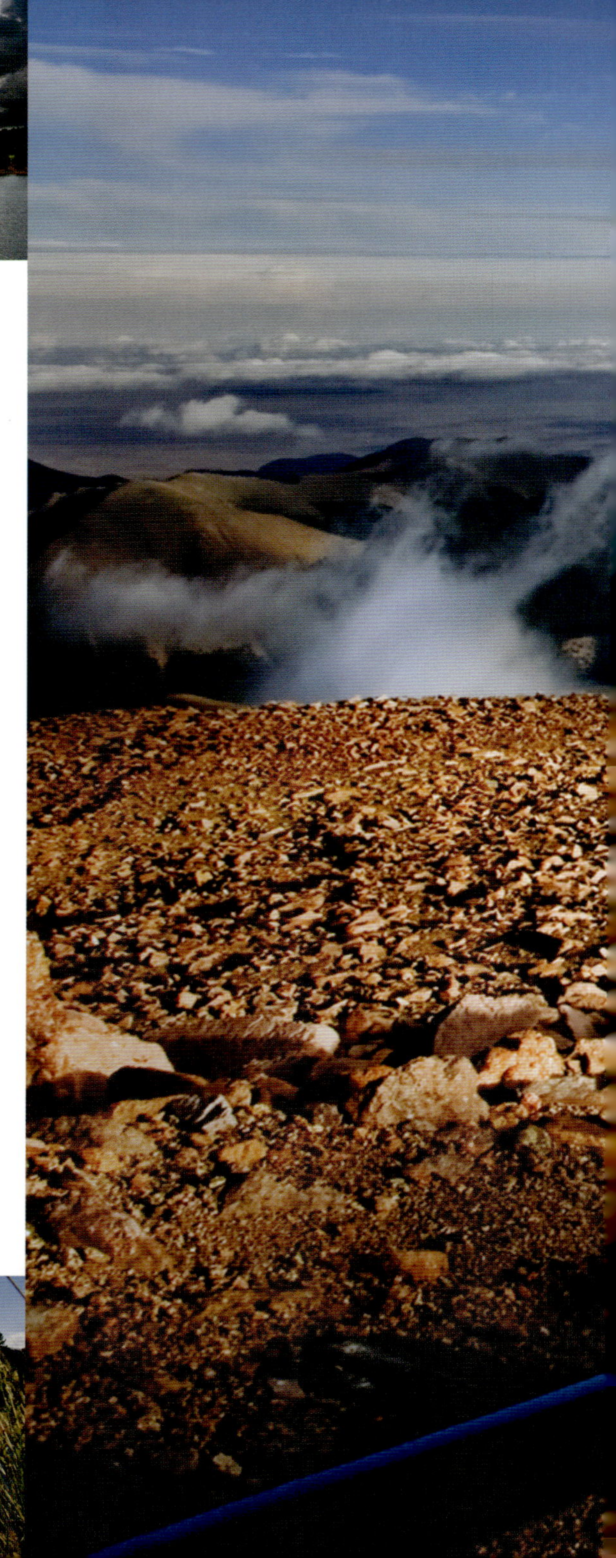

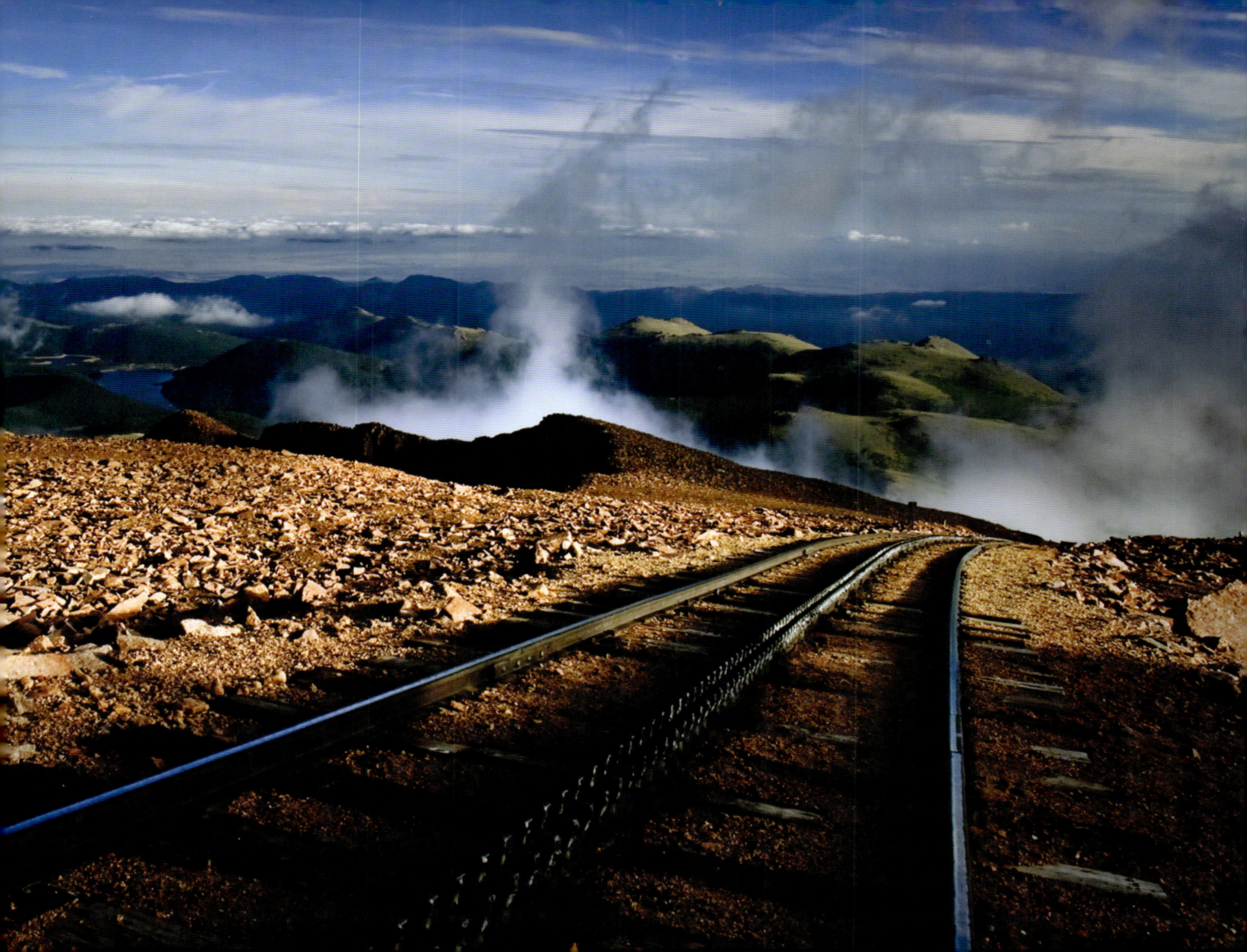

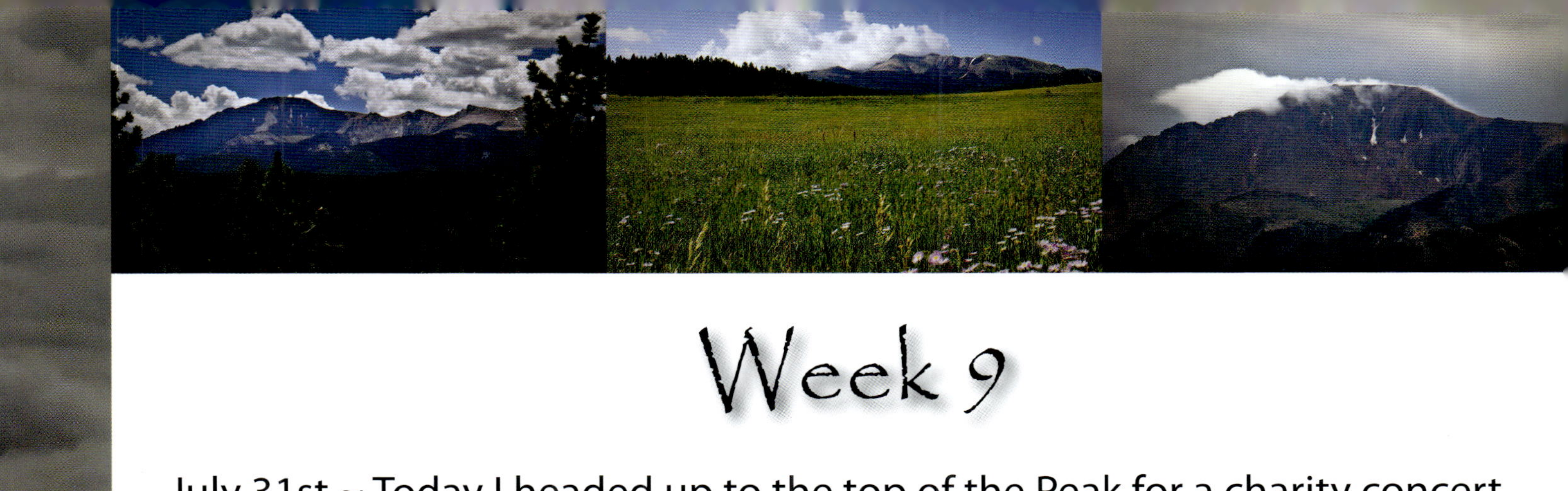

Week 9

July 31st ~ Today I headed up to the top of the Peak for a charity concert, and in a very uncharacteristic fashion, I was late! I was only 20 minutes late, but I missed the show and while very disappointed, it only took a moment for me to be excited again. I was totally amazed by the majesty of the clouds ~ you just had to be up there to understand how incredible they were. I started to climb around on the rocks and look for the perfect shot to express what it was like today when I stumbled on some flowers and small rock that said "We miss you and love you dad." ~ I'm a dad myself and was moved by the simple stone. As I moved out to the rocks in front of the cog trains, I saw this person sitting on the rock and thought it looked like it might be someone's dad looking down from heaven…

Week 10

August 6th ~ If you have ever been about 5 miles North of Woodland Park, driving South on HWY 67 towards the Peak, there is a split second when you come over the hill, that the Peak looks larger than life. I have seen this view hundreds of times and tried to capture it on several occasions. I have hiked up and down the walking path, stomped through tall grass on the other side of the road, even walked right down the middle of the highway. The pictures I took never really captured what I was seeing when I was driving. I decided to set up this shot while driving, and what a challenge! I rigged it so my camera was hanging out the front of my truck window and I used a remote to snap continuous pictures as I drove over the hill. I had to adjust the rigging a few times and after 4 takes, I finally got the shot that shows off this amazing view!

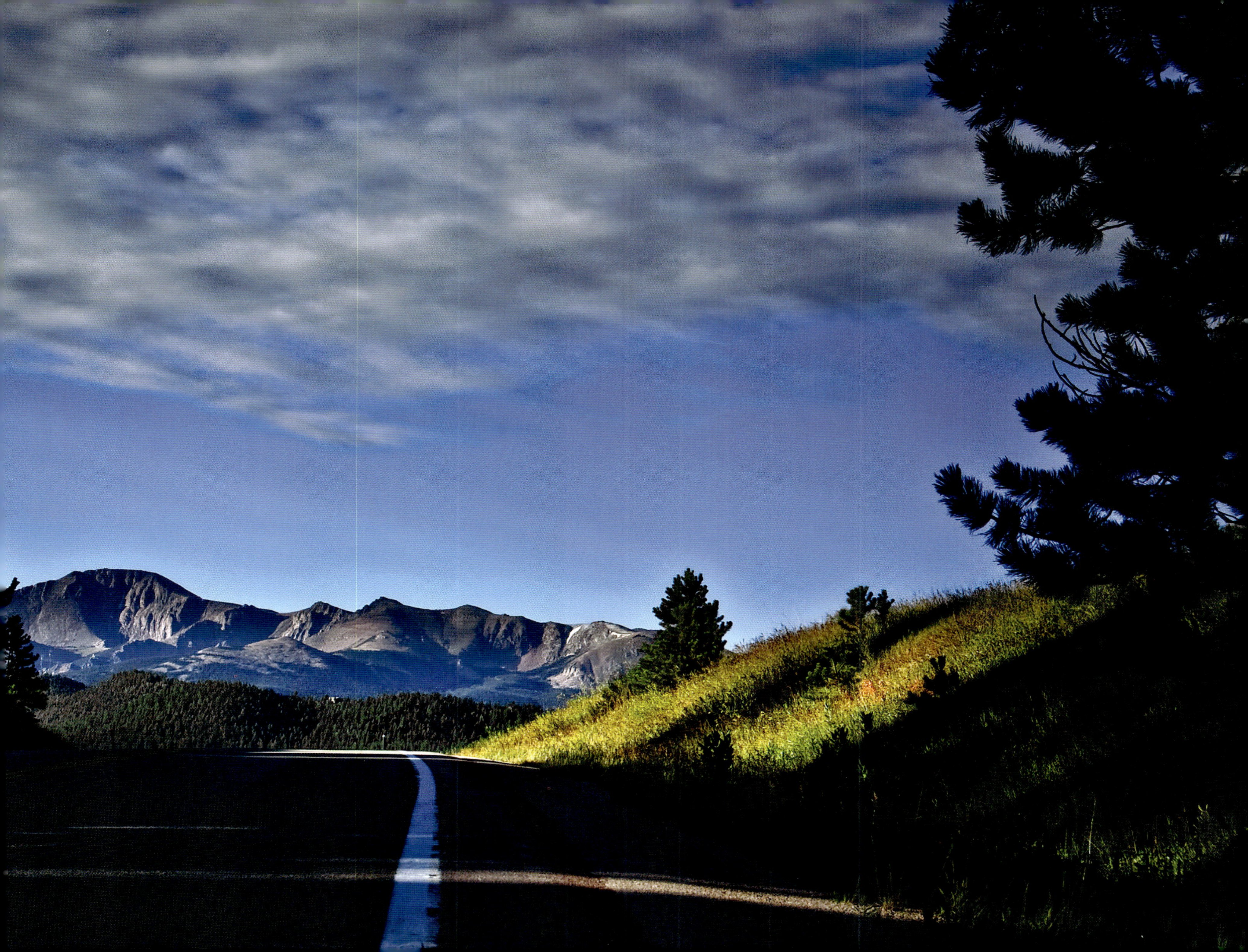

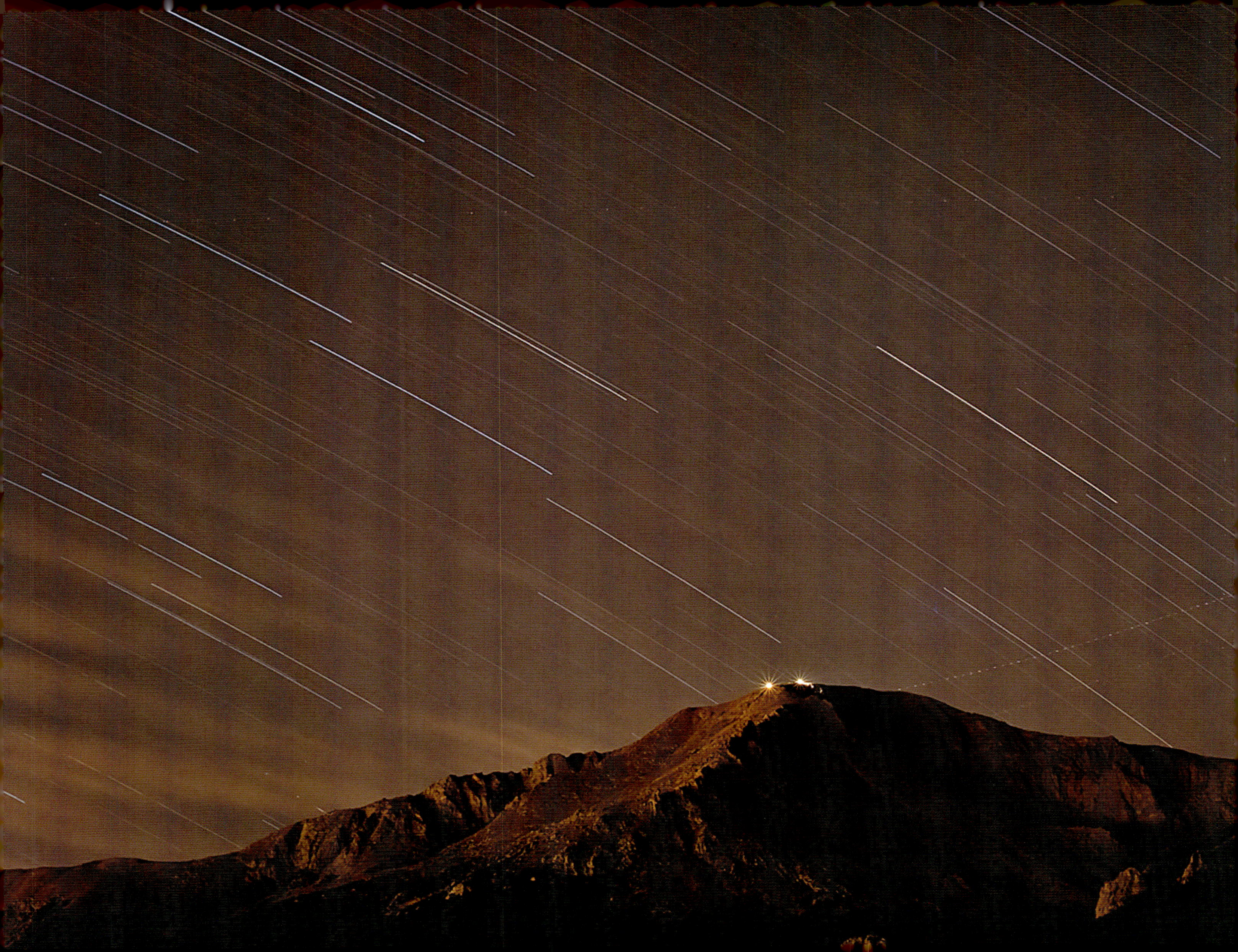

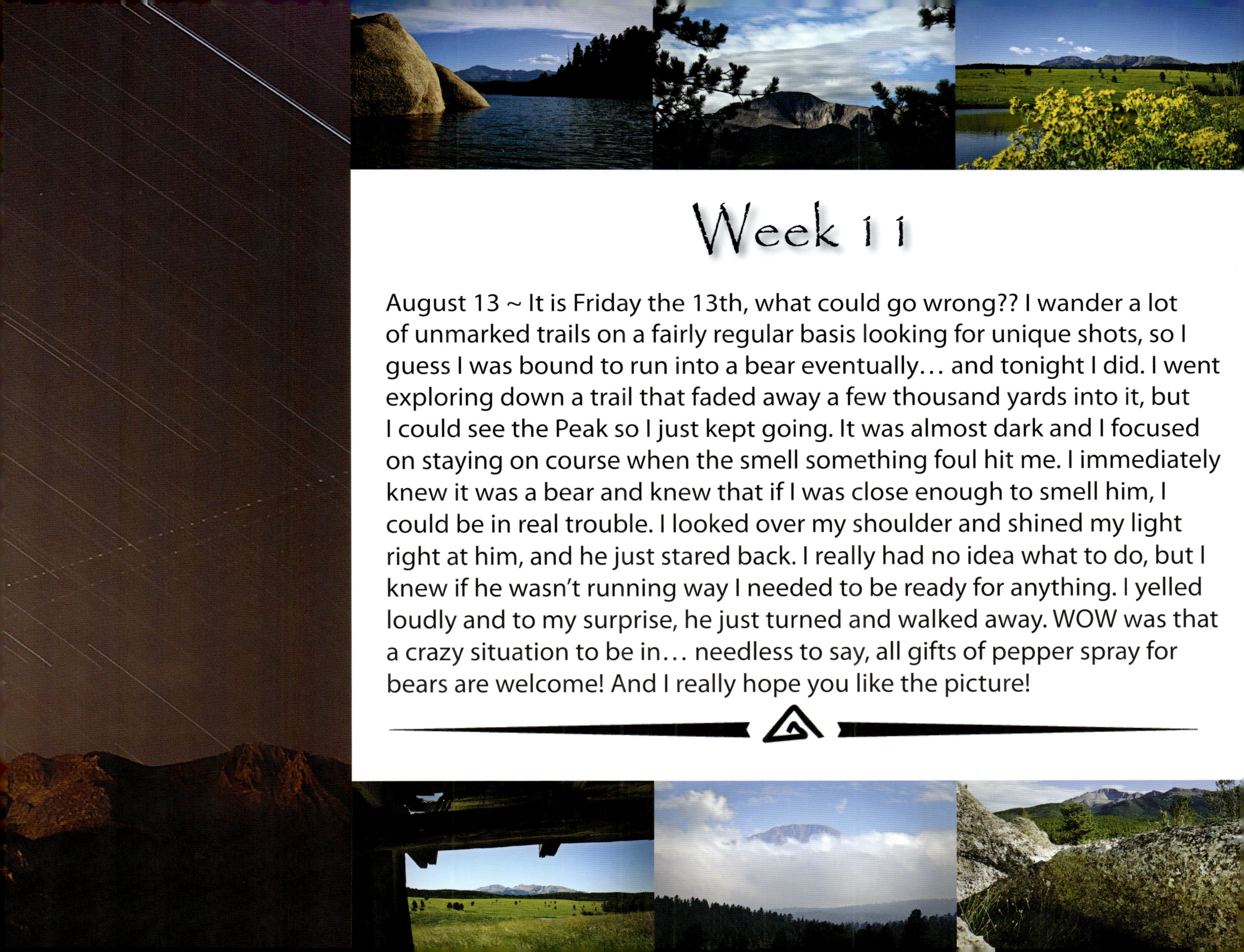

Week 11

August 13 ~ It is Friday the 13th, what could go wrong?? I wander a lot of unmarked trails on a fairly regular basis looking for unique shots, so I guess I was bound to run into a bear eventually… and tonight I did. I went exploring down a trail that faded away a few thousand yards into it, but I could see the Peak so I just kept going. It was almost dark and I focused on staying on course when the smell something foul hit me. I immediately knew it was a bear and knew that if I was close enough to smell him, I could be in real trouble. I looked over my shoulder and shined my light right at him, and he just stared back. I really had no idea what to do, but I knew if he wasn't running way I needed to be ready for anything. I yelled loudly and to my surprise, he just turned and walked away. WOW was that a crazy situation to be in… needless to say, all gifts of pepper spray for bears are welcome! And I really hope you like the picture!

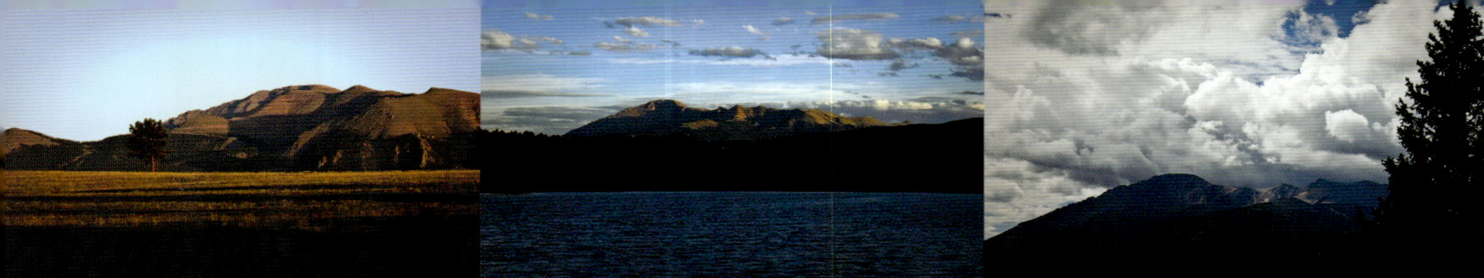

Week 12

August 22nd ~ Even though getting up early enough to catch a sunrise over the Garden of the Gods is ALWAYS worth the effort, getting going that early on a Sunday is the hardest thing ever! A lot of people ask how long it takes for me to do this each day, and it really depends on how much prep is needed for the shot. On a day like this where I know where I am going and have it all planned out, it can take as little as an hour and a half. I spend an hour driving to and from the location, 3o minutes setting up ~ and 1/40 of a second capturing the shot! When the sun comes up around 6:00am, that means I have to get moving pretty early… and for a guy that loves to sleep in on the weekends, this is a real indicator of my passion for this project!

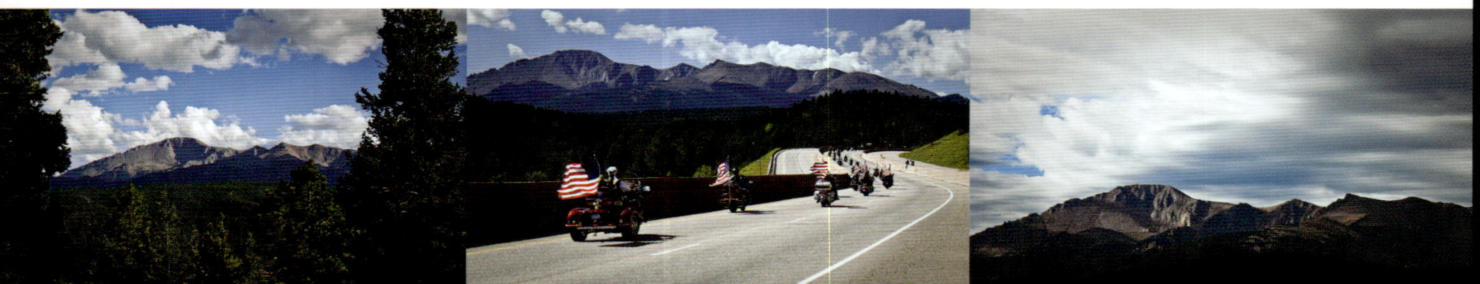

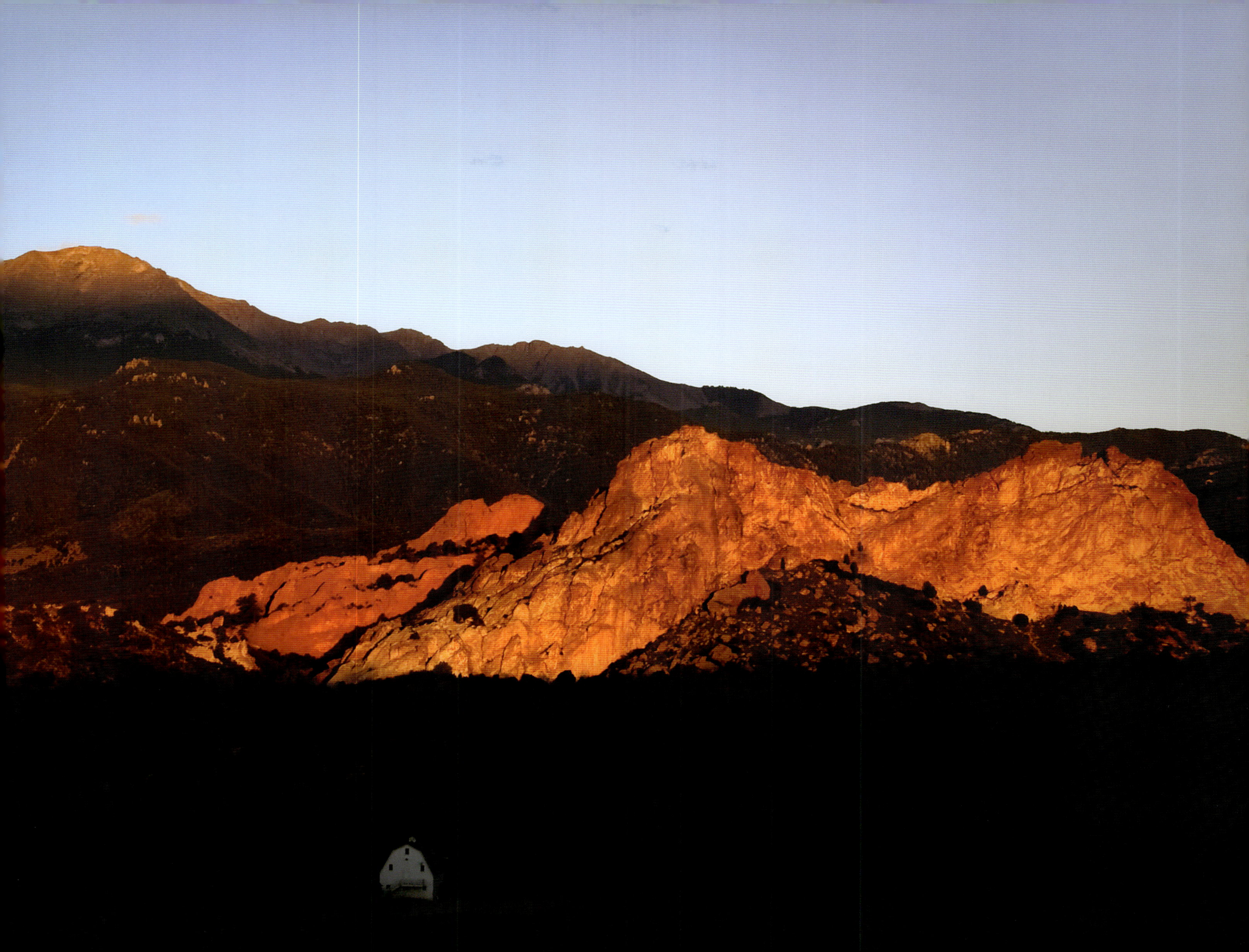

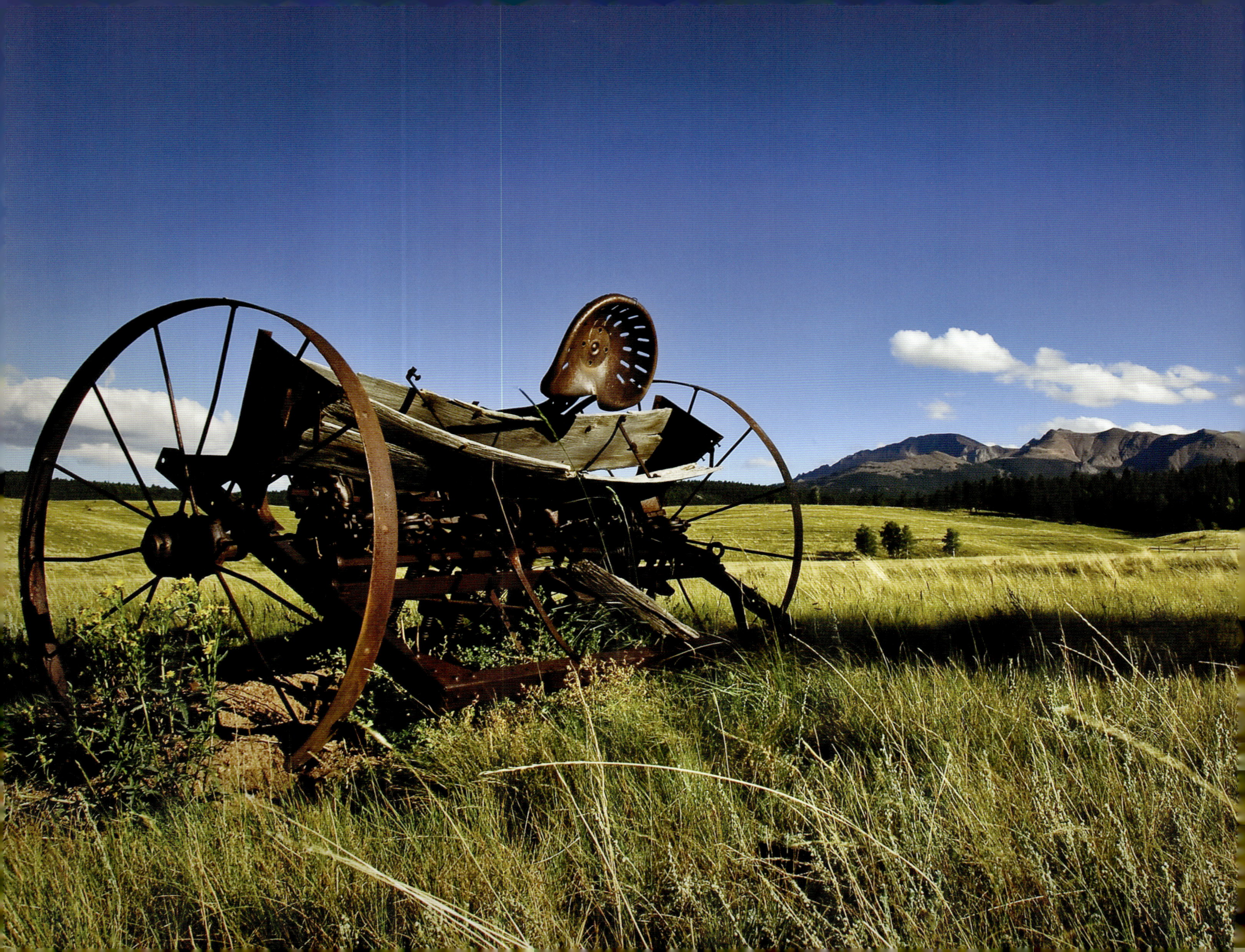

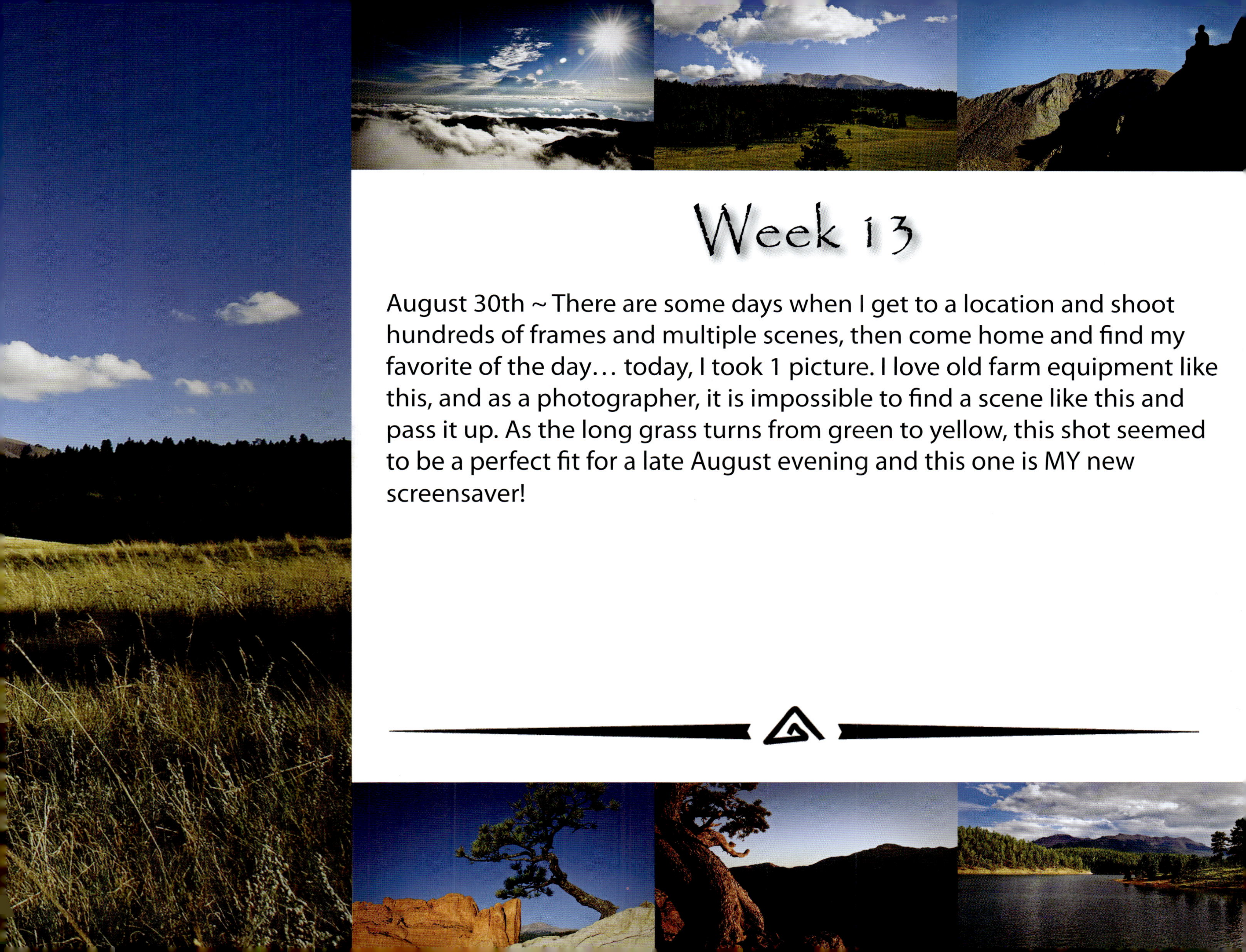

Week 13

August 30th ~ There are some days when I get to a location and shoot hundreds of frames and multiple scenes, then come home and find my favorite of the day... today, I took 1 picture. I love old farm equipment like this, and as a photographer, it is impossible to find a scene like this and pass it up. As the long grass turns from green to yellow, this shot seemed to be a perfect fit for a late August evening and this one is MY new screensaver!

Chapter 2

Fall

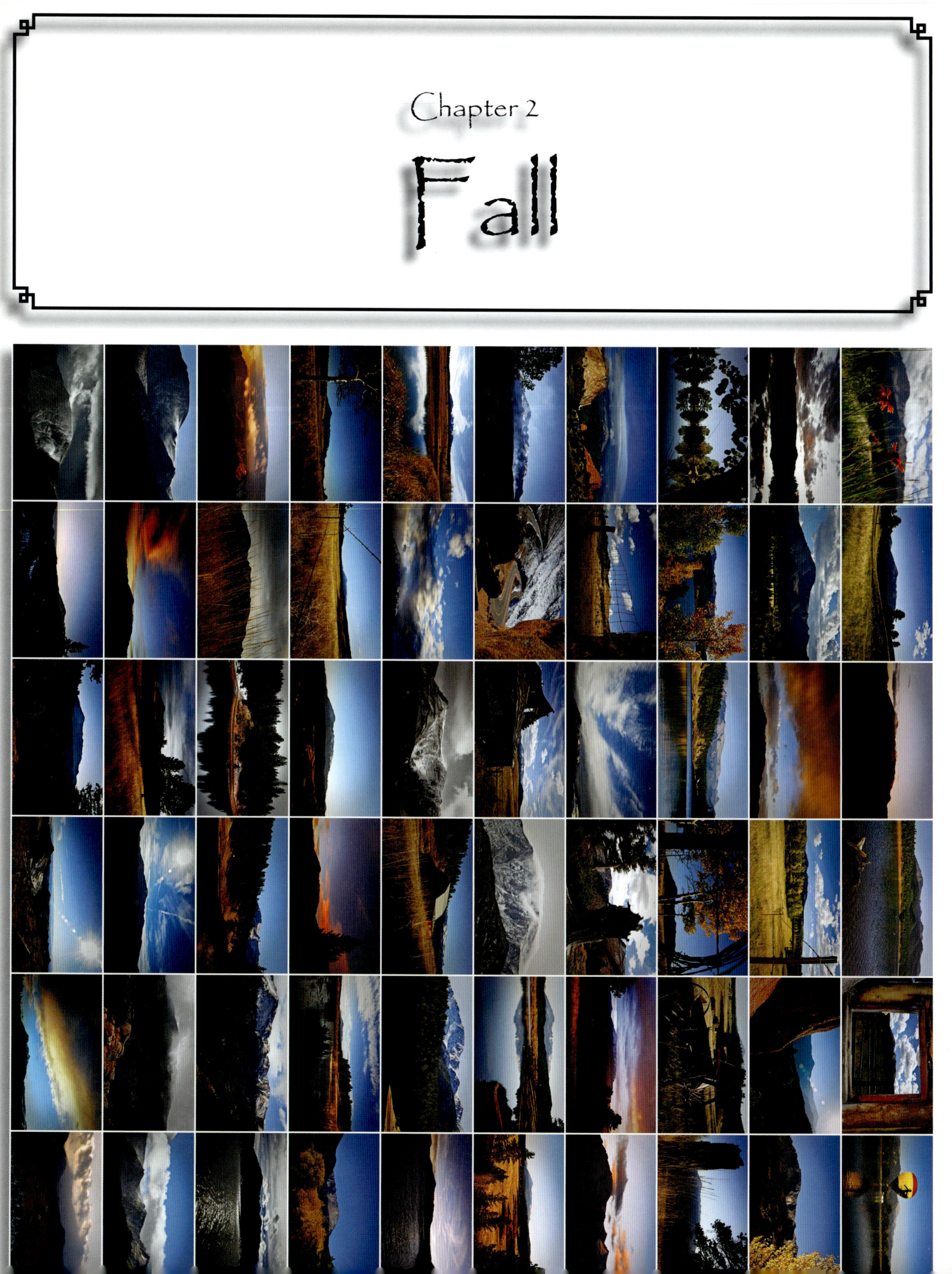

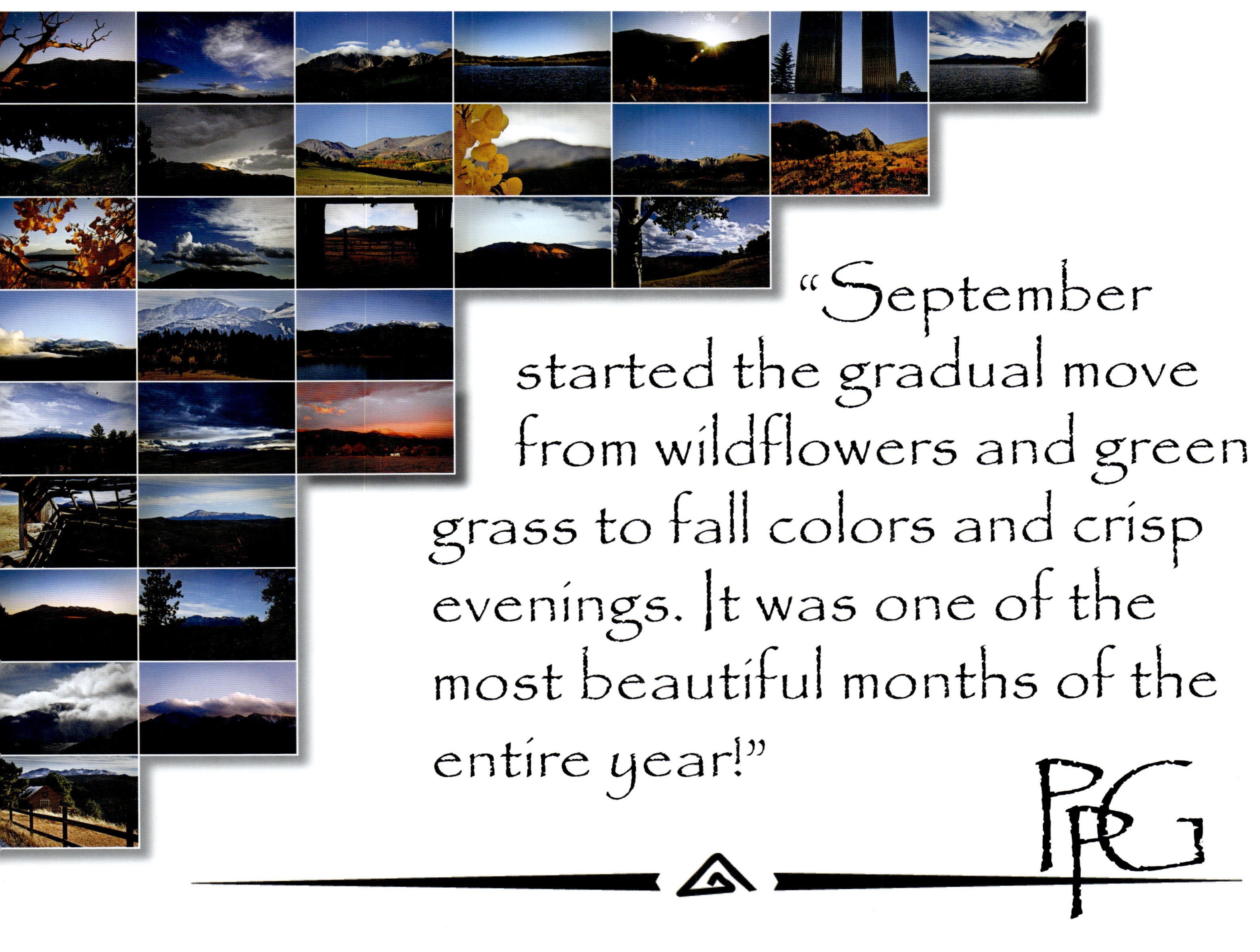
"September started the gradual move from wildflowers and green grass to fall colors and crisp evenings. It was one of the most beautiful months of the entire year!"
PPG

Week 14

September 3rd ~ Ok, maybe I was a little premature with the "fall" word on the first post of the month, but you have to admit there is a chill in the air up here! Just the thought of our long winter ahead made me want to get out and hike tonight. So I hiked all the way around Crystal Reservoir this evening. As I was walking and taking picture after picture, I realized that the cool weather had driven everyone away, and I was the only one on that lake tonight. Once I got home I had to go through the 300+ pictures I had taken and this one photo caught my eye ~ an old tree stump all by itself in the crystal clear water. I laughed for a second and realized that just like this old stump, I was the only thing floating around the reservoir tonight!

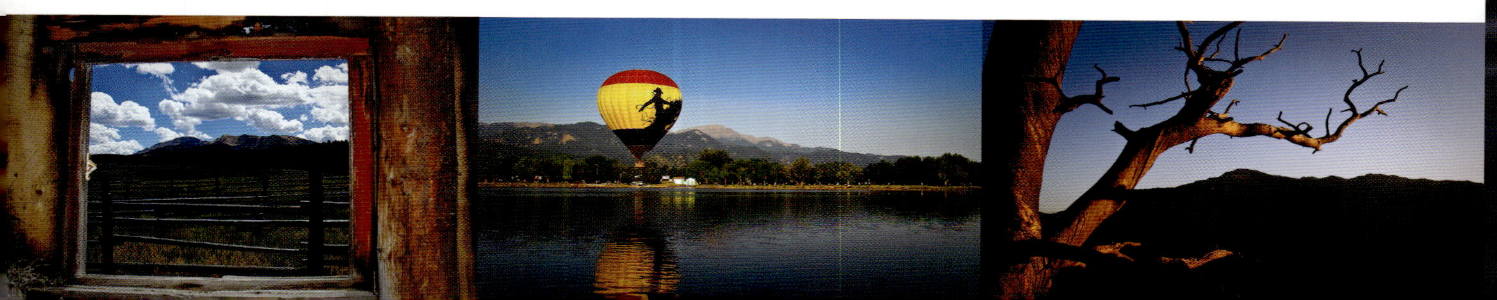

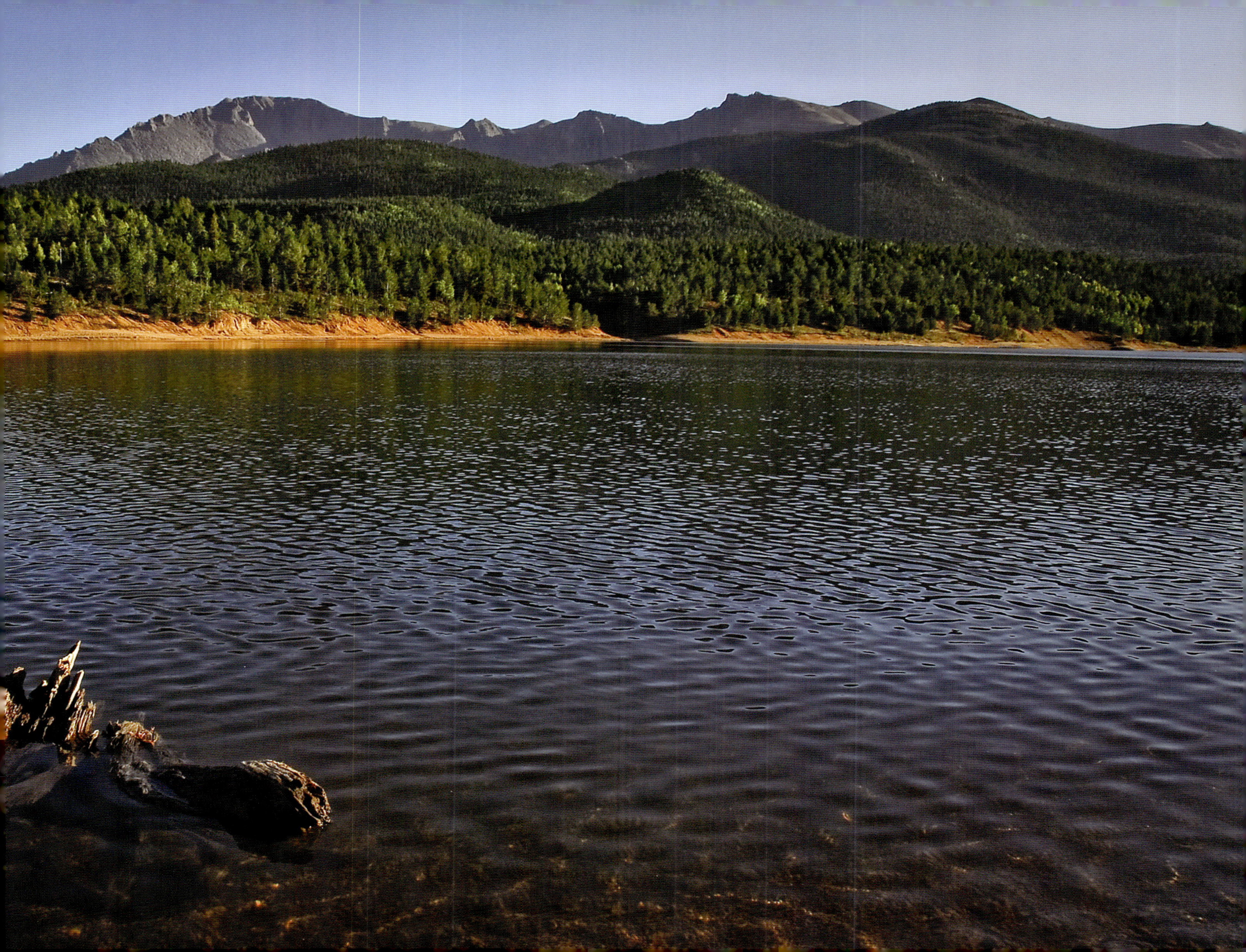

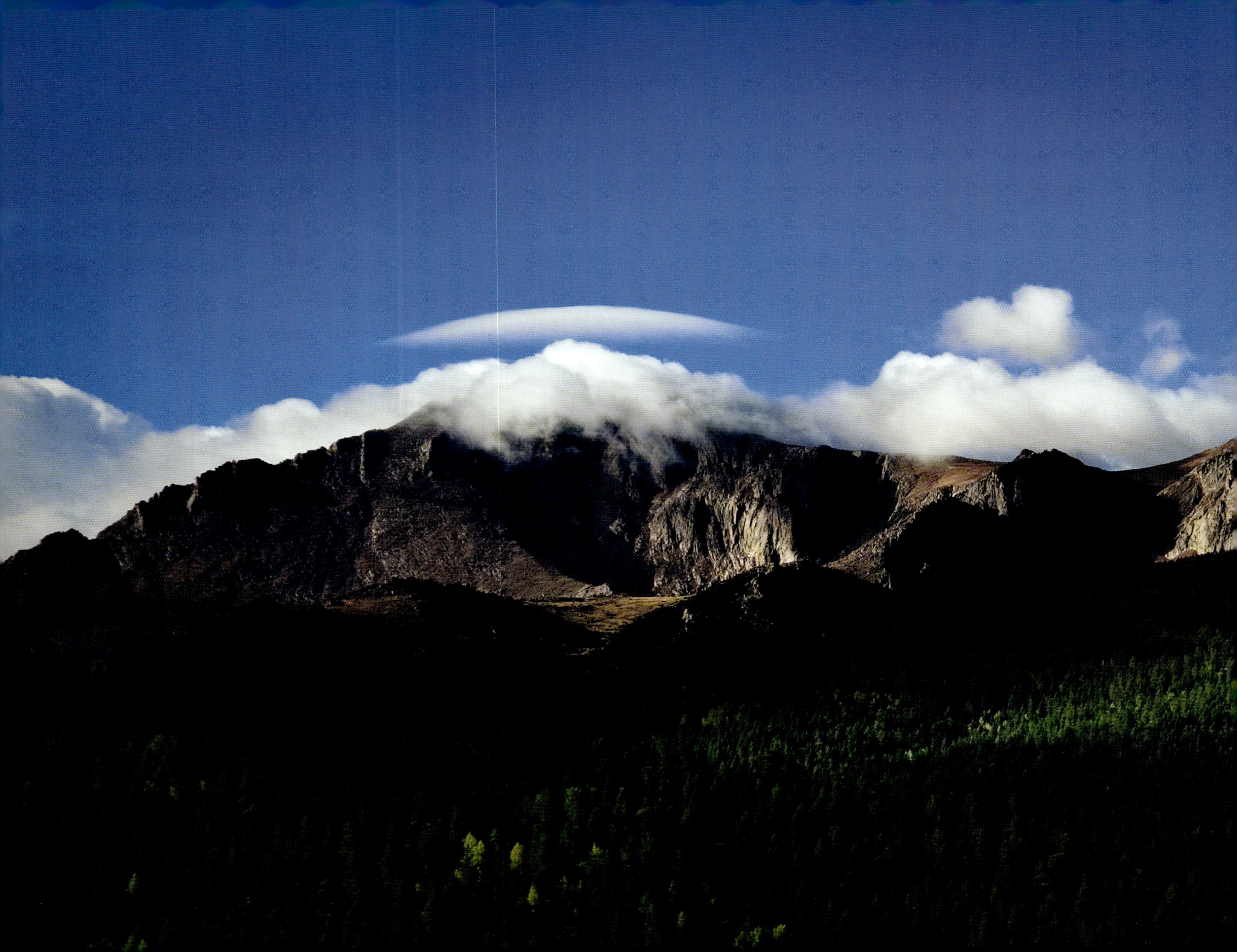

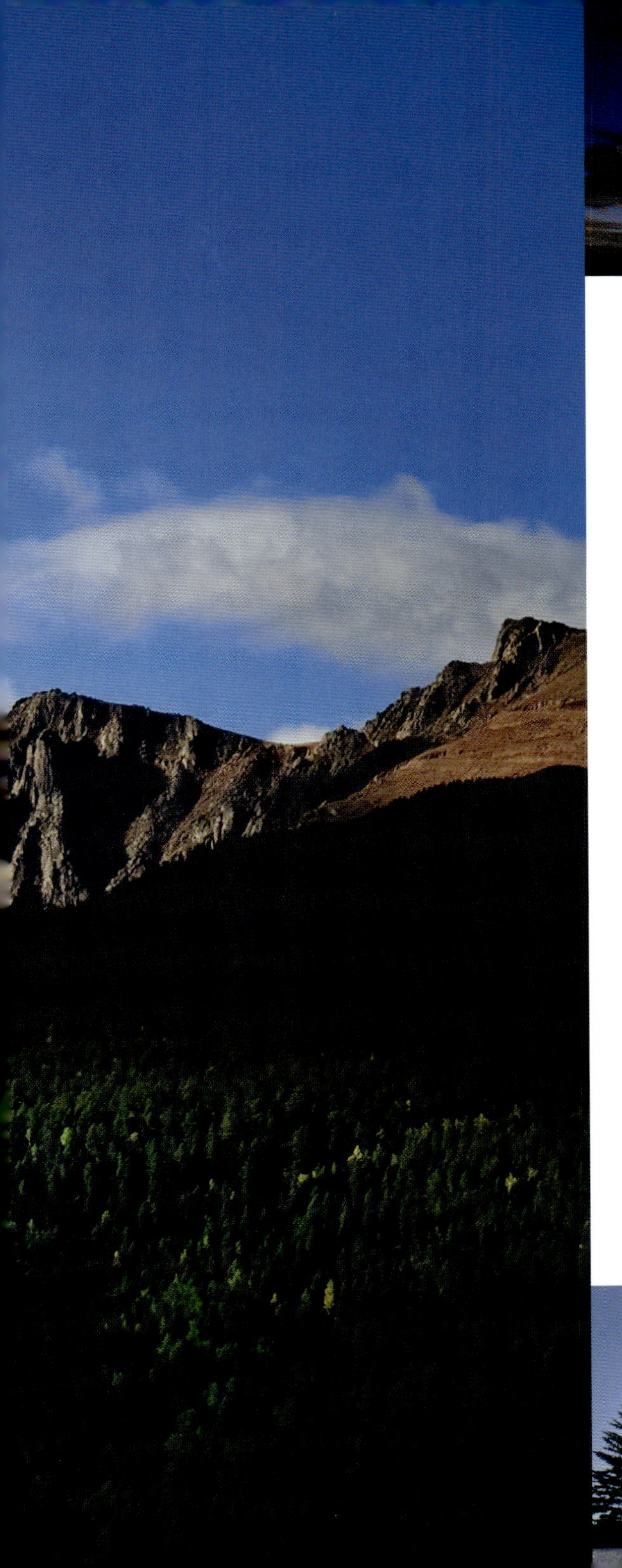

Week 15

September 8th ~ Last year I drove my son to school every day and on my way out of the parking lot, I would sit in traffic waiting my turn at the 4 way stop and watch the Peak. Seeing the Peak every morning like that was a big part of my inspiration for this project and as I dropped him off today, the view of the Peak brought me back to that time. The changing trees were lit up, the sun was low in the morning sky, and as I was setting up for this shot a "cloud cap" started to form right over the summit. I love it when it changes like this right before my eyes!

Week 16

September 18 ~ After yesterday's summer like picture, I thought I should find a way to show off the fall colors up on the Pikes Peak Highway… a little dose of a late September day in Pike National Forest. When you are taking a picture of something as large as the Peak, even a grove of aspens can look small. It took me a while to figure out the best way to capture what I wanted in a shot like this, and I think this really shows the colors. What I love most about the aspens is that when the sunlight shines on an aspen tree, the leaves light up like someone just plugged it into a wall outlet ~ it truly glows!

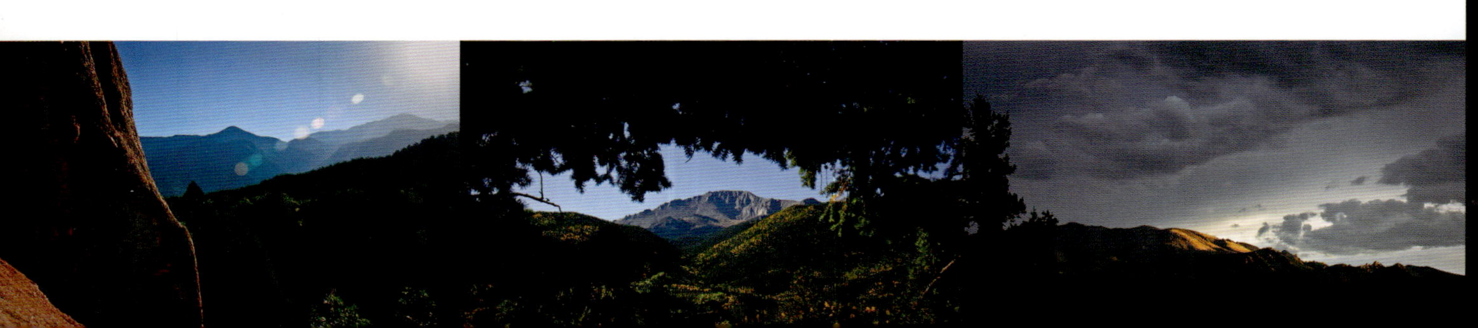

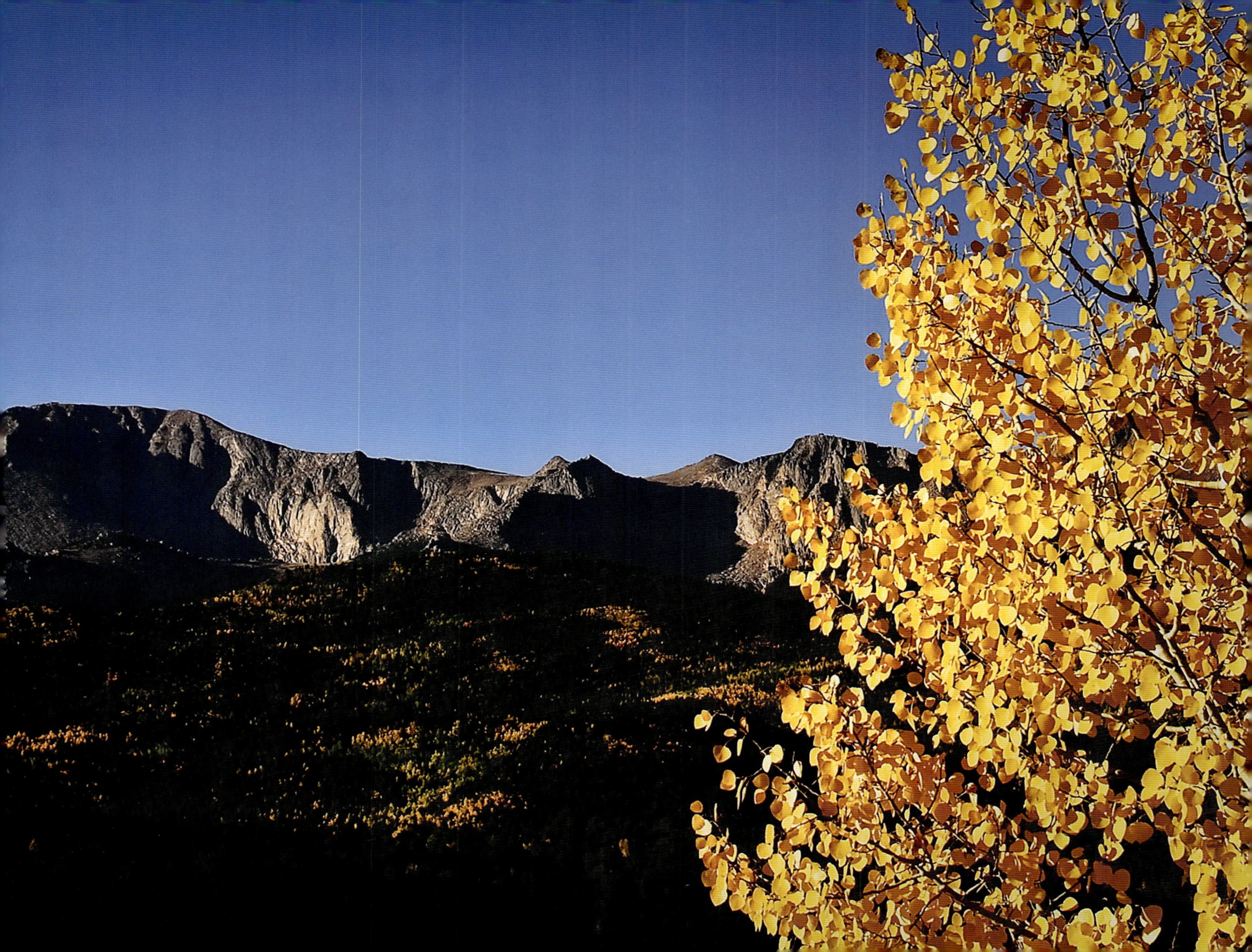

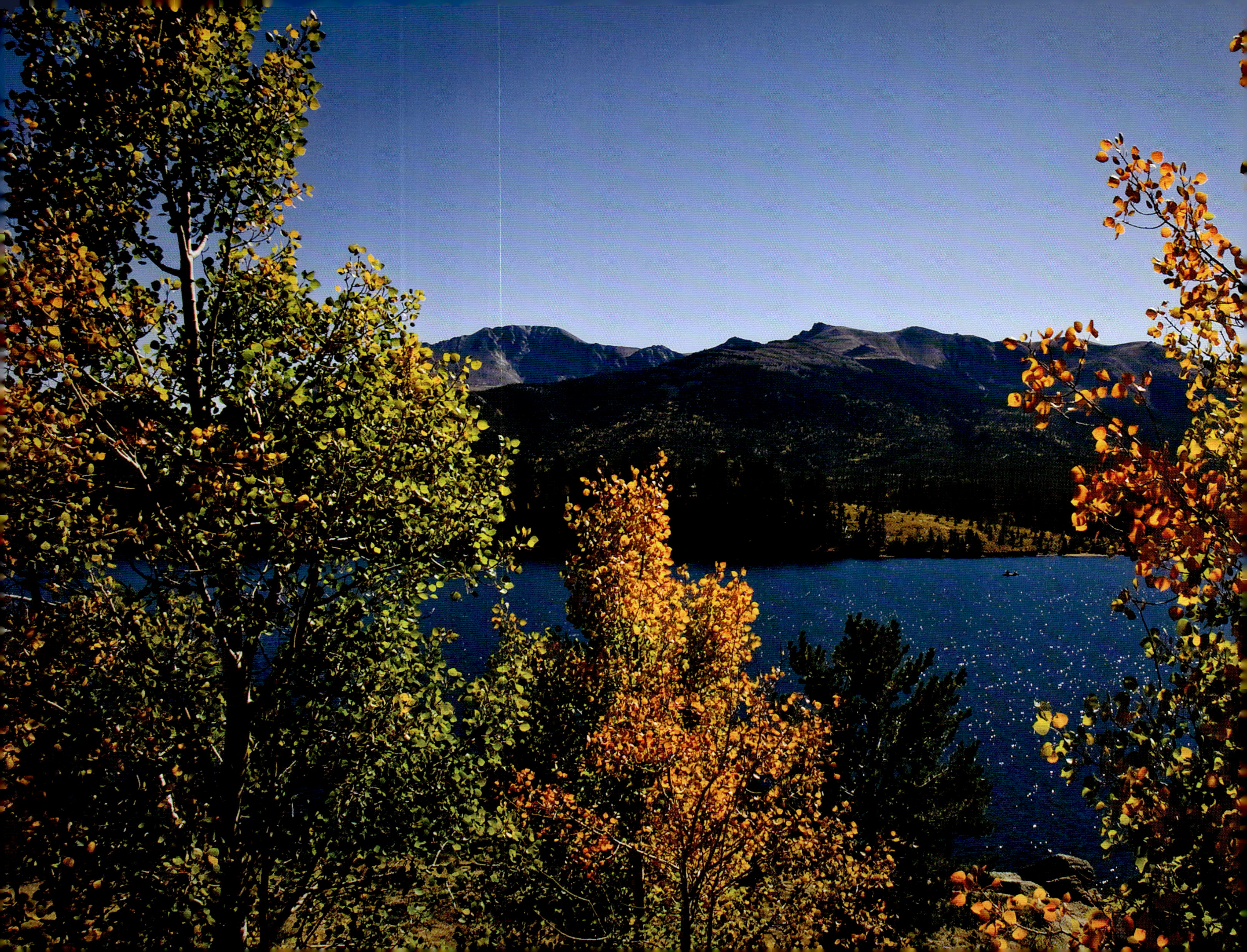

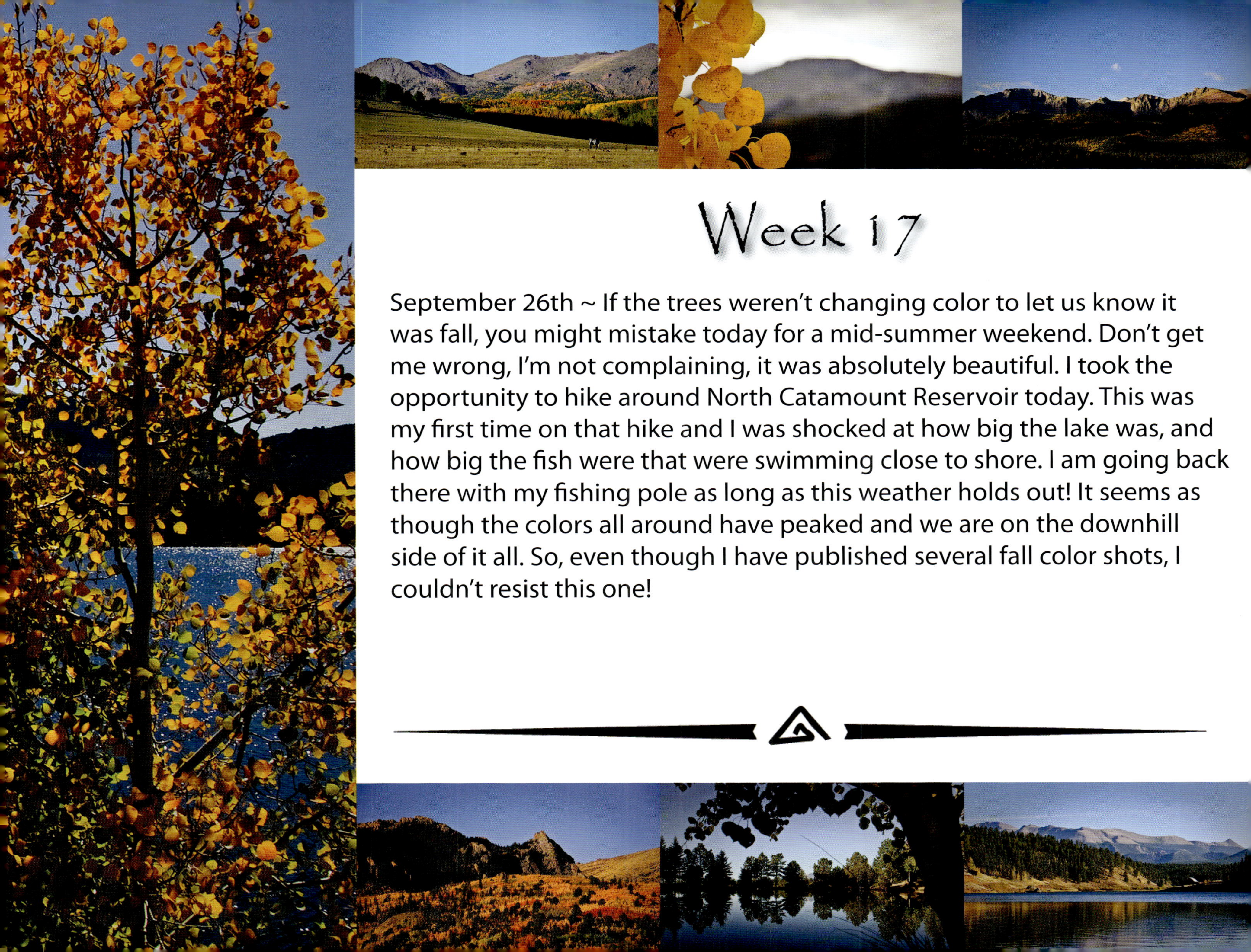

Week 17

September 26th ~ If the trees weren't changing color to let us know it was fall, you might mistake today for a mid-summer weekend. Don't get me wrong, I'm not complaining, it was absolutely beautiful. I took the opportunity to hike around North Catamount Reservoir today. This was my first time on that hike and I was shocked at how big the lake was, and how big the fish were that were swimming close to shore. I am going back there with my fishing pole as long as this weather holds out! It seems as though the colors all around have peaked and we are on the downhill side of it all. So, even though I have published several fall color shots, I couldn't resist this one!

Week 18

October 1st ~ I can't believe I am starting the fifth month of this project today! Tonight was one of those beautifully crisp fall nights that make you dig for your favorite light jacket… it made me feel like I was ready for the snow to start falling at any time. One of my daughters came to visit tonight and she went out with me on my photo shoot/hike. We had such a great time! I love it when my kids come with me to take photos; we seem to discover things they have never seen or done right in our own backyard. One of the reasons I love this project so much is that it is such a gift to be able to show someone beauty that has been around them their entire lives yet never seen ~ but it is magical when it is your own kids.

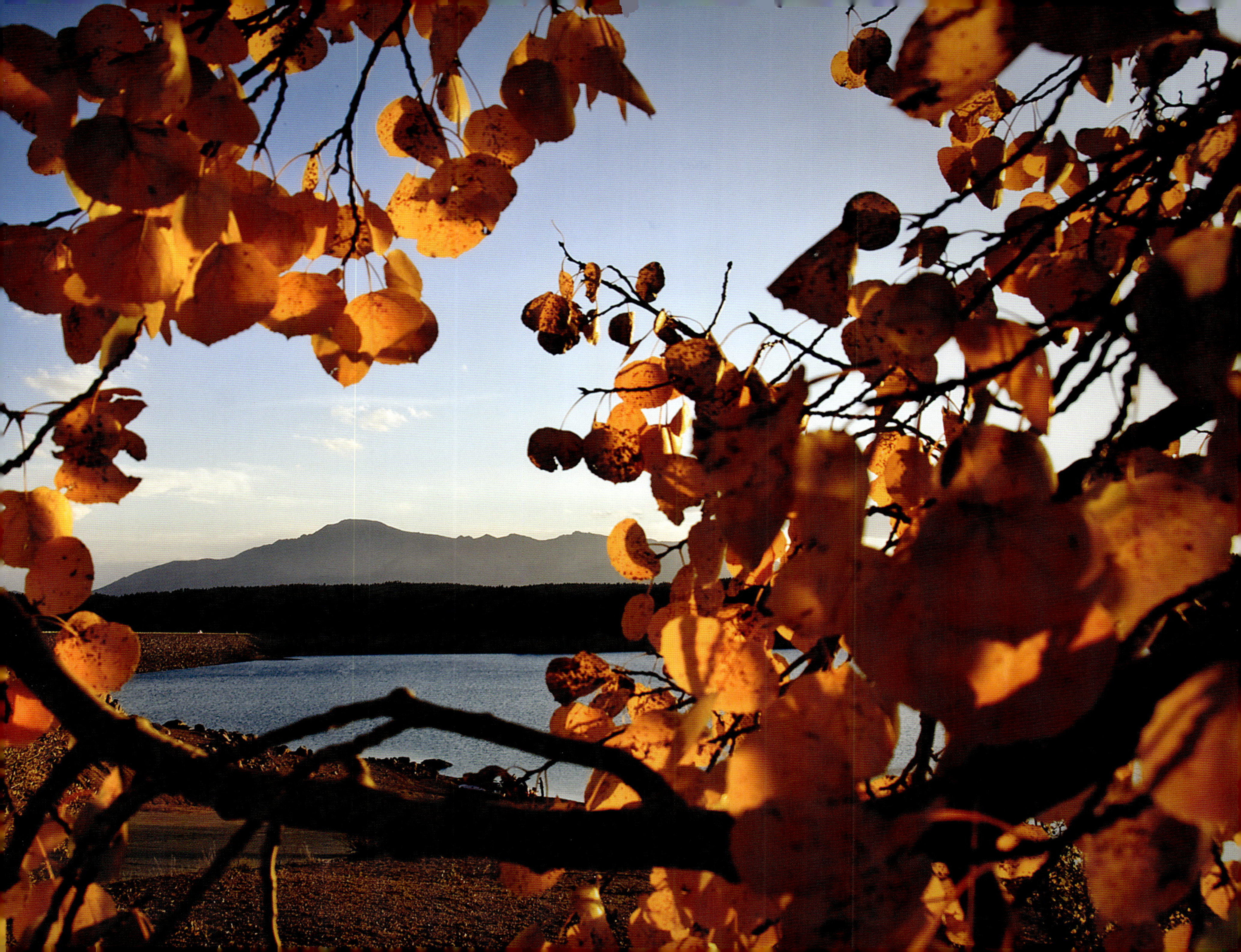

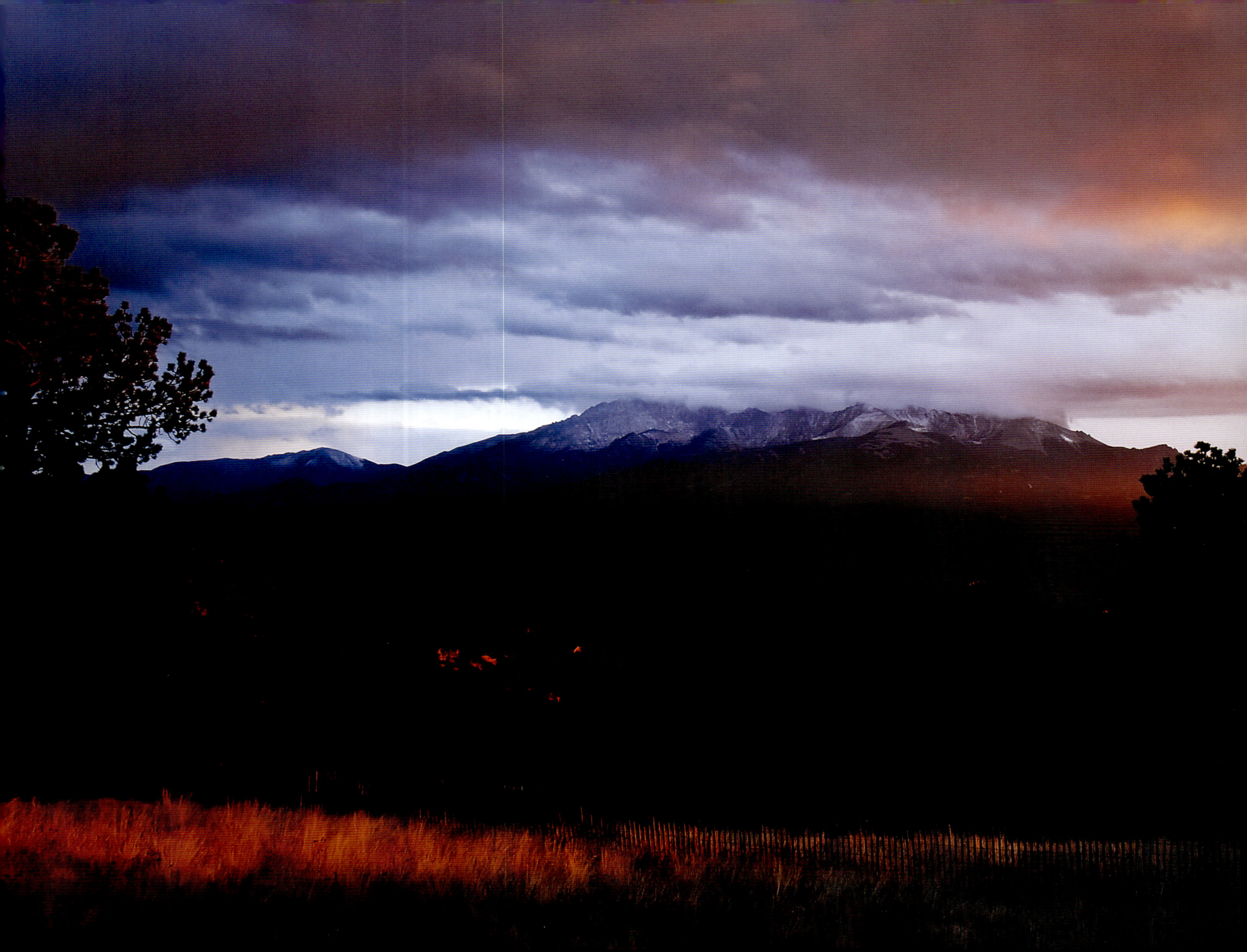

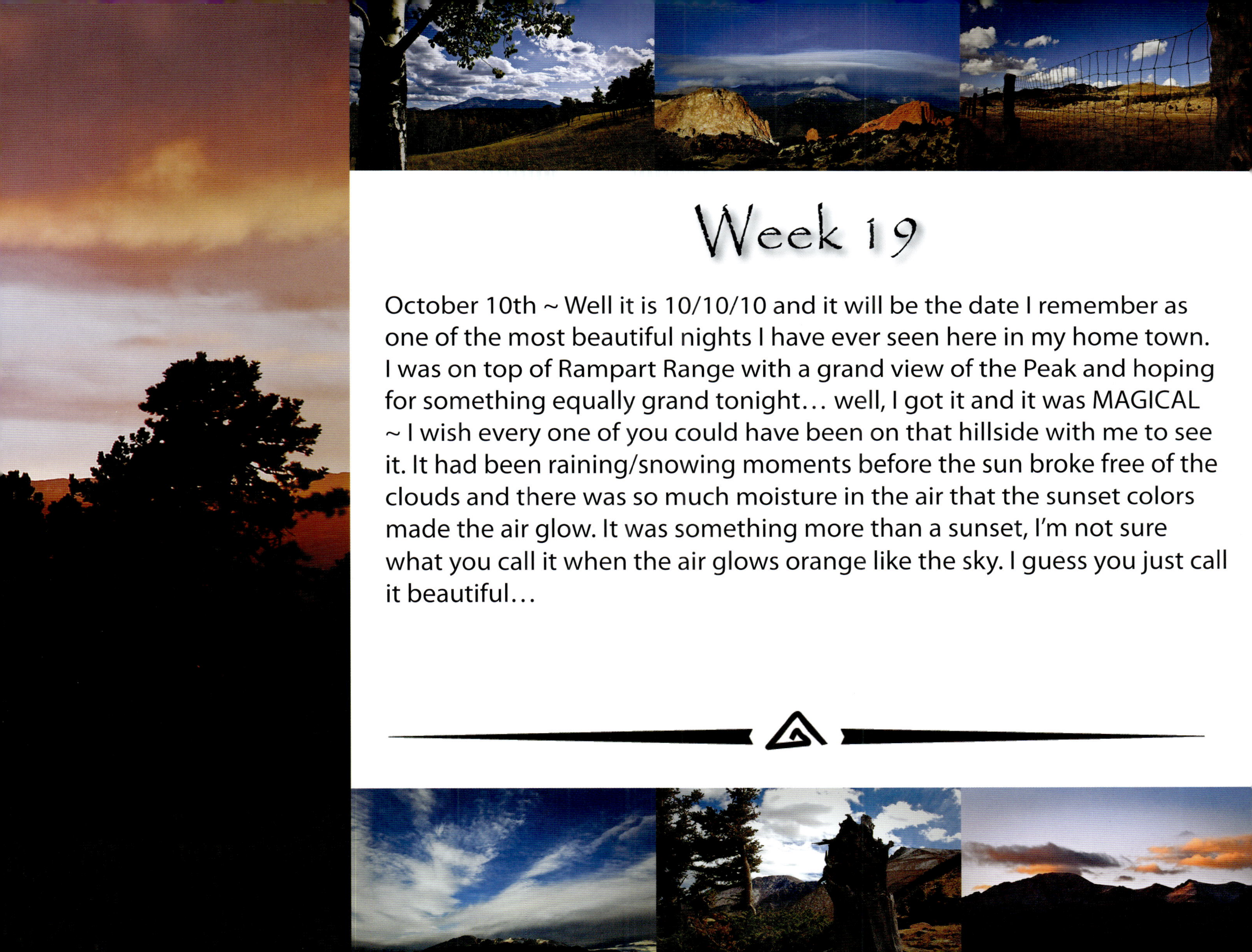

Week 19

October 10th ~ Well it is 10/10/10 and it will be the date I remember as one of the most beautiful nights I have ever seen here in my home town. I was on top of Rampart Range with a grand view of the Peak and hoping for something equally grand tonight… well, I got it and it was MAGICAL ~ I wish every one of you could have been on that hillside with me to see it. It had been raining/snowing moments before the sun broke free of the clouds and there was so much moisture in the air that the sunset colors made the air glow. It was something more than a sunset, I'm not sure what you call it when the air glows orange like the sky. I guess you just call it beautiful…

Week 20

October 13th ~ I don't take shots in the middle of the day as a general rule, but today the mid day sun made the new snow seem like you could just reach out and scoop up a snowball. And there was something about the lighting and the snow that made the Peak seem larger than life. So I decided to try to find a way to capture that. I went to a few locations I had been scouting, and when I got to this one I knew it would be my shot. What I loved about this shot was the way the foreground is in such contrast to the Peak behind it. There are two totally different seasons going on in this photo and it captures October in the Rockies. Blizzards one day, sunny and 75 the next… I love this time of year!

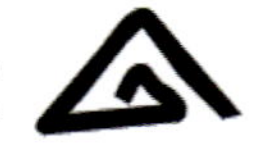

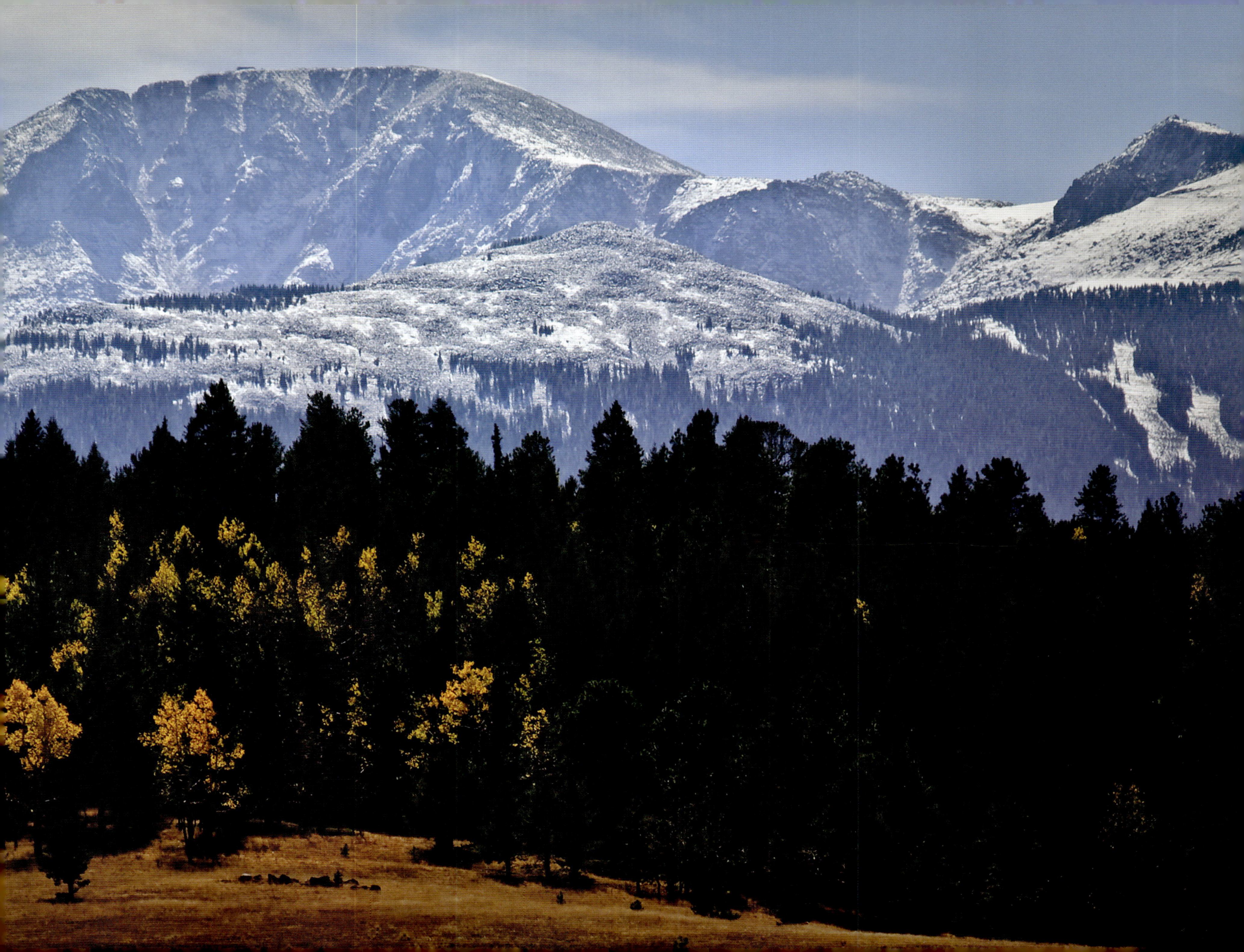

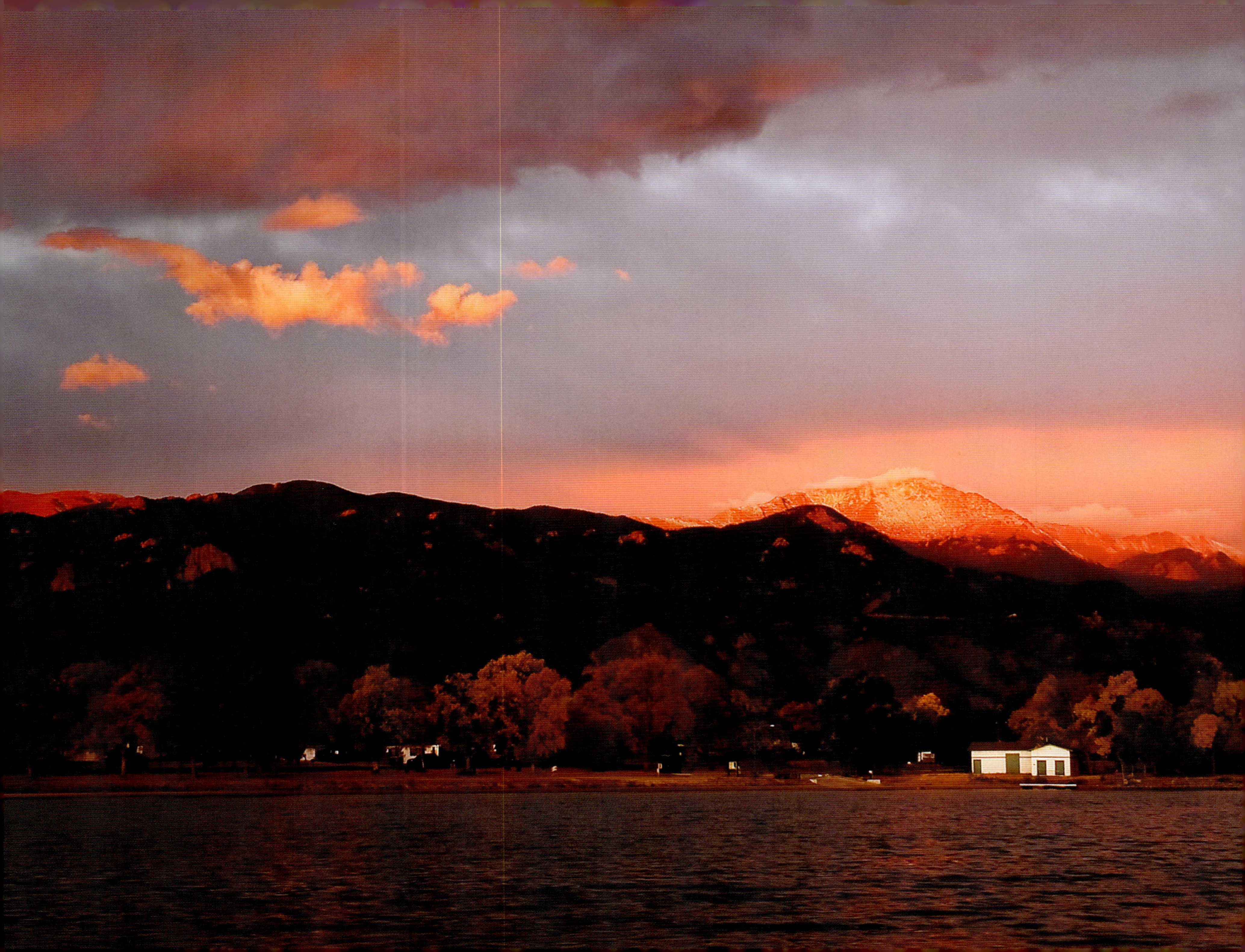

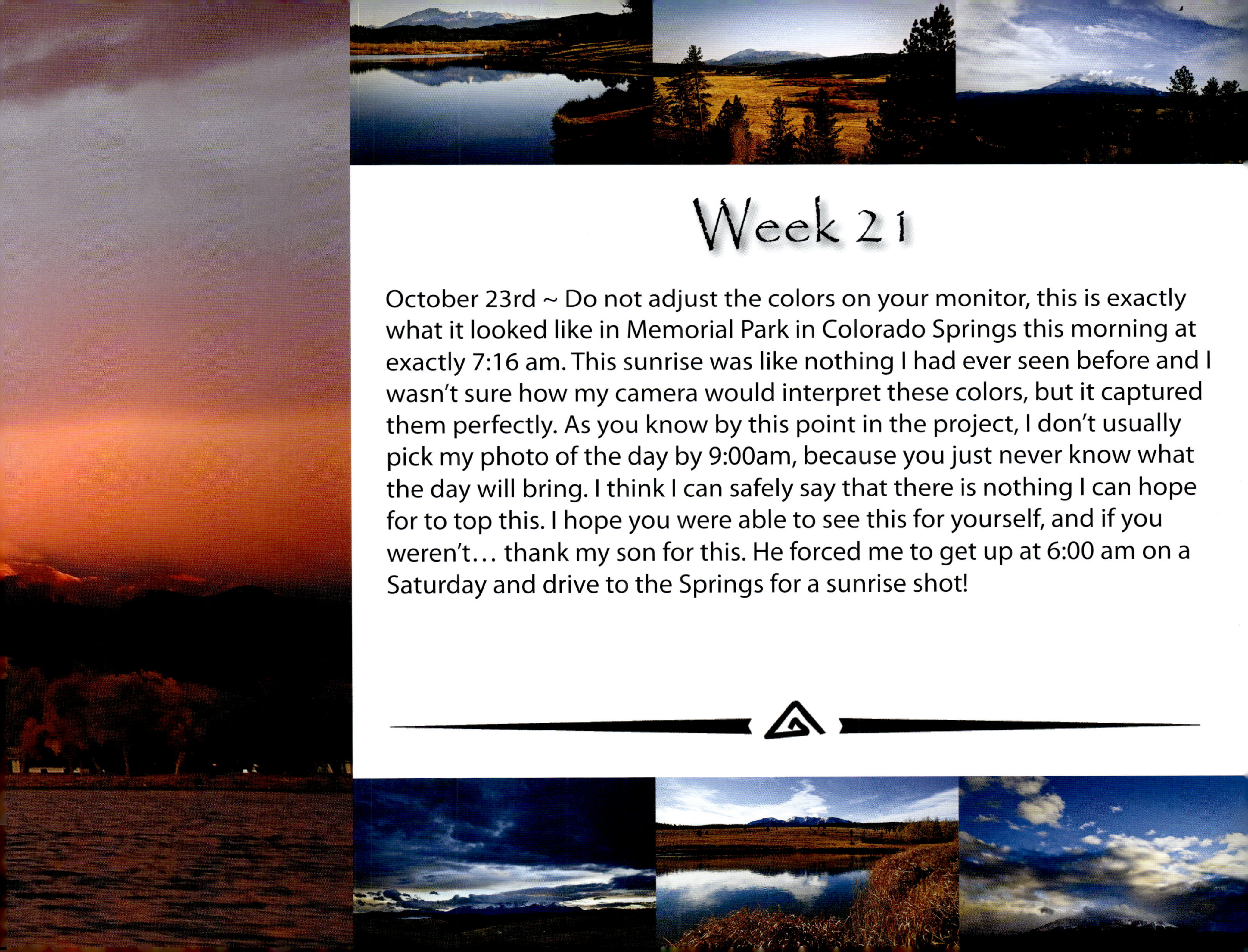

Week 21

October 23rd ~ Do not adjust the colors on your monitor, this is exactly what it looked like in Memorial Park in Colorado Springs this morning at exactly 7:16 am. This sunrise was like nothing I had ever seen before and I wasn't sure how my camera would interpret these colors, but it captured them perfectly. As you know by this point in the project, I don't usually pick my photo of the day by 9:00am, because you just never know what the day will bring. I think I can safely say that there is nothing I can hope for to top this. I hope you were able to see this for yourself, and if you weren't… thank my son for this. He forced me to get up at 6:00 am on a Saturday and drive to the Springs for a sunrise shot!

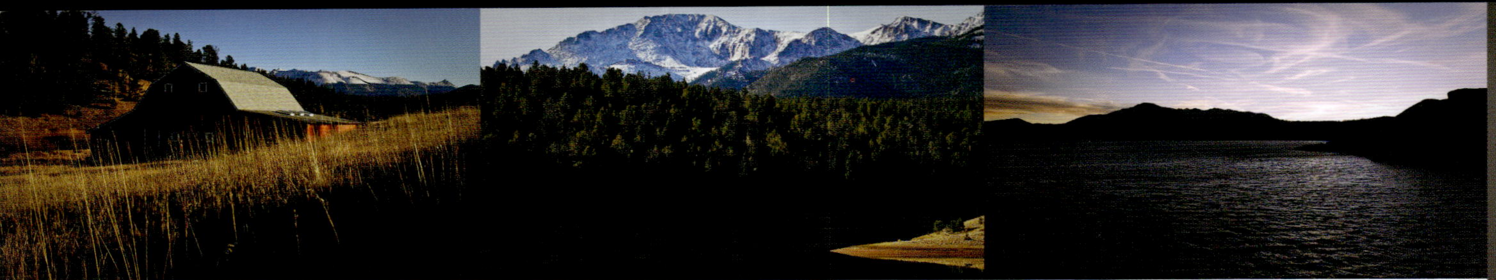

Week 22

October 26th ~ I think I spoke too soon last night when I mentioned how cold it was, because today it was below zero on top of the Peak and the wind blew with gusts well over 50 mph up there. I thought about how to capture this (and not be up there to do it) and decided to head to a location that would get me good and close…and show the snow that fell yesterday blowing off the mountain today. Since Halloween is right around the corner, I thought the Devil's Playground would be the perfect feature to focus my camera on. People ask me all the time where it gets its name from, and it comes from the way lightning jumps from rock to rock in the boulder fields of this formation. Pikes Peak is one of the most active lightning regions in the US, and the area known as Devil's Playground is one of the most active on the mountain.

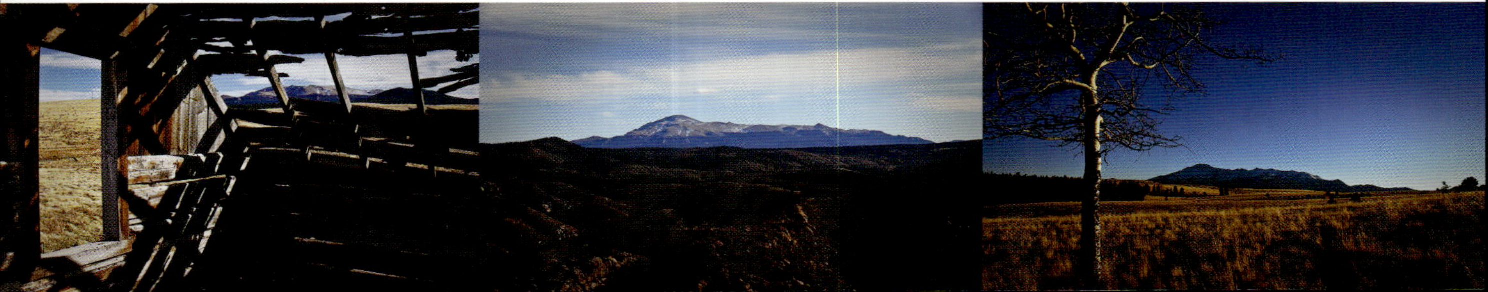

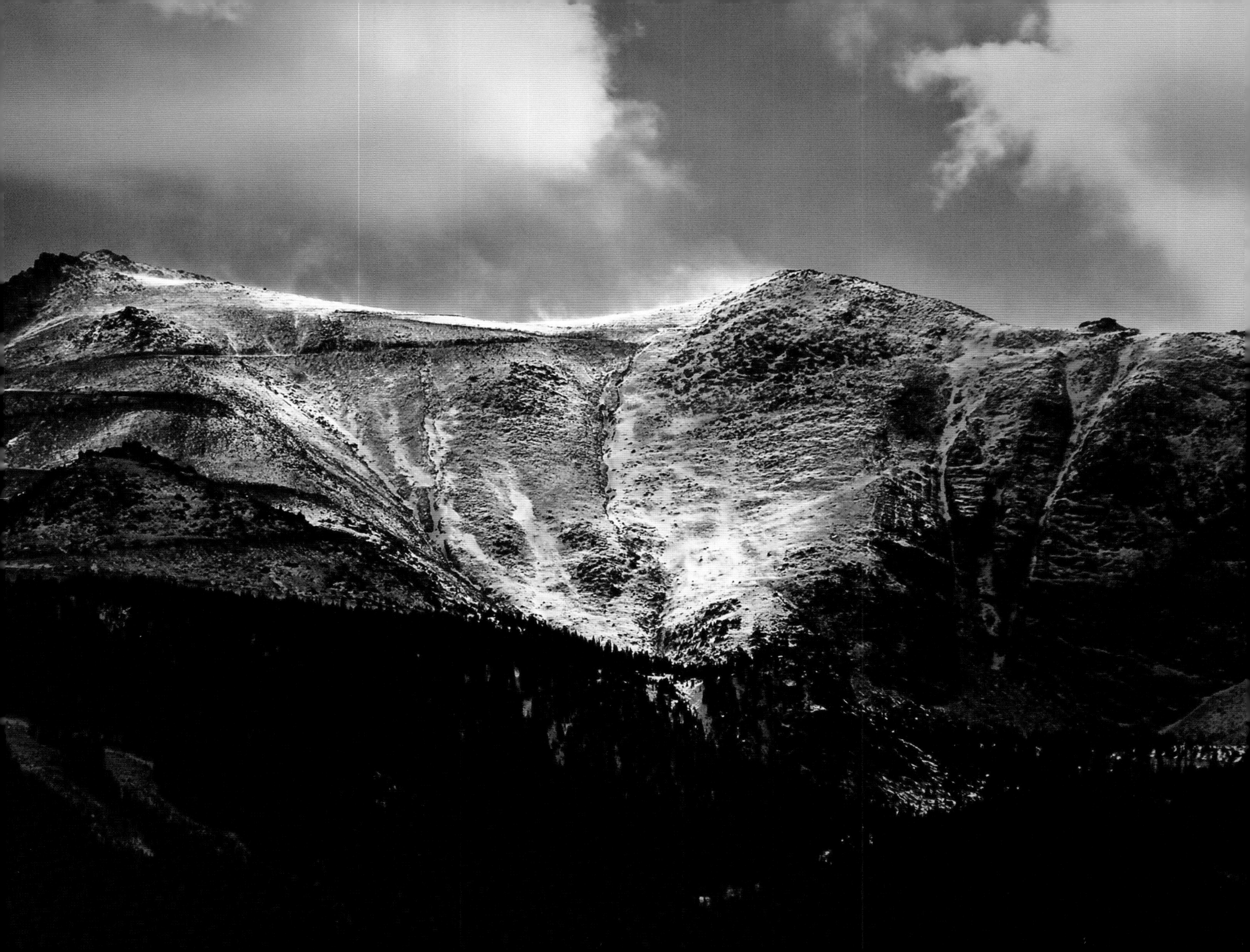

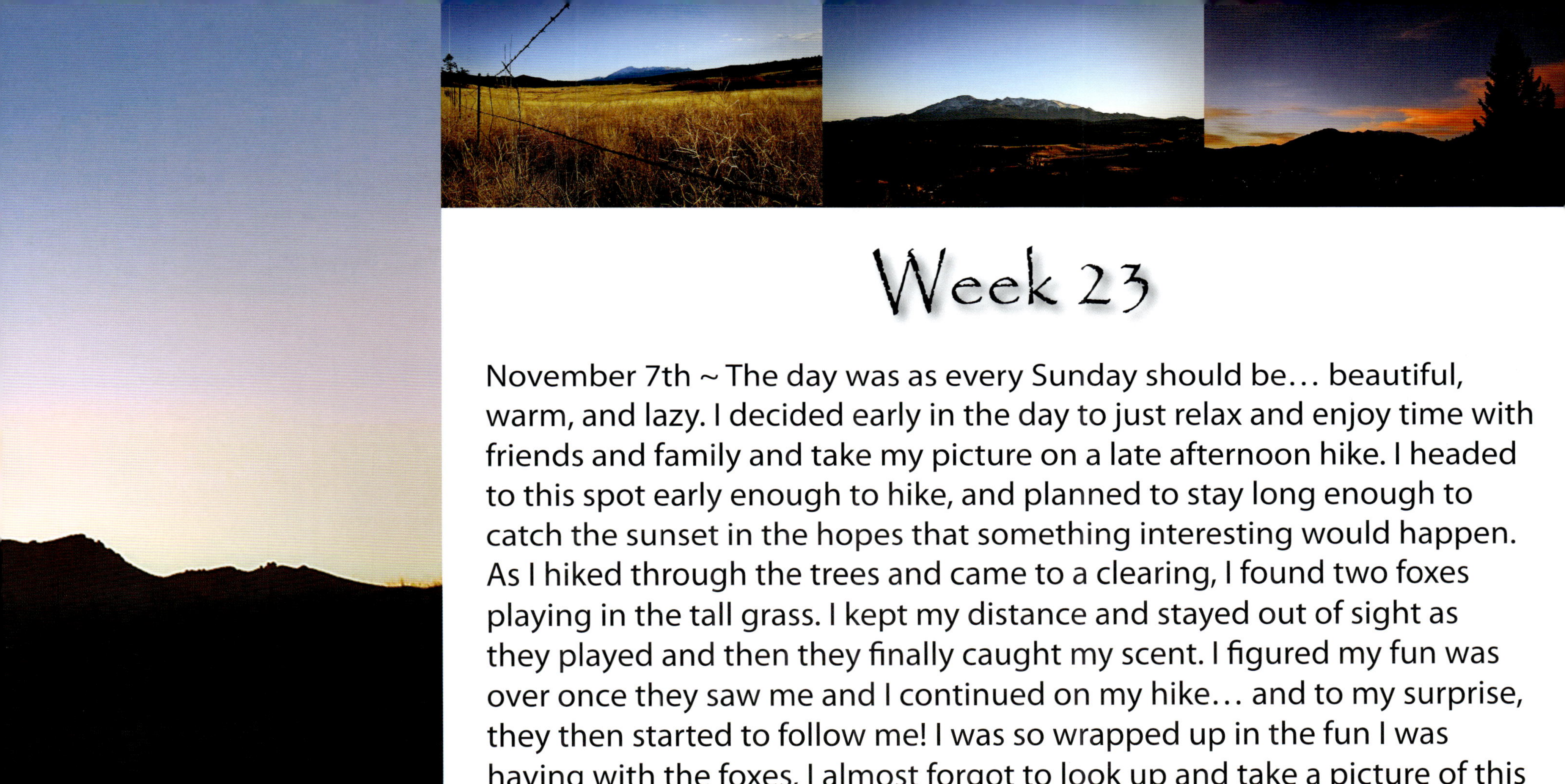

Week 23

November 7th ~ The day was as every Sunday should be… beautiful, warm, and lazy. I decided early in the day to just relax and enjoy time with friends and family and take my picture on a late afternoon hike. I headed to this spot early enough to hike, and planned to stay long enough to catch the sunset in the hopes that something interesting would happen. As I hiked through the trees and came to a clearing, I found two foxes playing in the tall grass. I kept my distance and stayed out of sight as they played and then they finally caught my scent. I figured my fun was over once they saw me and I continued on my hike… and to my surprise, they then started to follow me! I was so wrapped up in the fun I was having with the foxes, I almost forgot to look up and take a picture of this wonderfully serene sunset.

Week 24

November 9th ~ This morning was my first attempt at a sunrise shot since we rolled the clocks back. I went North so I could catch a South-East view and be sure to get a little color. The colors peaked over the Springs and I caught both: the colors and the cloud capped mountain in a great photo… then headed back home. As I was driving back the cloud cap over the mountain created a second sunrise of sorts. I drove like crazy to get to a spot with a clear view and was lucky to capture the second sunrise of the morning. I wasn't sure what to expect when I went out this morning, but I sure wasn't expecting two sunrises!

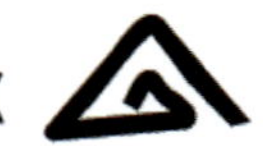

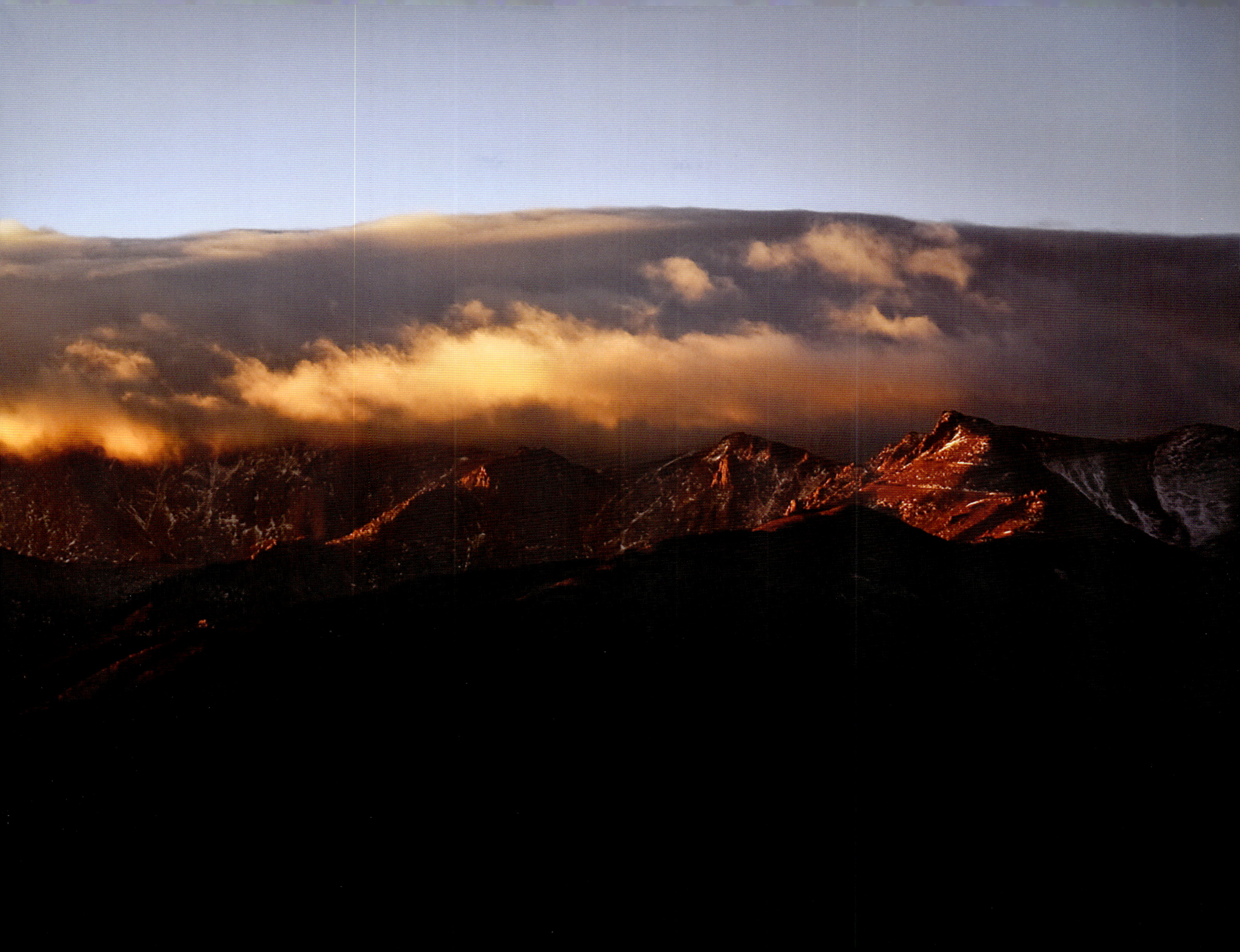

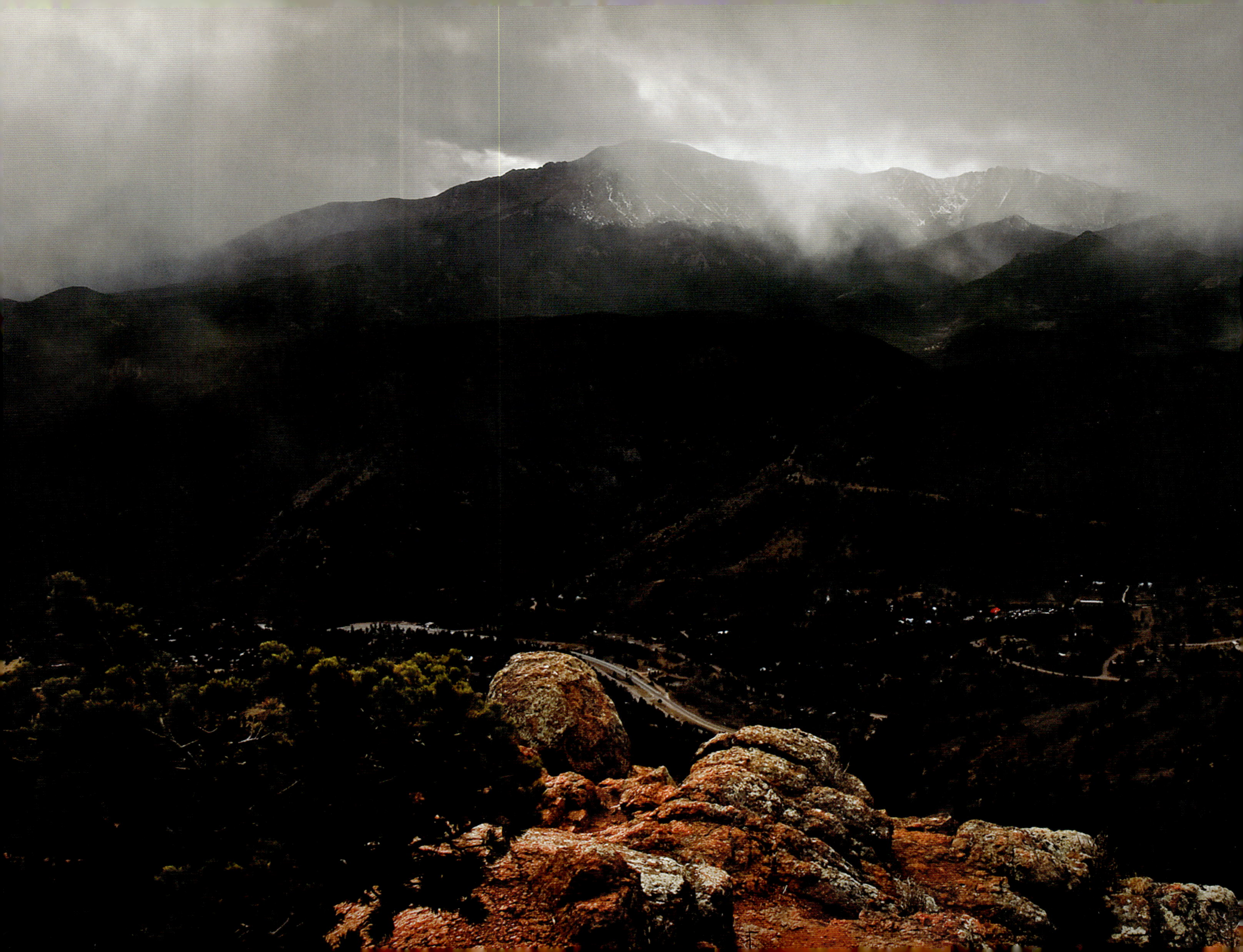

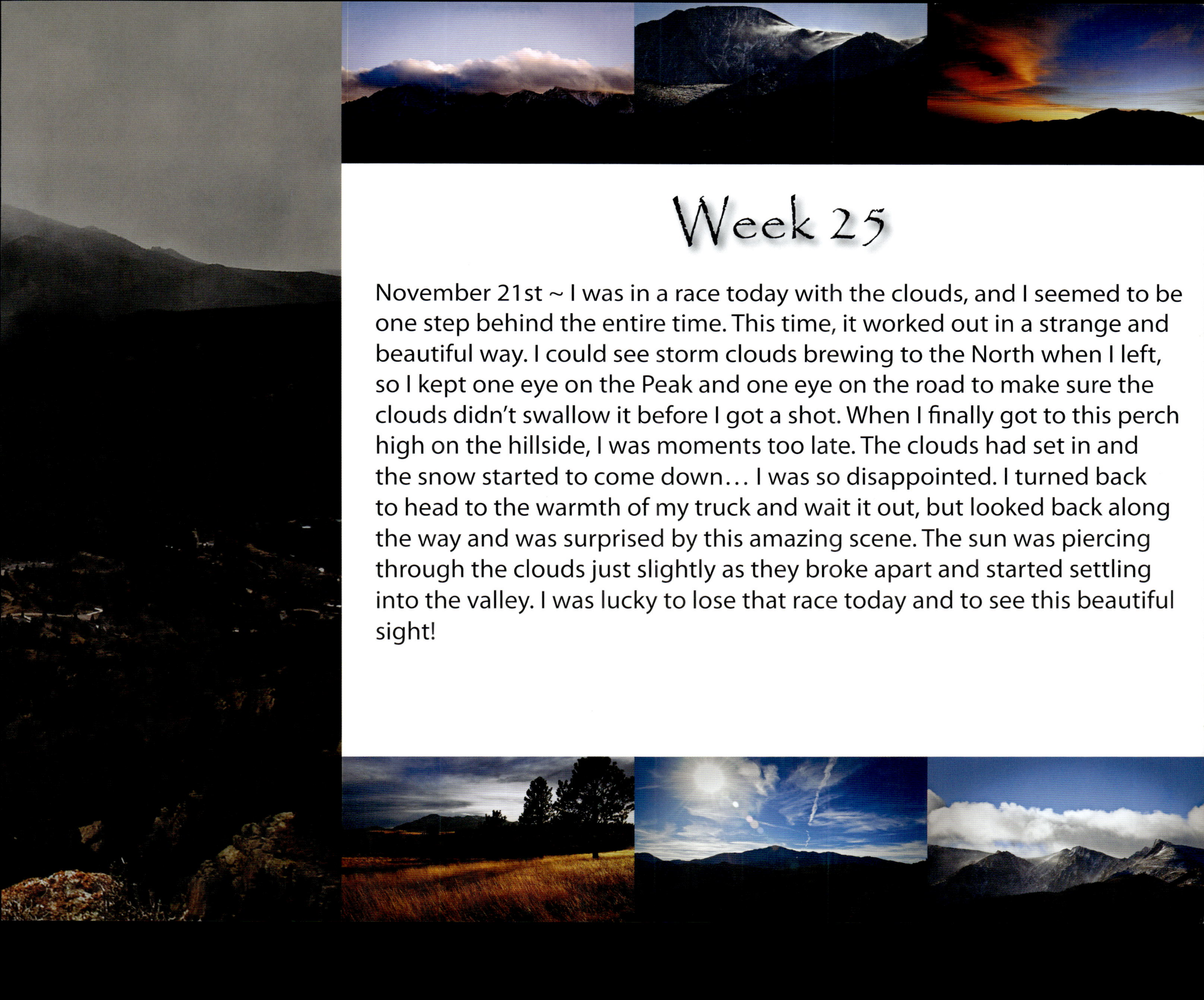

Week 25

November 21st ~ I was in a race today with the clouds, and I seemed to be one step behind the entire time. This time, it worked out in a strange and beautiful way. I could see storm clouds brewing to the North when I left, so I kept one eye on the Peak and one eye on the road to make sure the clouds didn't swallow it before I got a shot. When I finally got to this perch high on the hillside, I was moments too late. The clouds had set in and the snow started to come down… I was so disappointed. I turned back to head to the warmth of my truck and wait it out, but looked back along the way and was surprised by this amazing scene. The sun was piercing through the clouds just slightly as they broke apart and started settling into the valley. I was lucky to lose that race today and to see this beautiful sight!

Week 26

November 23rd ~ The changing seasons have created a lot of new challenges for me with this project, and at this point I think the biggest challenge is the changing light. As a photographer, lighting is everything, so it has forced me to get out and explore how the lighting impacts some old locations and pushes me to find new ones. It is a bit of a rediscovery and today I went to a spot I had been to many times before, but never noticed this view. The out-building and the fence line were a perfect addition to the shot and I loved the way all of the elements came together in this scene. What I loved most about this shot is that I am 177 days into this project and still finding new and interesting locations right in my own back yard.

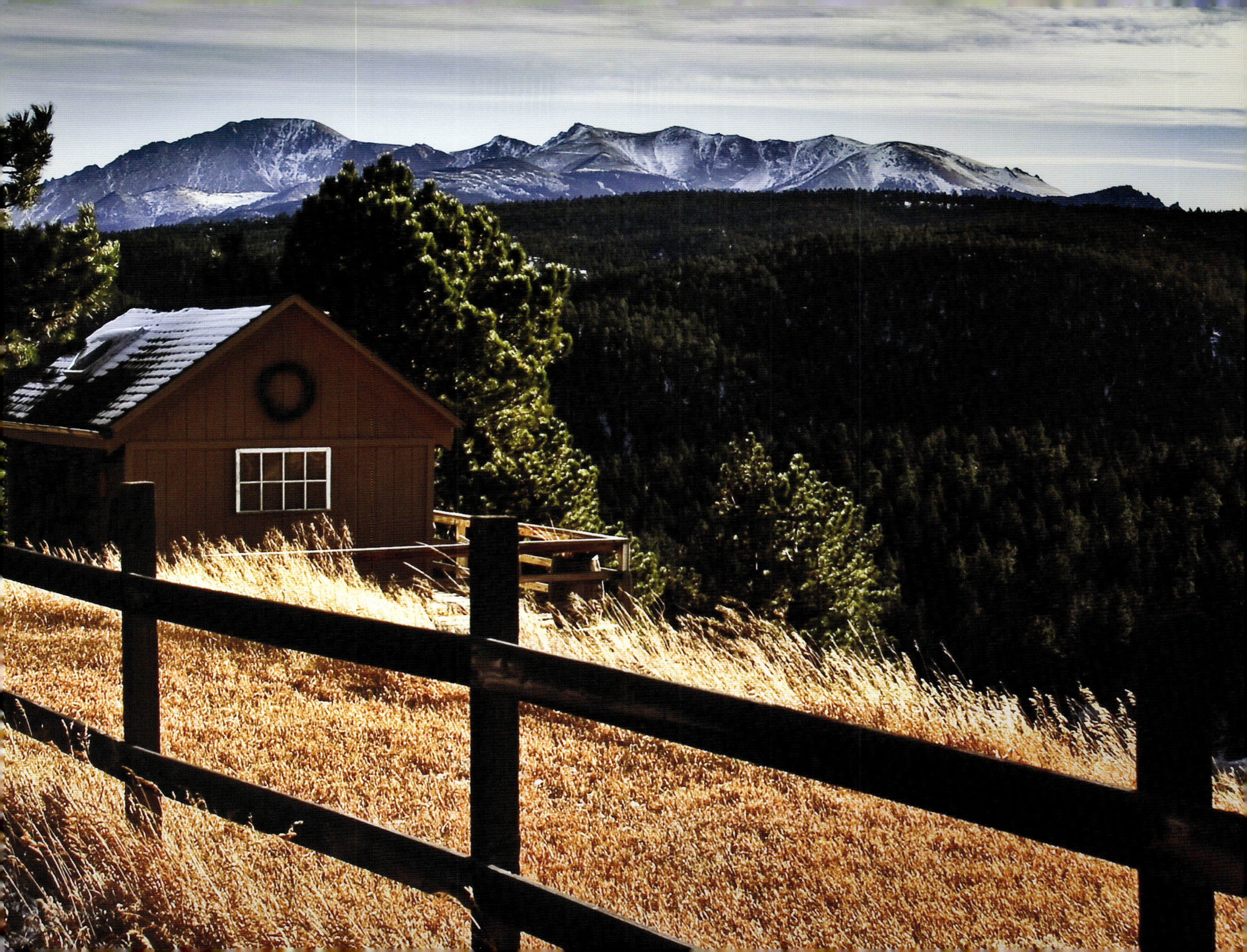

Chapter 3

Winter

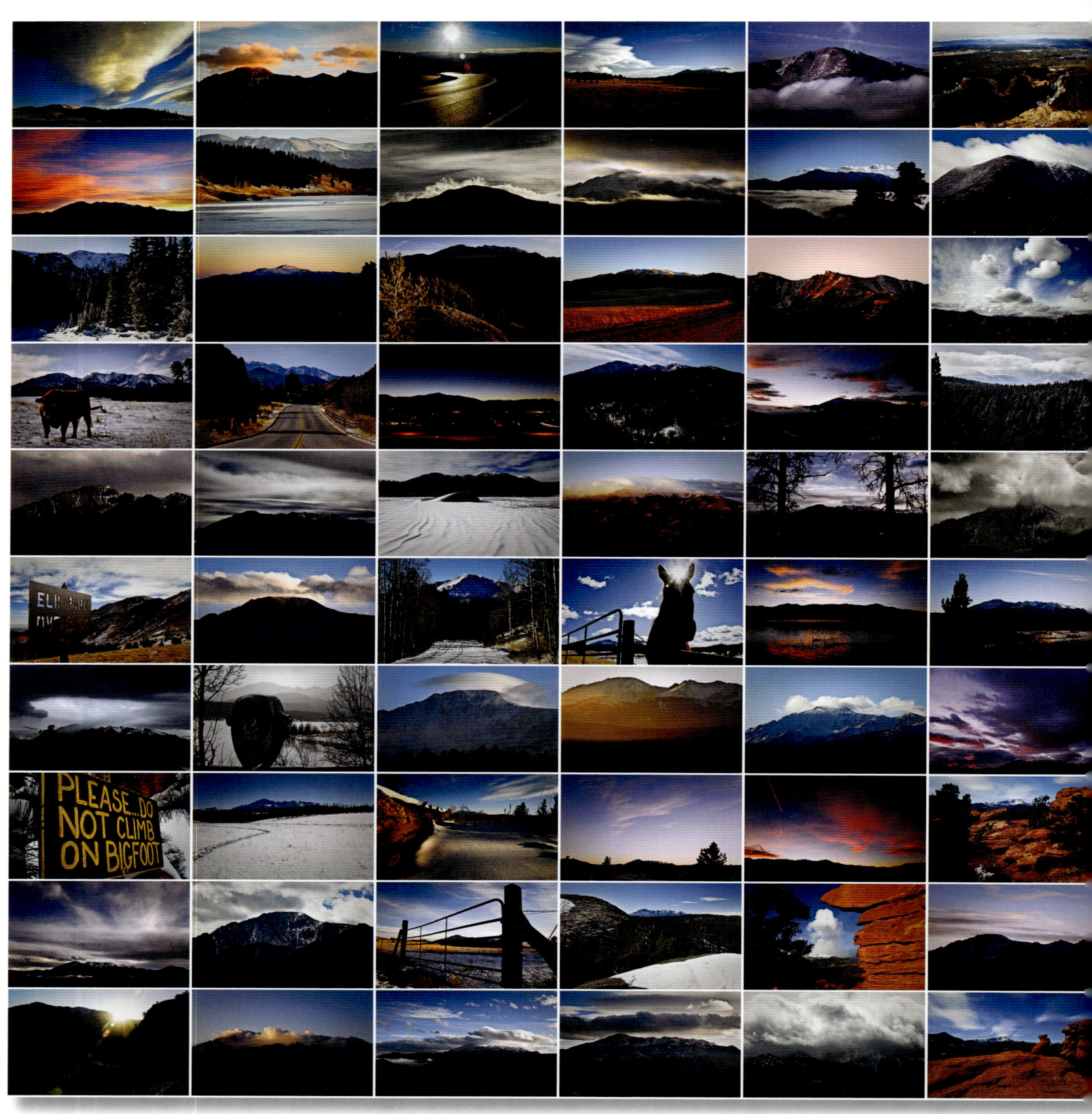

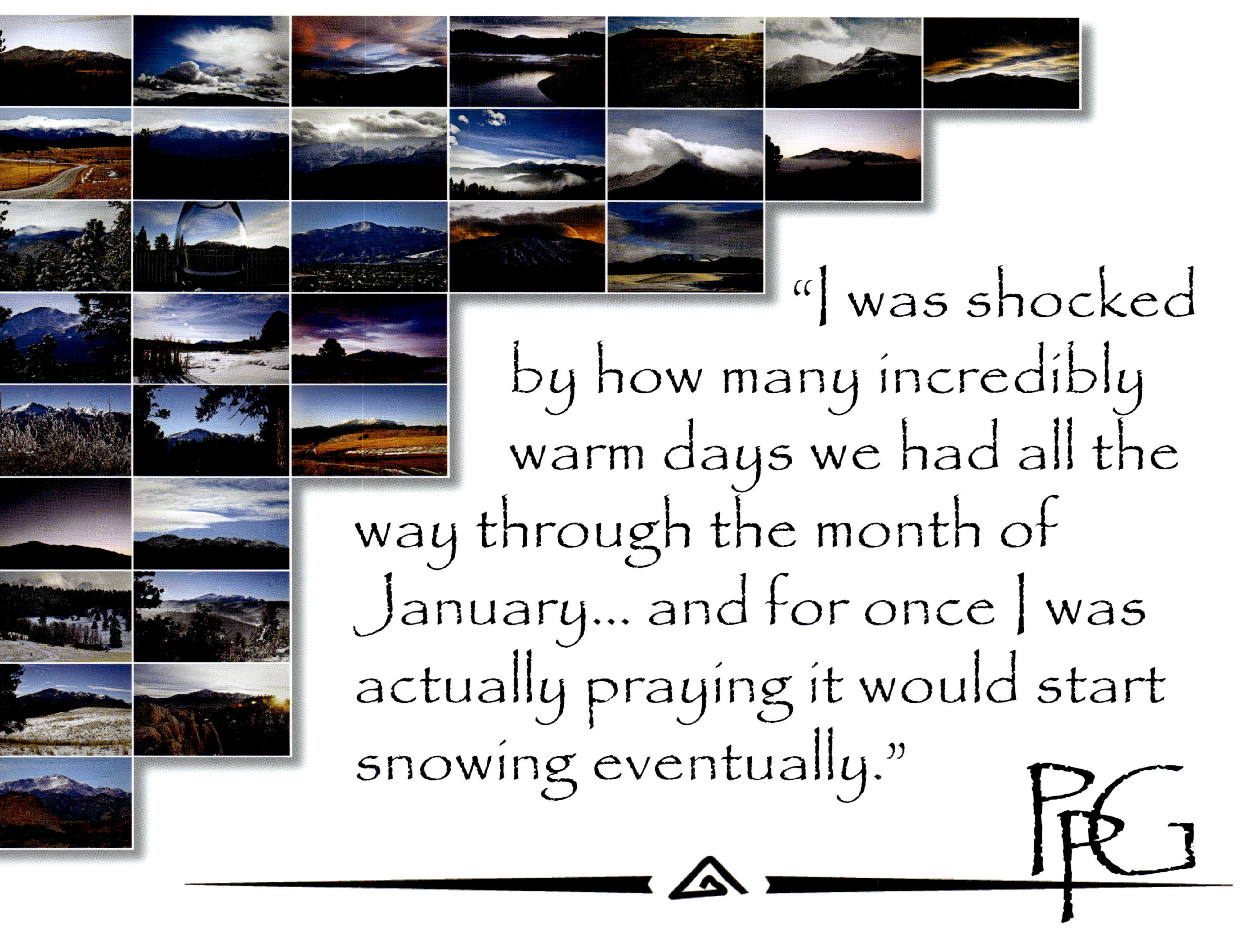
"I was shocked by how many incredibly warm days we had all the way through the month of January... and for once I was actually praying it would start snowing eventually."
PPG

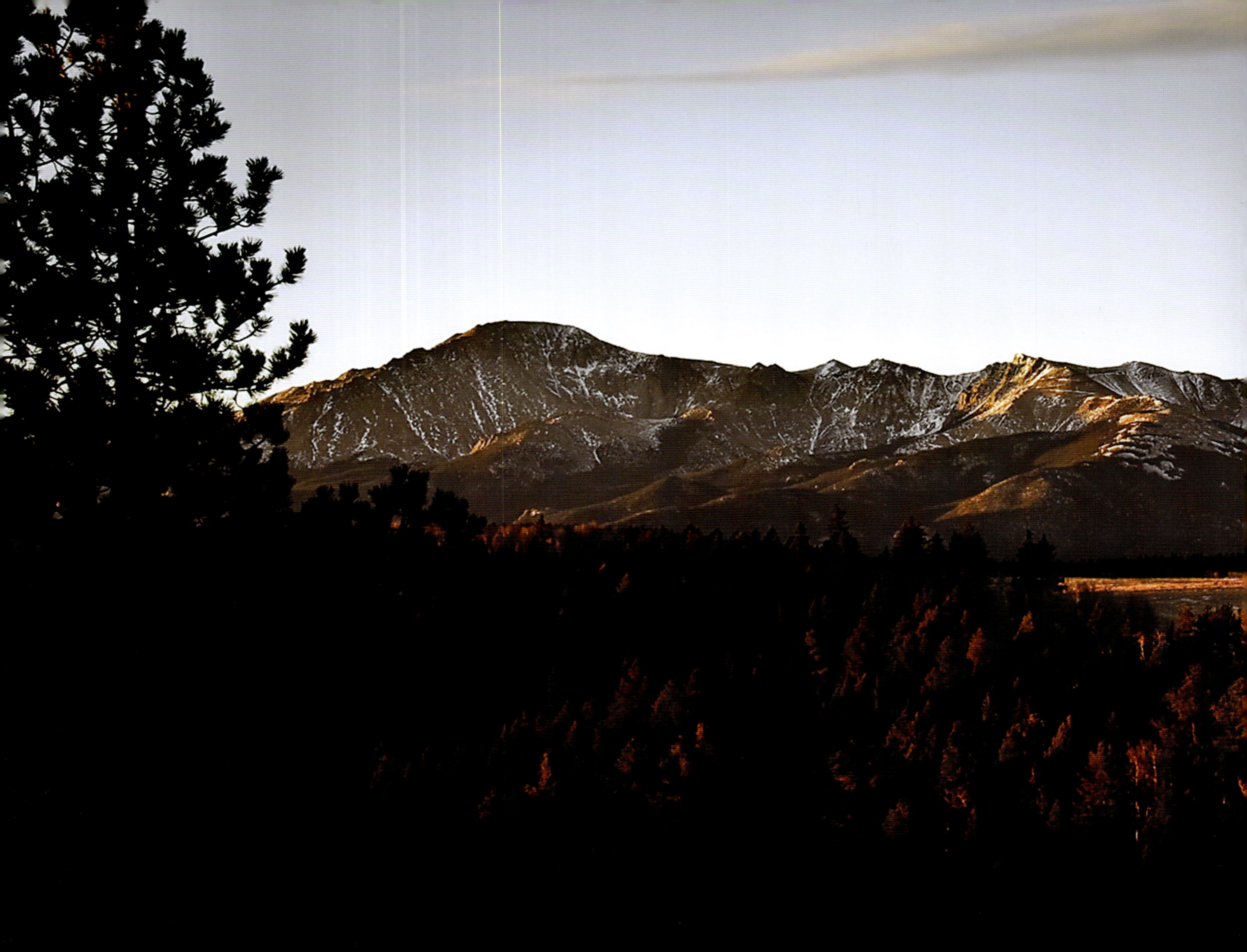

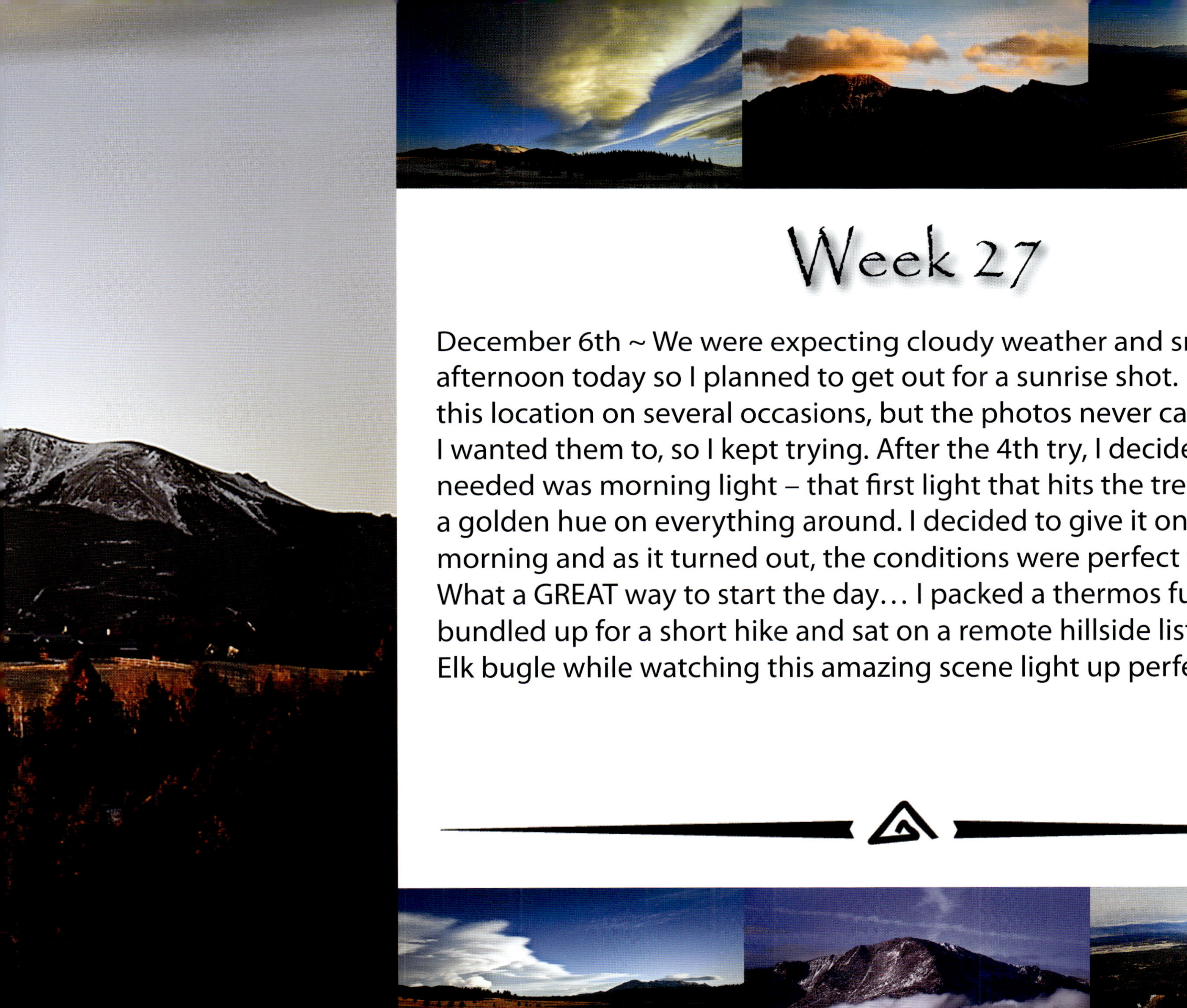

Week 27

December 6th ~ We were expecting cloudy weather and snow by the afternoon today so I planned to get out for a sunrise shot. I had been to this location on several occasions, but the photos never came out the way I wanted them to, so I kept trying. After the 4th try, I decided that what I needed was morning light – that first light that hits the tree tops and cast a golden hue on everything around. I decided to give it one more try this morning and as it turned out, the conditions were perfect for this scene! What a GREAT way to start the day… I packed a thermos full of coffee, got bundled up for a short hike and sat on a remote hillside listening to the Elk bugle while watching this amazing scene light up perfectly.

Week 28

December 8th ~ When I heard that it was going to be warmer here in the Rockies than it would be in some parts of Florida, I knew I needed to go for a hike! While it was nice and warm for a December day, clouds setting in made it kind of a dreary day… it was like a blanket of gray over our normally deep blue skies. With those kind of conditions, I decided to hike to a new location and find a big view just in case the clouds stuck around. Once I found my spot I took some great shots and decided to wait out the sunset on the off chance something interesting would happen. Something interesting happened alright, and the only word I can think of to describe tonight's sunset is – epic! I really hope you saw this in person tonight. It was one for the record books!

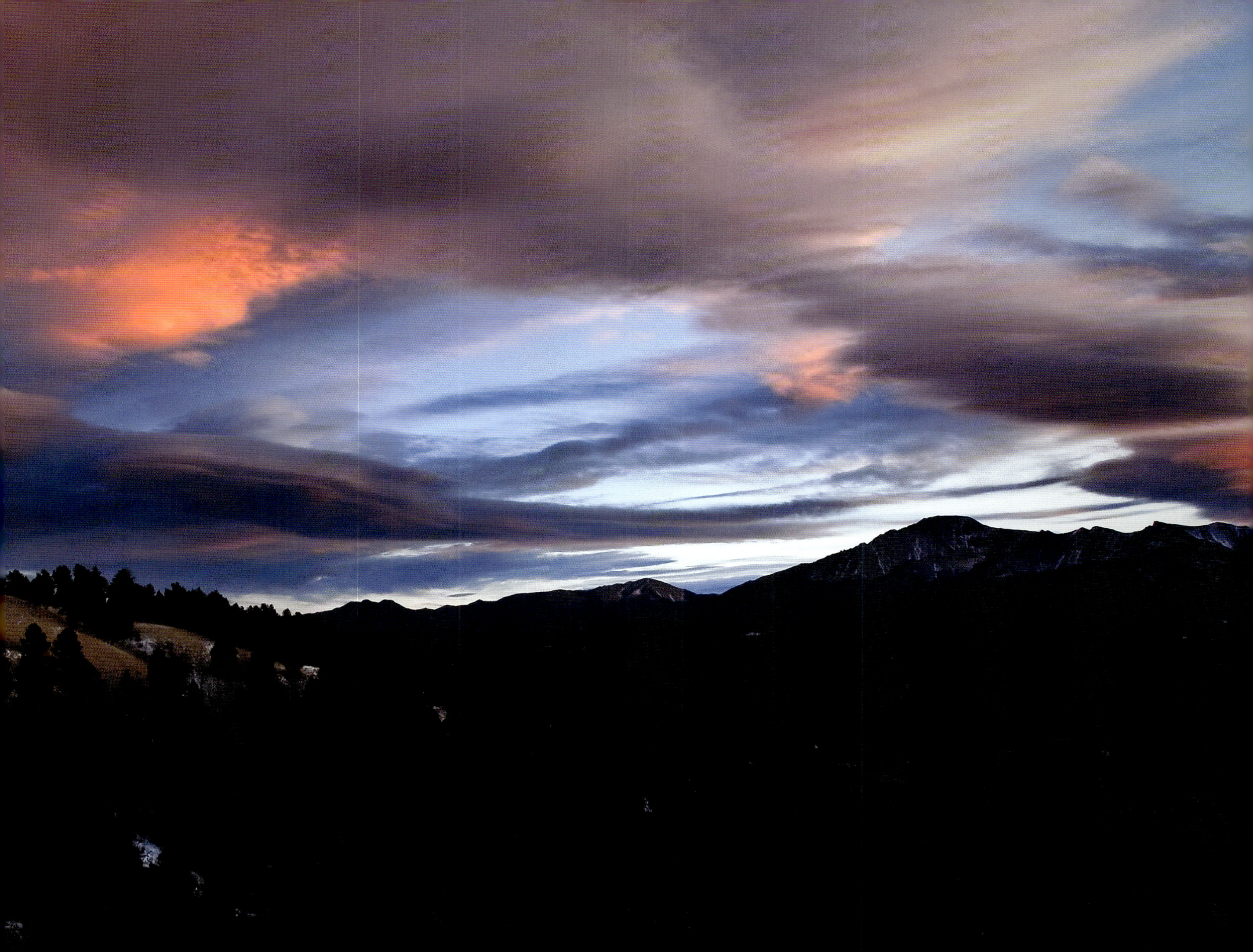

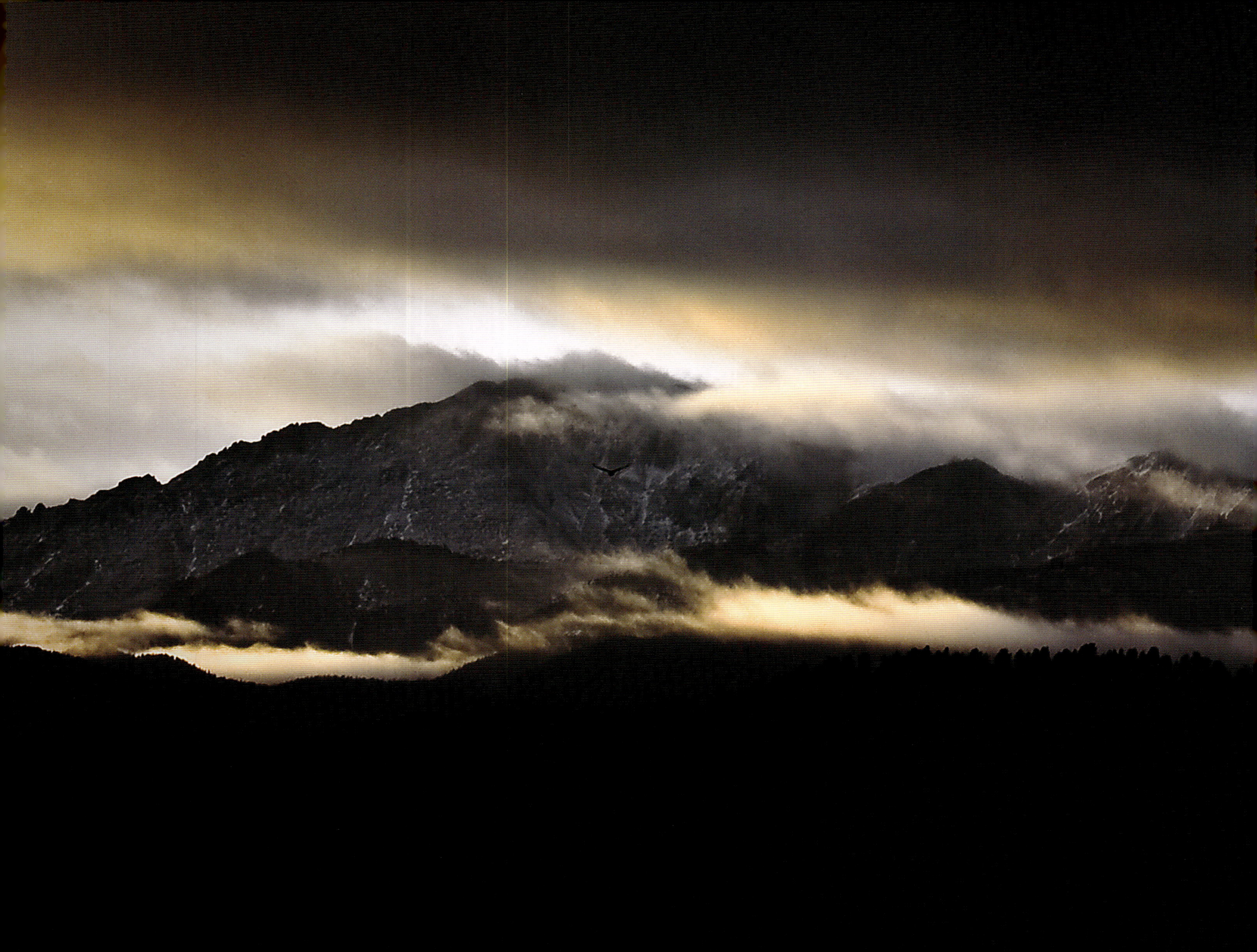

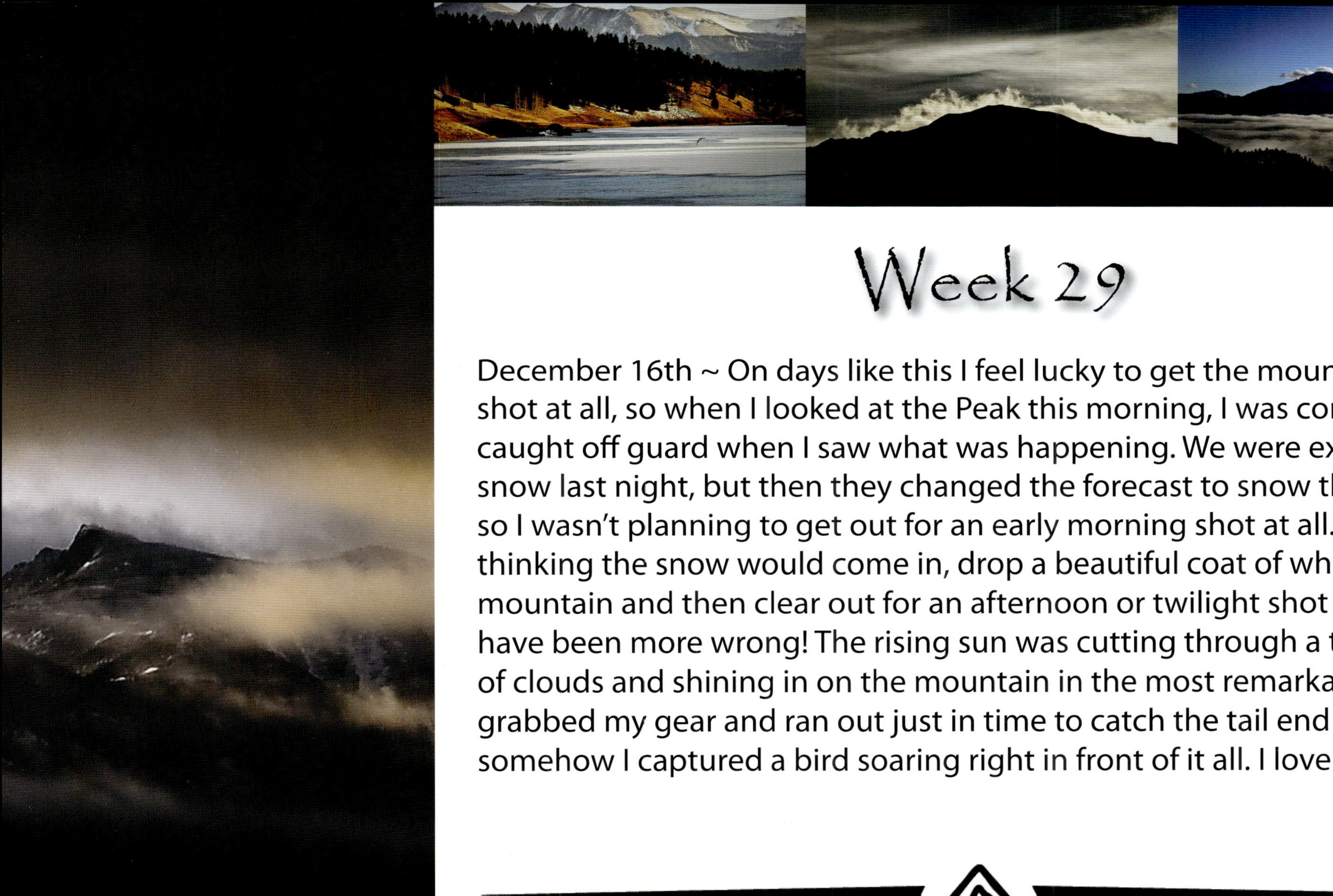

Week 29

December 16th ~ On days like this I feel lucky to get the mountain in a shot at all, so when I looked at the Peak this morning, I was completely caught off guard when I saw what was happening. We were expecting snow last night, but then they changed the forecast to snow this morning, so I wasn't planning to get out for an early morning shot at all. I was thinking the snow would come in, drop a beautiful coat of white on the mountain and then clear out for an afternoon or twilight shot ~ I couldn't have been more wrong! The rising sun was cutting through a thin strip of clouds and shining in on the mountain in the most remarkable way. I grabbed my gear and ran out just in time to catch the tail end of it… and somehow I captured a bird soaring right in front of it all. I love this shot!

Week 30

December 21st ~ Today is the first day of Winter and the 4th day in a row of the cloud cap over the Peak. As the clouds lifted just a little this afternoon, a dusting of snow was revealed and it actually looked like winter for a few minutes! I was so glad to see the snow, it makes for such a great contrast in the photo and it makes the shot seem almost black and white. I waited patiently for the clouds to thin out just enough to act like a lamp shade, diffusing the harsh mid day sun and casting soft light onto the fresh snow. The intensity of the afternoon sun was the key to this shot and even though I took several interesting shots today, I knew this was going to be my pick from the minute I saw it through my camera!

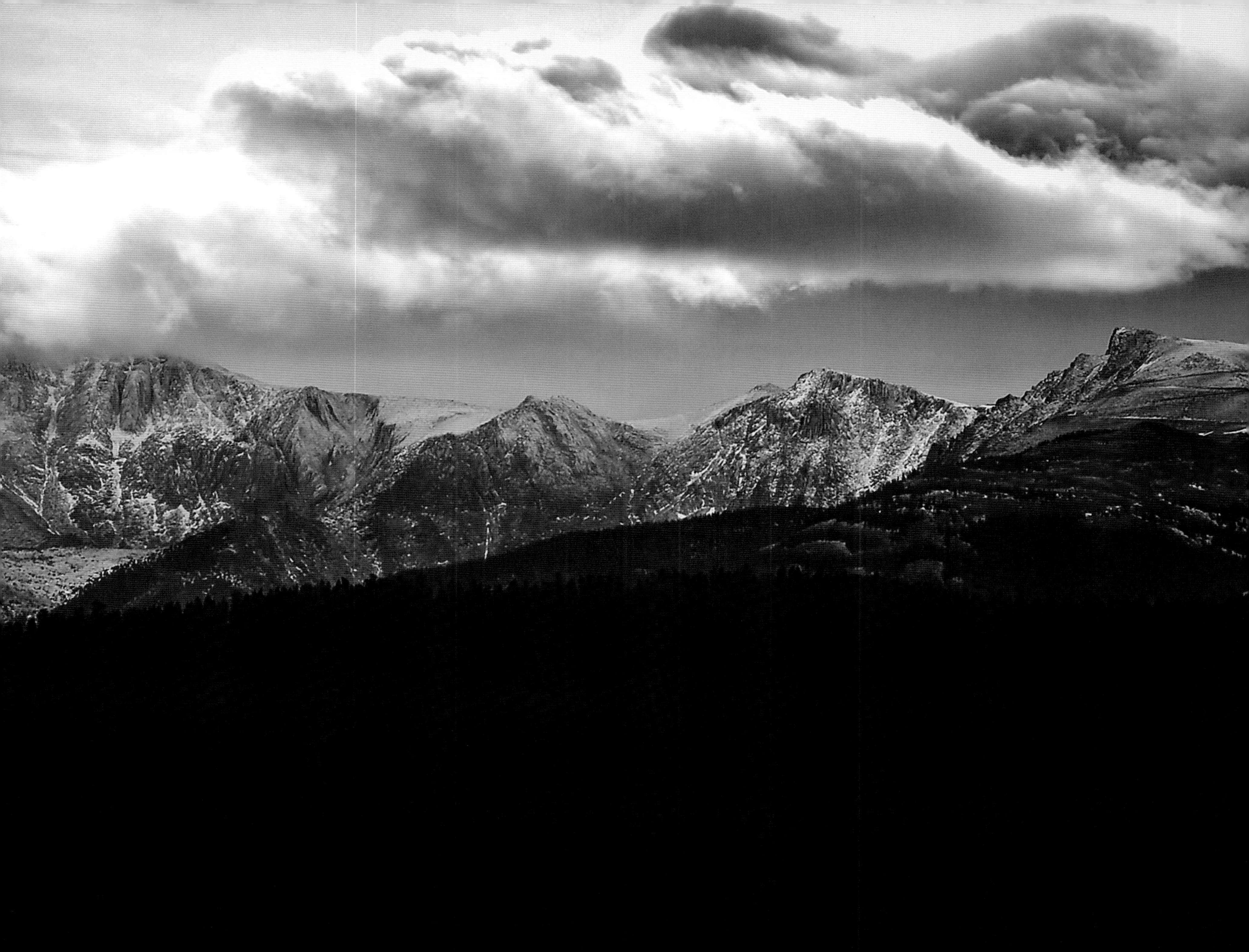

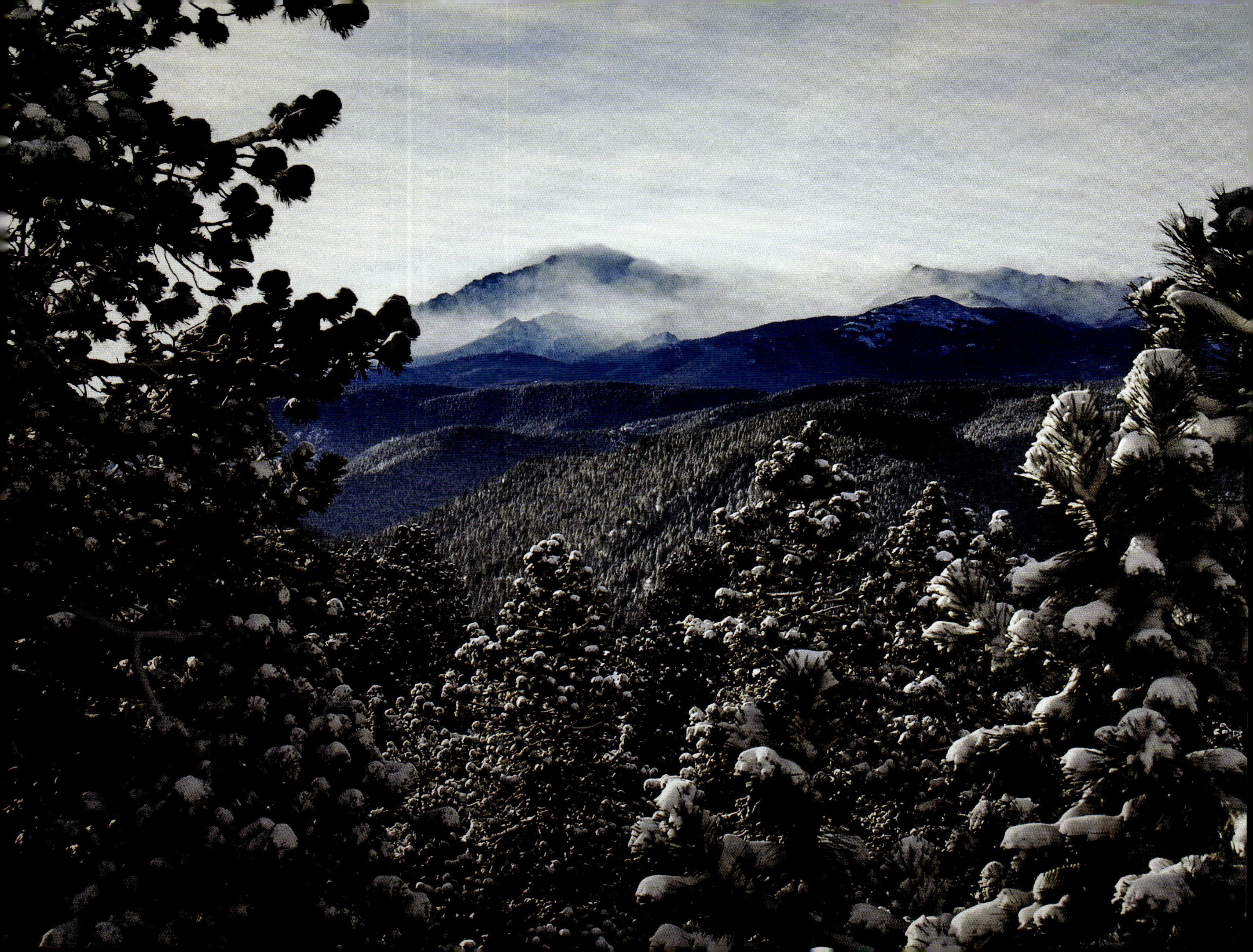

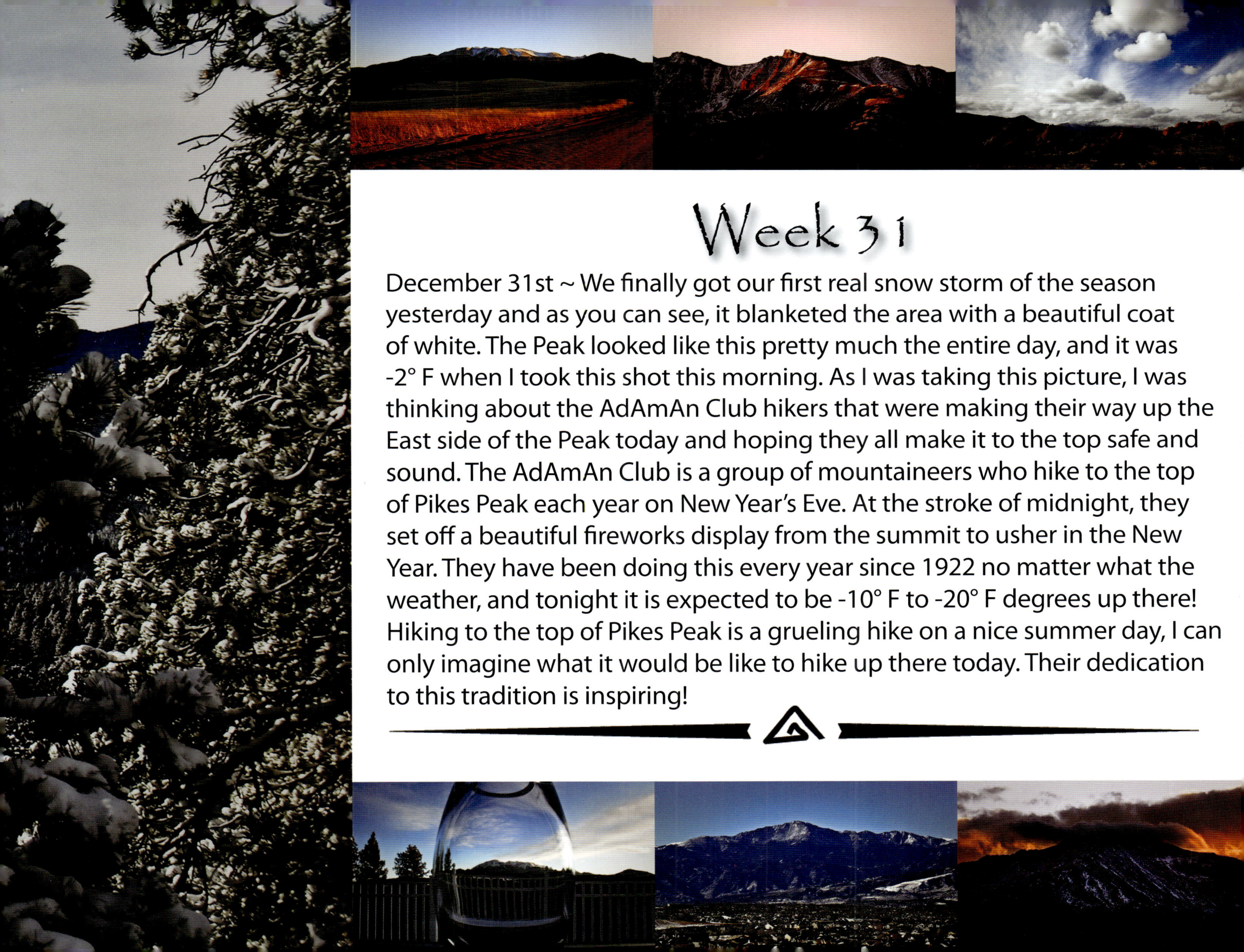

Week 31

December 31st ~ We finally got our first real snow storm of the season yesterday and as you can see, it blanketed the area with a beautiful coat of white. The Peak looked like this pretty much the entire day, and it was -2° F when I took this shot this morning. As I was taking this picture, I was thinking about the AdAmAn Club hikers that were making their way up the East side of the Peak today and hoping they all make it to the top safe and sound. The AdAmAn Club is a group of mountaineers who hike to the top of Pikes Peak each year on New Year's Eve. At the stroke of midnight, they set off a beautiful fireworks display from the summit to usher in the New Year. They have been doing this every year since 1922 no matter what the weather, and tonight it is expected to be -10° F to -20° F degrees up there! Hiking to the top of Pikes Peak is a grueling hike on a nice summer day, I can only imagine what it would be like to hike up there today. Their dedication to this tradition is inspiring!

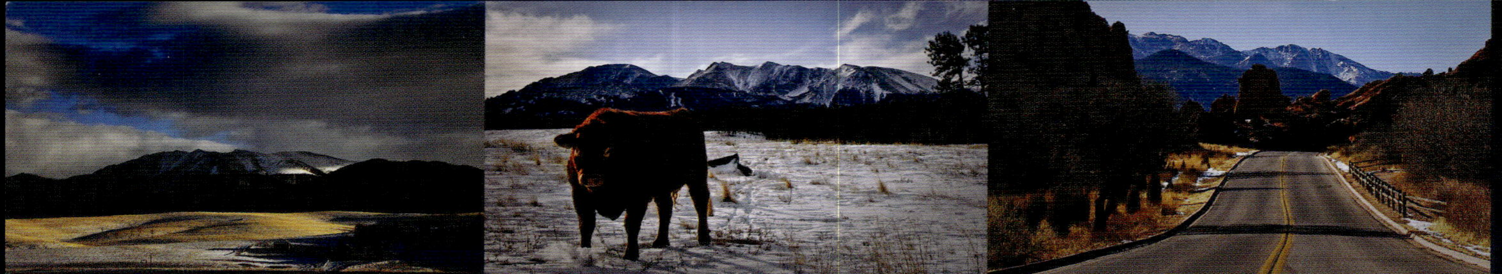

Week 32

January 7th ~ Today I started taking pictures at first light, and finished my day catching the last light of the evening. I wasn't planning on taking a picture this late in the day, but that seems to be when I get some of my favorite shots… when I don't expect them. I expected to use my shot from early morning, but today all the conditions were right for a shot like this, and there was no risk of failure, because I had my shots from earlier. Having a back up picture is what allows me to take chances on shots like this, and at the same time I have been waiting for a day with zero clouds, little to no moonlight and the time to get out to a location like this. All of these things came together for me tonight and I absolutely love this shot!

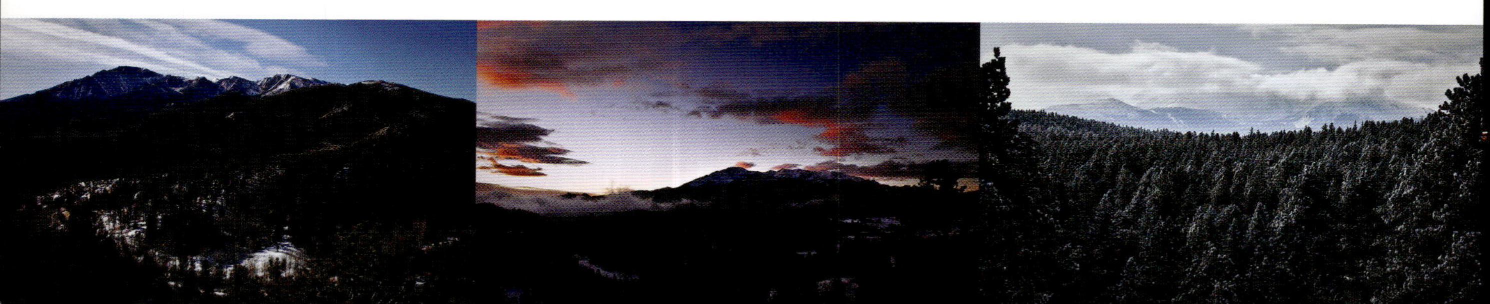

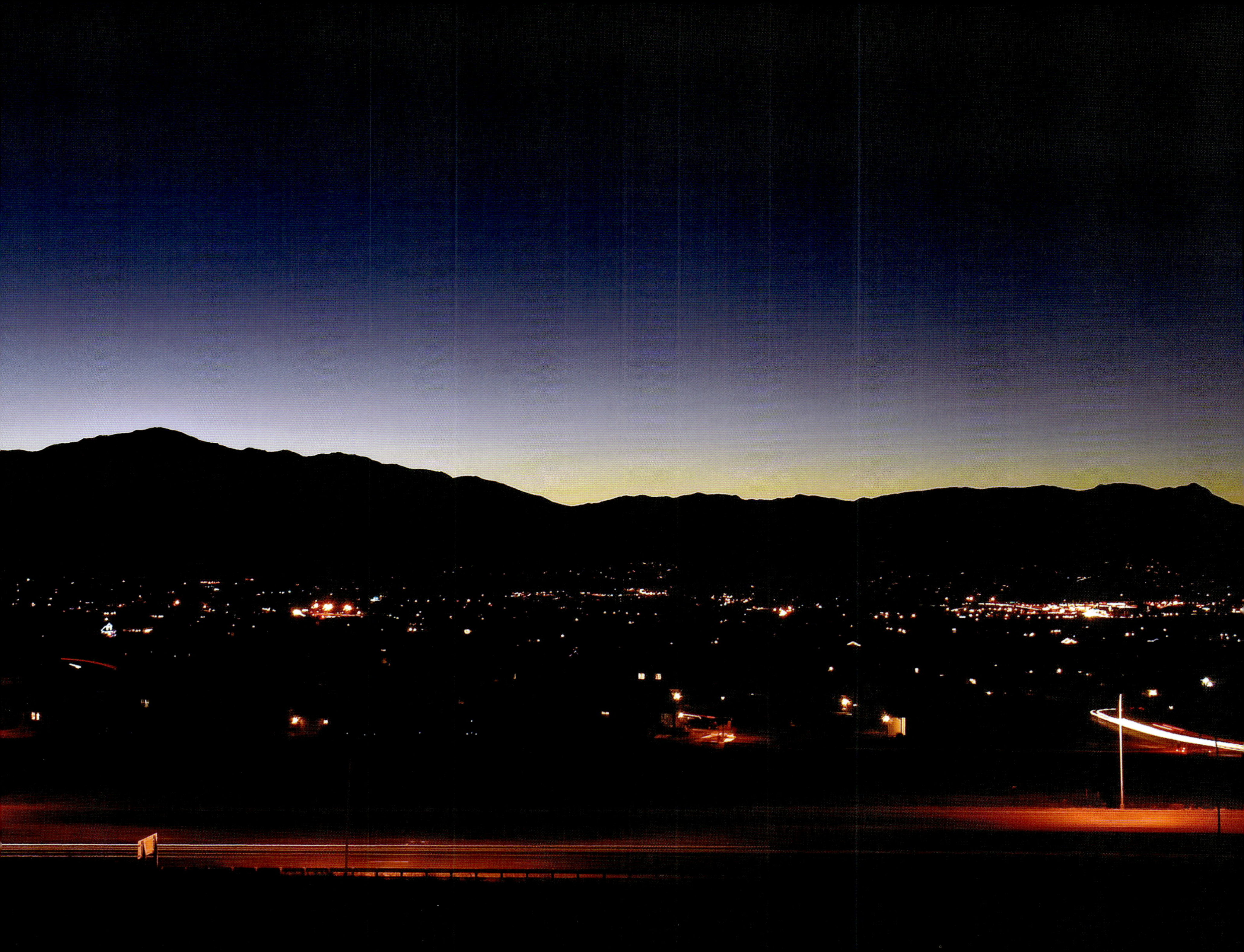

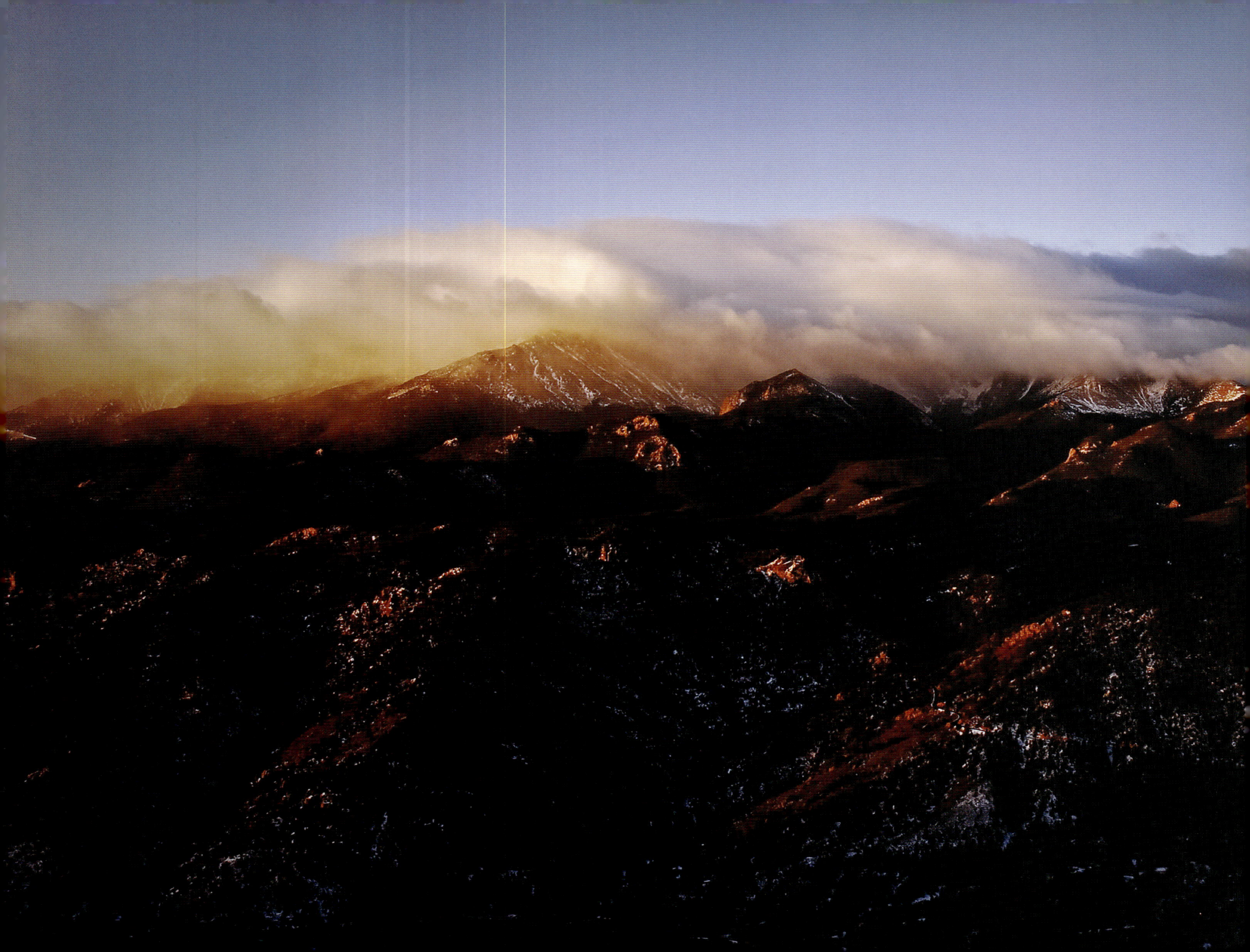

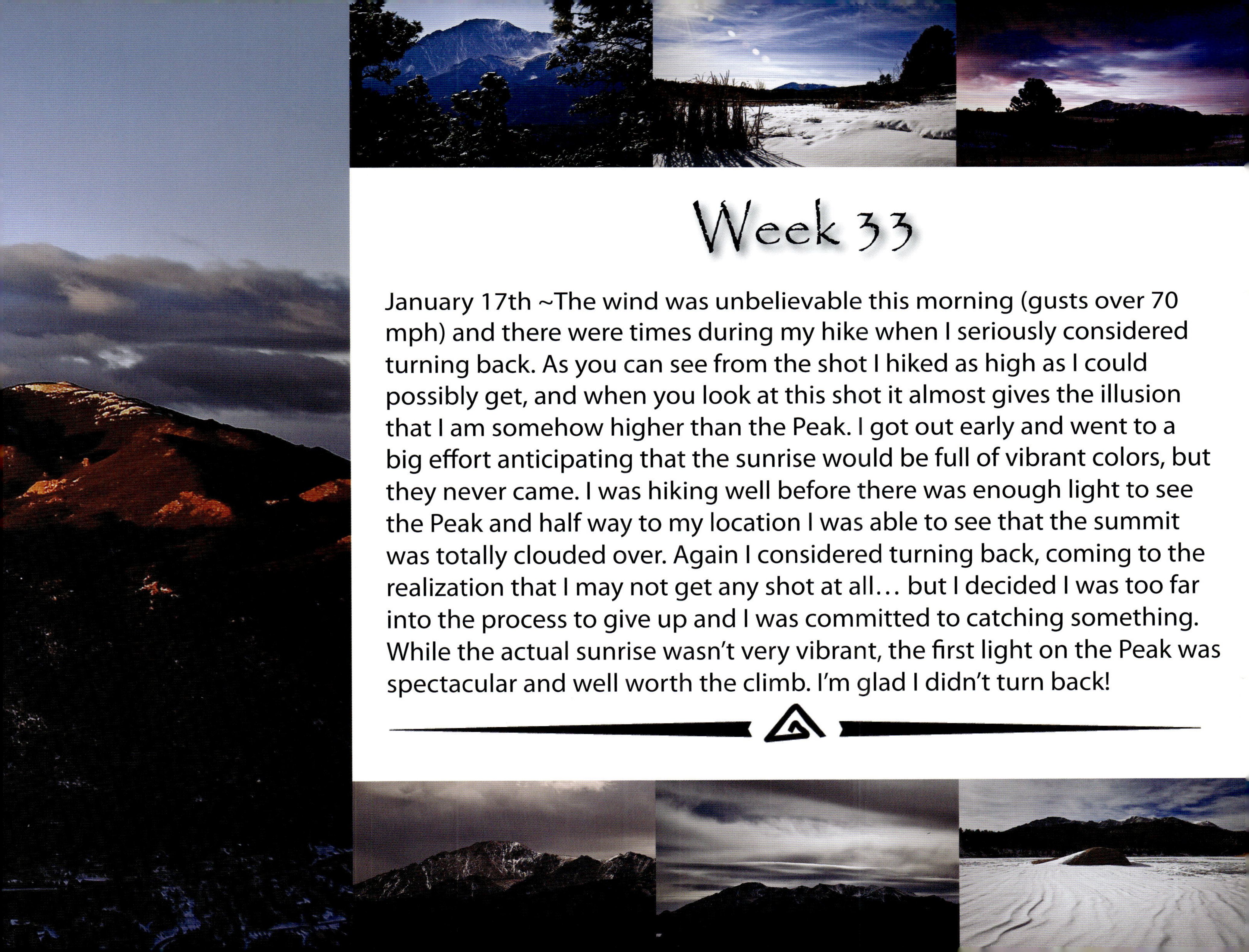

Week 33

January 17th ~The wind was unbelievable this morning (gusts over 70 mph) and there were times during my hike when I seriously considered turning back. As you can see from the shot I hiked as high as I could possibly get, and when you look at this shot it almost gives the illusion that I am somehow higher than the Peak. I got out early and went to a big effort anticipating that the sunrise would be full of vibrant colors, but they never came. I was hiking well before there was enough light to see the Peak and half way to my location I was able to see that the summit was totally clouded over. Again I considered turning back, coming to the realization that I may not get any shot at all… but I decided I was too far into the process to give up and I was committed to catching something. While the actual sunrise wasn't very vibrant, the first light on the Peak was spectacular and well worth the climb. I'm glad I didn't turn back!

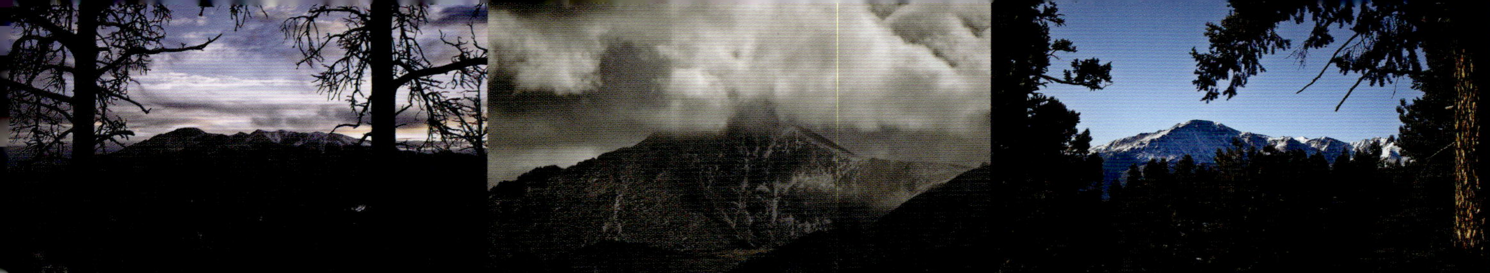

Week 34

January 20th ~ One of my favorite winter scenes is when everything gets coated with ice crystals from the fog – it is truly amazing. We had some snow last night, nothing major, but there were a few isolated spots high in the foothills that were protected from the wind and got more fog than snow. Although this isn't that full frosted scene that I would have loved to see this morning, it was a gift to be out there and have the chance to capture this photo. The big view of the entire mountain coupled with the deep blue sky are a backdrop that would make any photo magical. It is starting to feel like winter is finally here!

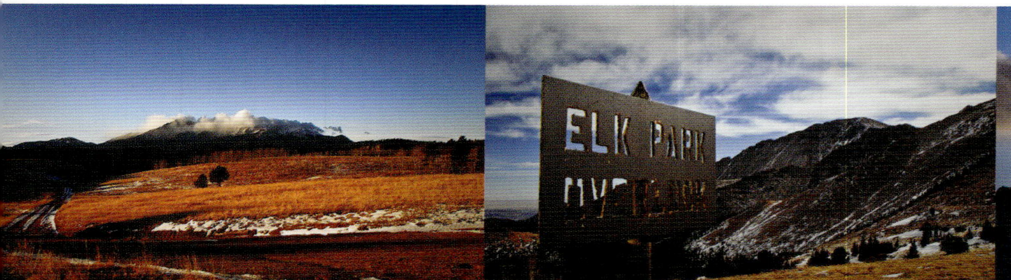

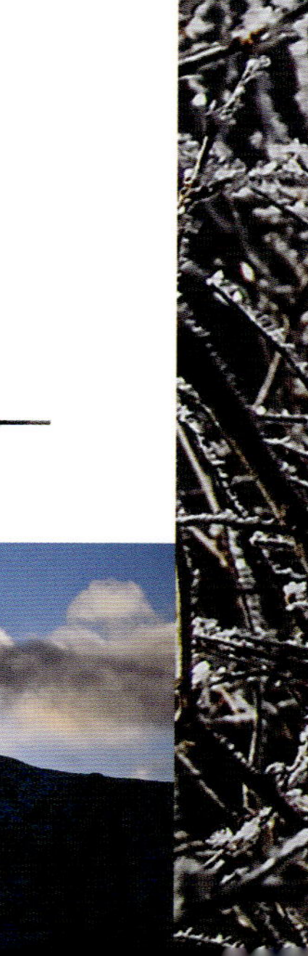

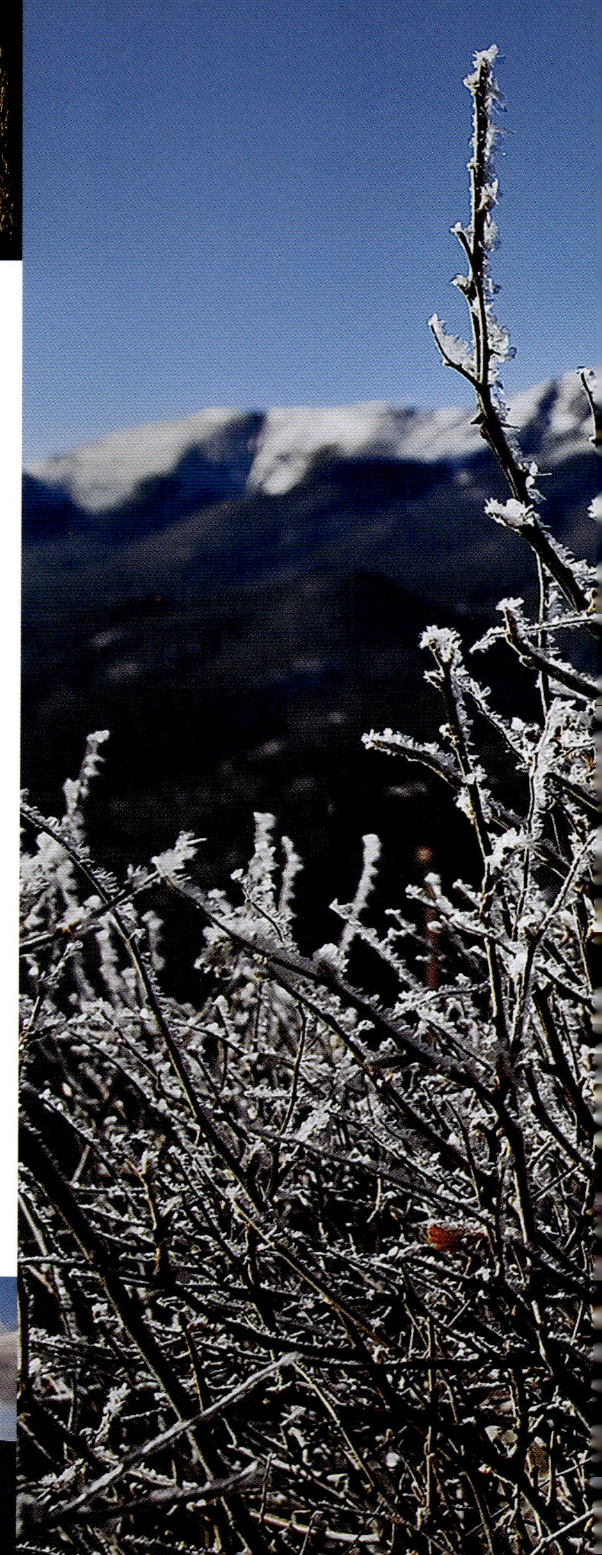

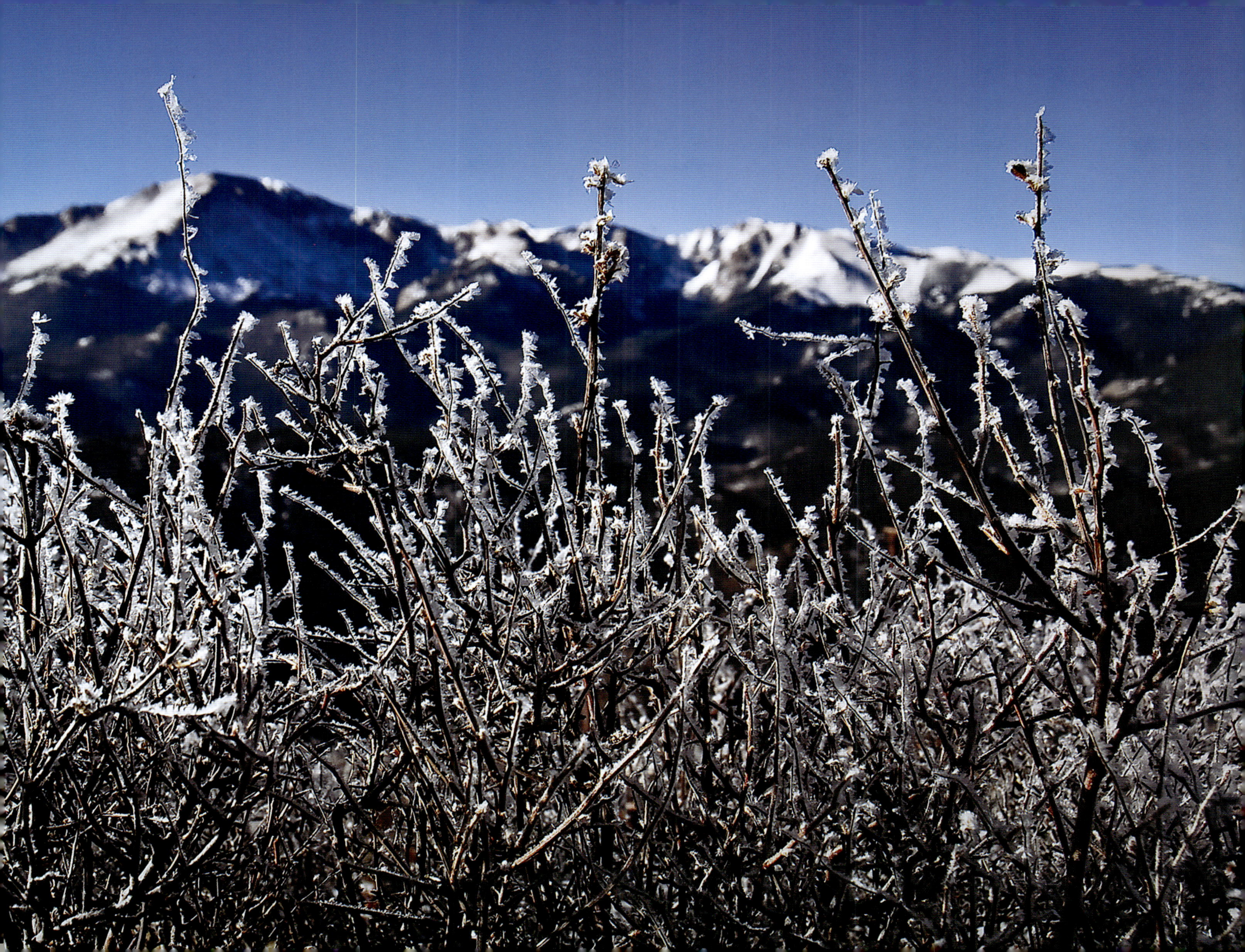

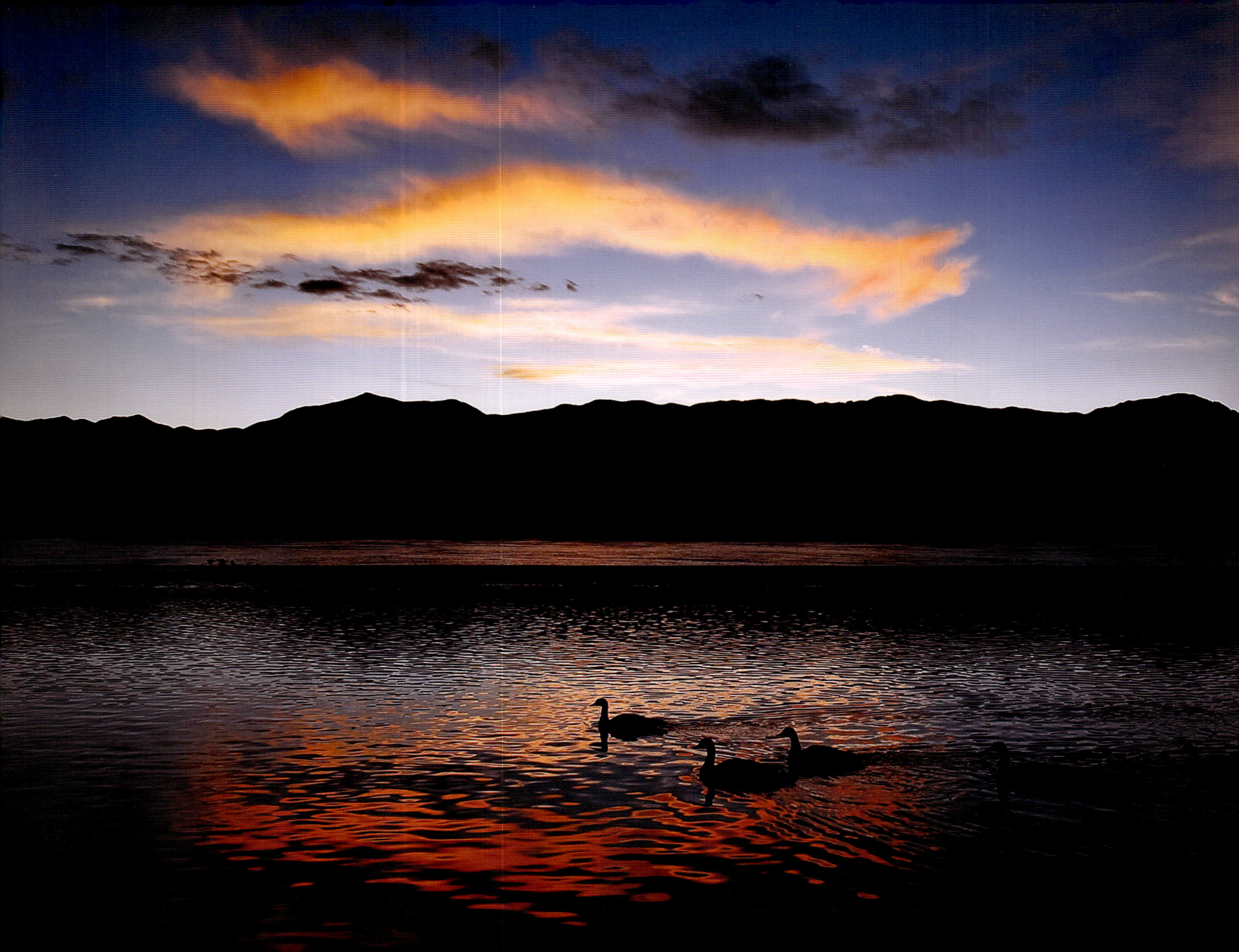

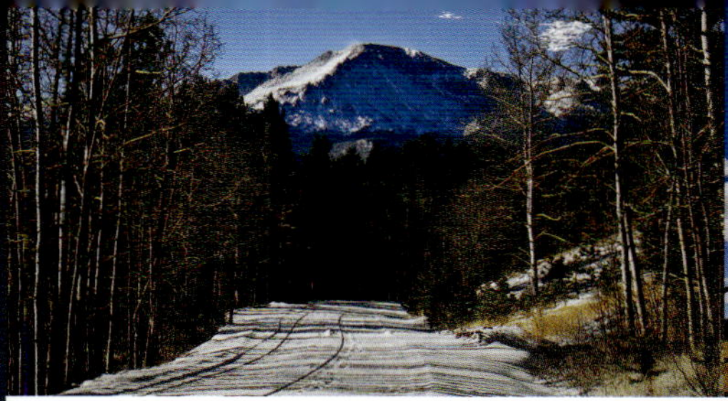

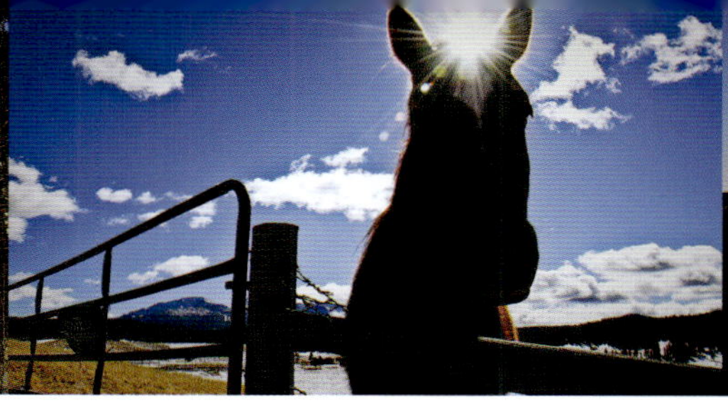

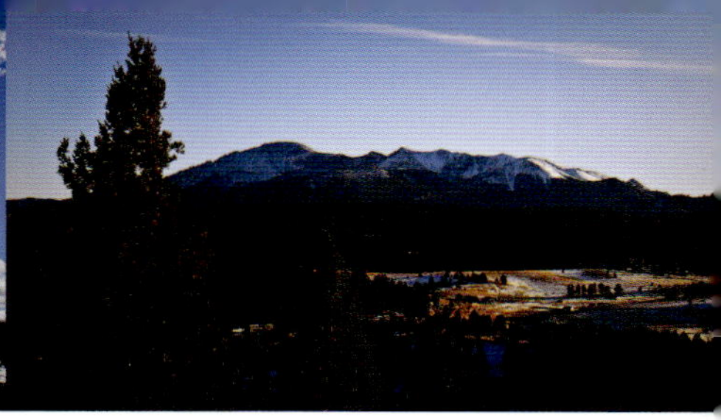

Week 35

January 27th ~ Colorado Springs has one of the most beautiful skylines of any city in Colorado, and tonight's sunset illustrated that in grand style. The weather was so warm today that I just had to get to the Springs for my photo and on a whim I decided to check and see if the lake in Memorial Park was still frozen over. I thought with all of this mild weather we have been getting there may be a chance that it melted some, and sure enough the South East end of the lake was thawed. Hanging out in the park, getting great shots of the Peak was a wonderful way to spend the evening, but when the sun went behind the mountain there was a hint of color that made me think it was about to get a lot better. It's been weeks since I have been able to catch a really dramatic sunset and tonight I was incredibly blessed to have been in the right place at the right time…

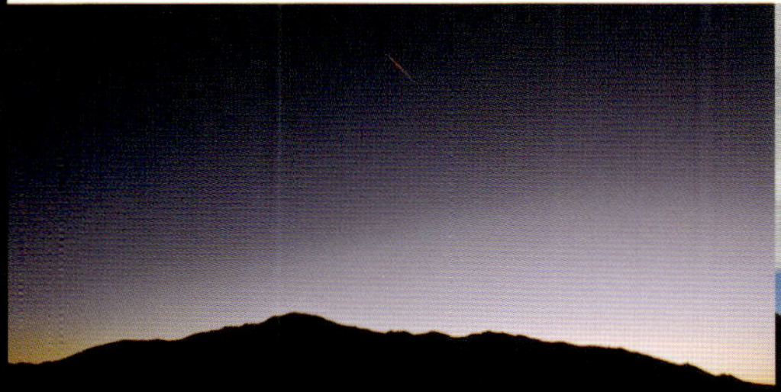

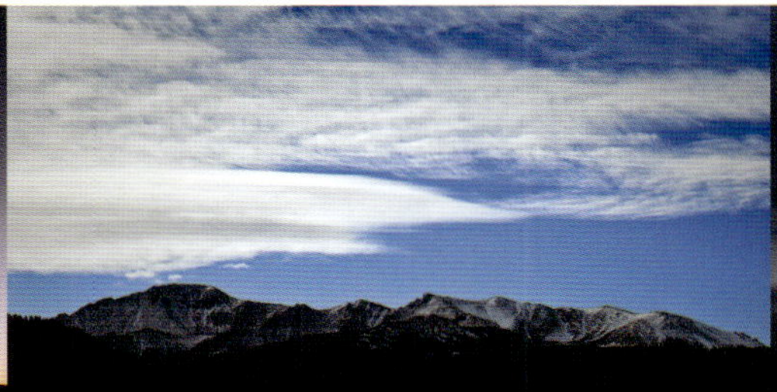

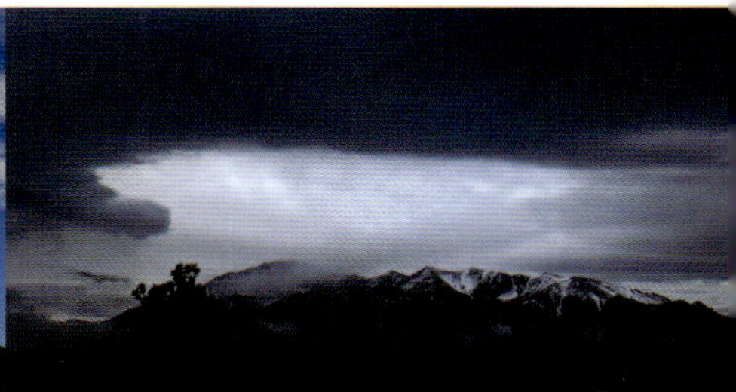

Week 36

February 7th ~ Since winter arrived here only 1 week ago, I haven't had too many "morning after the storm" shots thus far in the project and I really wanted to get something that showed how beautiful the Peak can be after a storm. Just before 8:00am, the wind started blowing and there was so much snow coming out of the trees that it was literally snowing again! I wanted to capture this in a photo, because it was spectacular to watch from street level and I knew if I could get up above it I would get that winter wonderland shot I was hoping for. A few moments after I got set up and started shooting, a giant wind rushed down the pass and it seemed to blow the snow out of every tree in the valley all at once… except the one I was sitting under. Well, that didn't last for long and the next thing I knew I was coated in snow and laughing out loud! A great morning indeed!

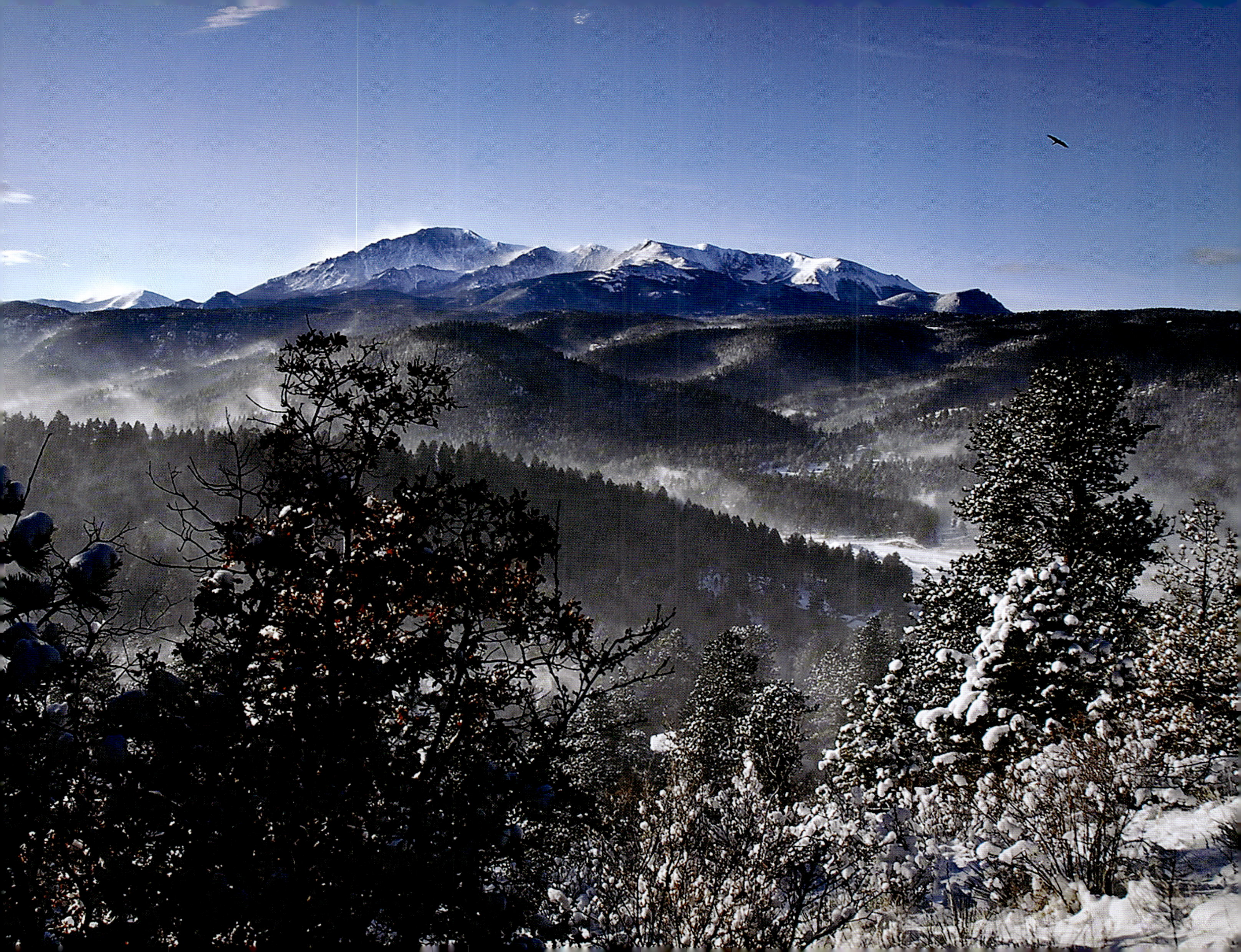

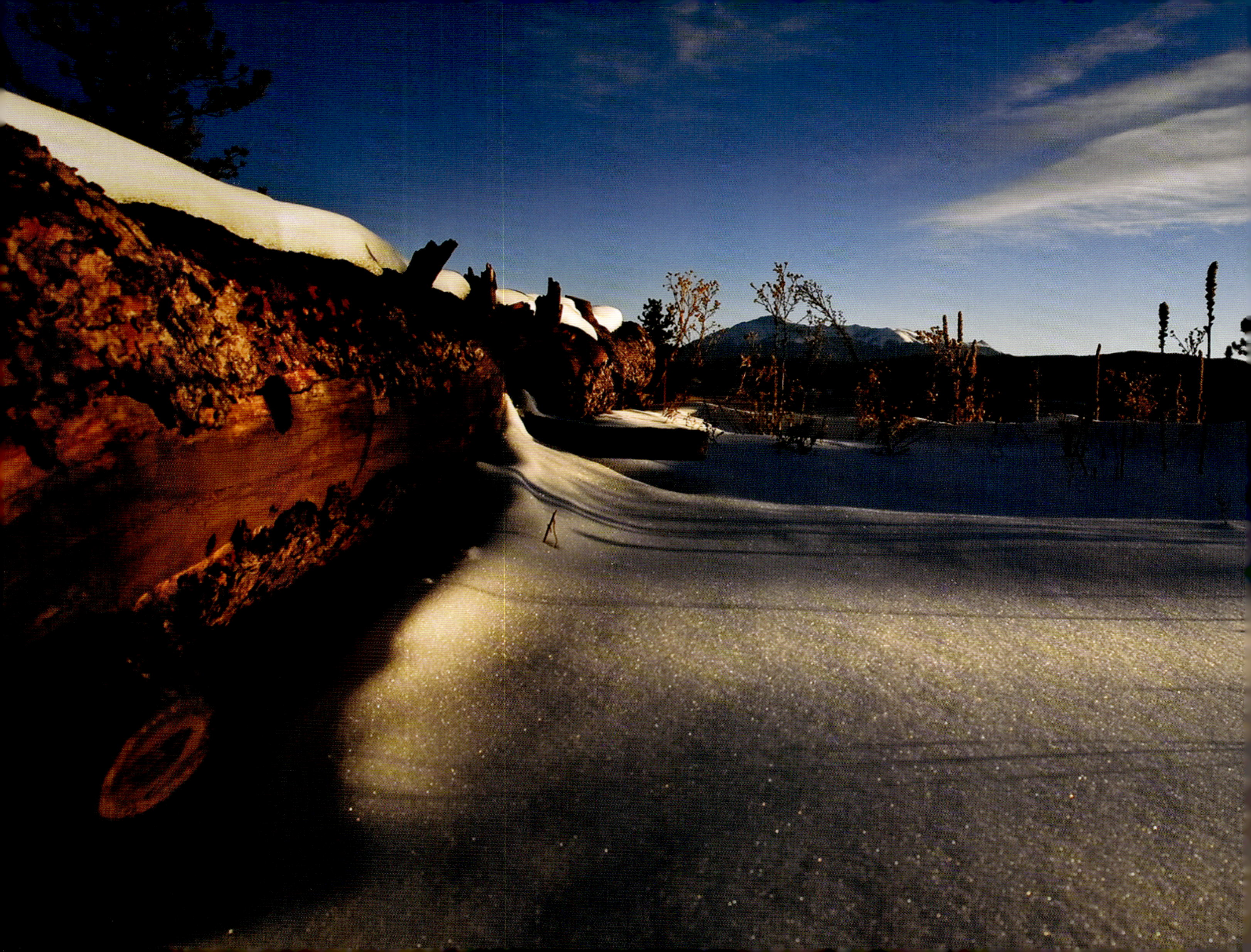

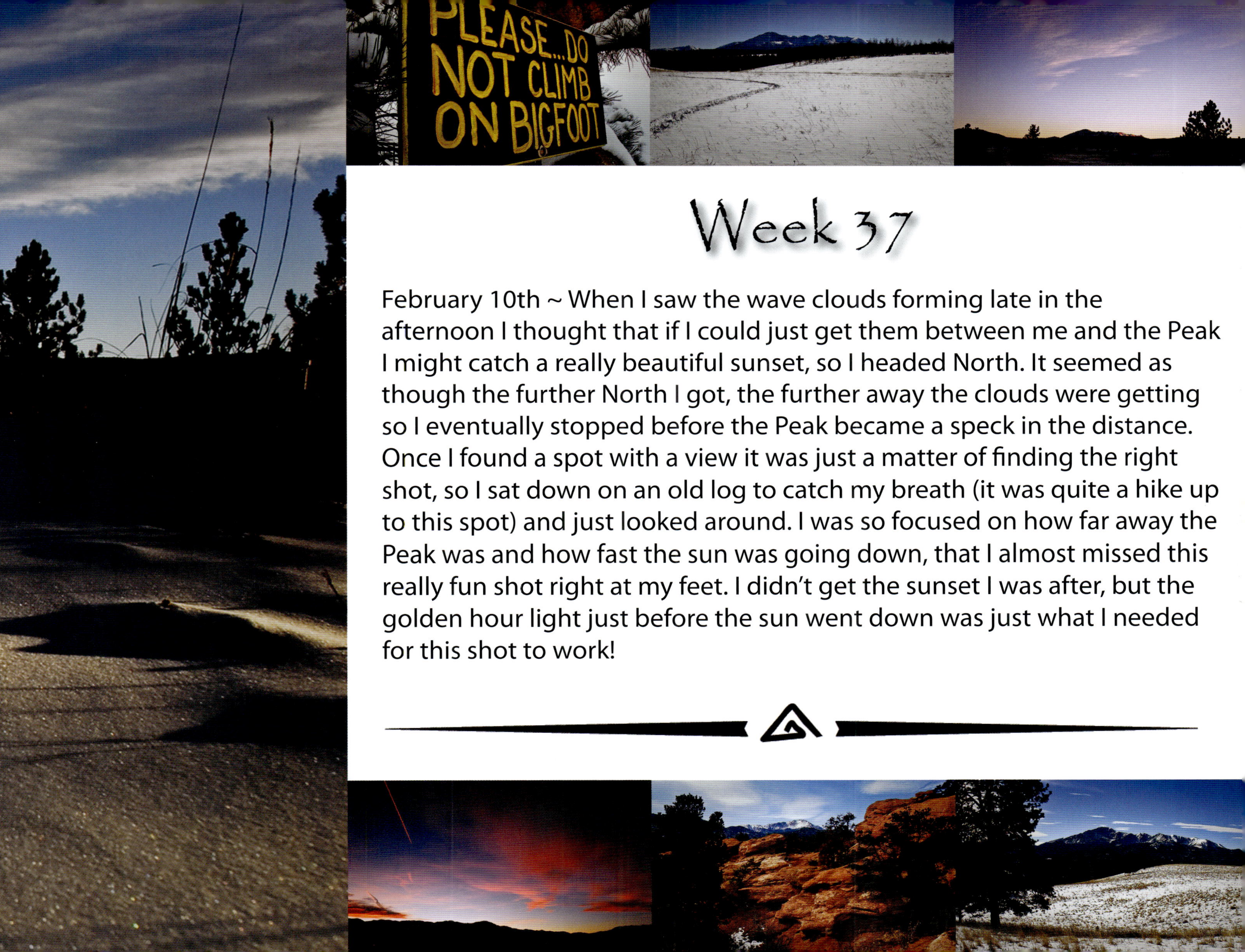

Week 37

February 10th ~ When I saw the wave clouds forming late in the afternoon I thought that if I could just get them between me and the Peak I might catch a really beautiful sunset, so I headed North. It seemed as though the further North I got, the further away the clouds were getting so I eventually stopped before the Peak became a speck in the distance. Once I found a spot with a view it was just a matter of finding the right shot, so I sat down on an old log to catch my breath (it was quite a hike up to this spot) and just looked around. I was so focused on how far away the Peak was and how fast the sun was going down, that I almost missed this really fun shot right at my feet. I didn't get the sunset I was after, but the golden hour light just before the sun went down was just what I needed for this shot to work!

Week 38

February 20th ~ Today is another milestone in the project – it is day 265. When I got out this morning it was too dark to see the Peak, but the full moon was still out and it gave me just enough light to get the sense that the summit was covered with clouds. I thought they might clear out by the time the sun came up or at least add something interesting to the shot, so I stuck with my plan. The roads were totally iced over from the rain and snow the night before and I had to drive so slow that it was too late for the sunrise, but it really didn't matter, because the clouds didn't start to rise until about an hour after that… and they rose in a way that made the Peak look like a belching volcano! All this time on the project and I had never seen anything like it and it was really neat to watch. Even though you can't see the summit in this picture, it was my absolute favorite of the entire day!

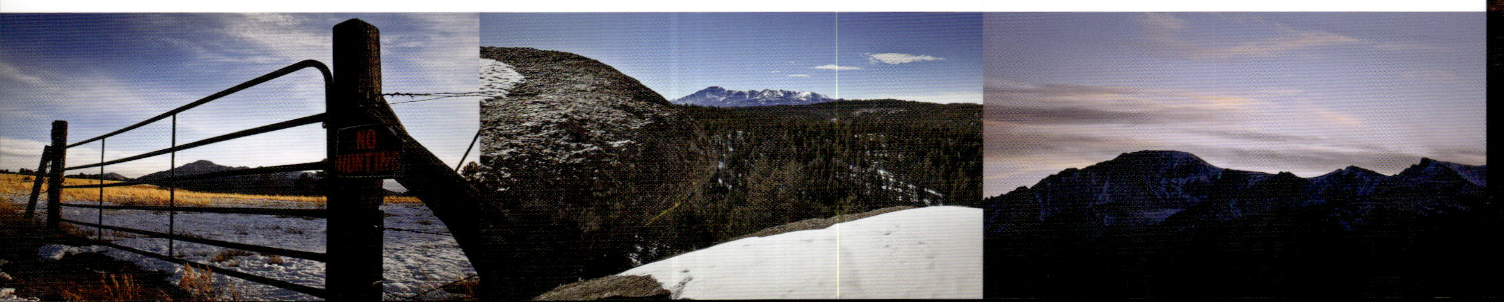

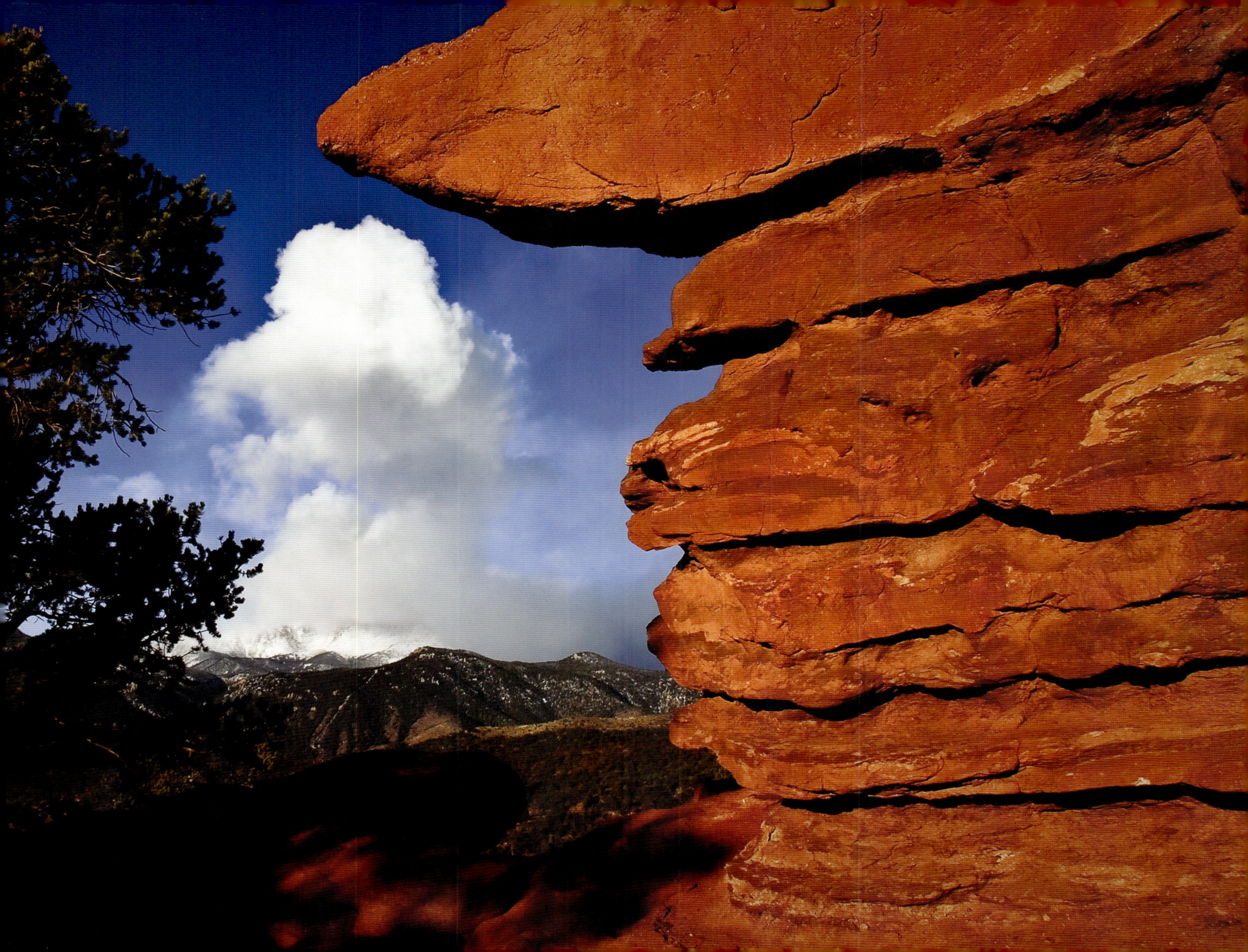

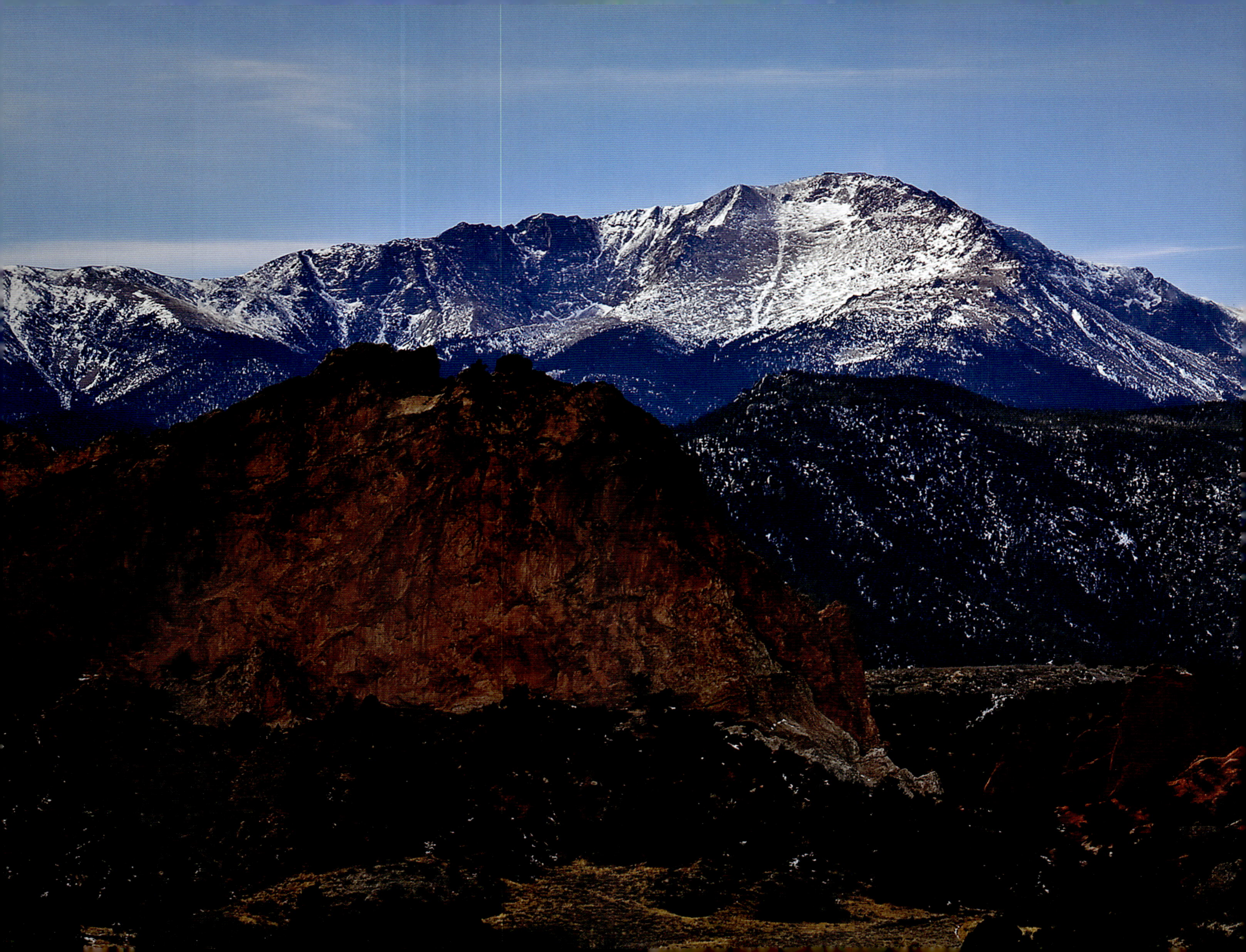

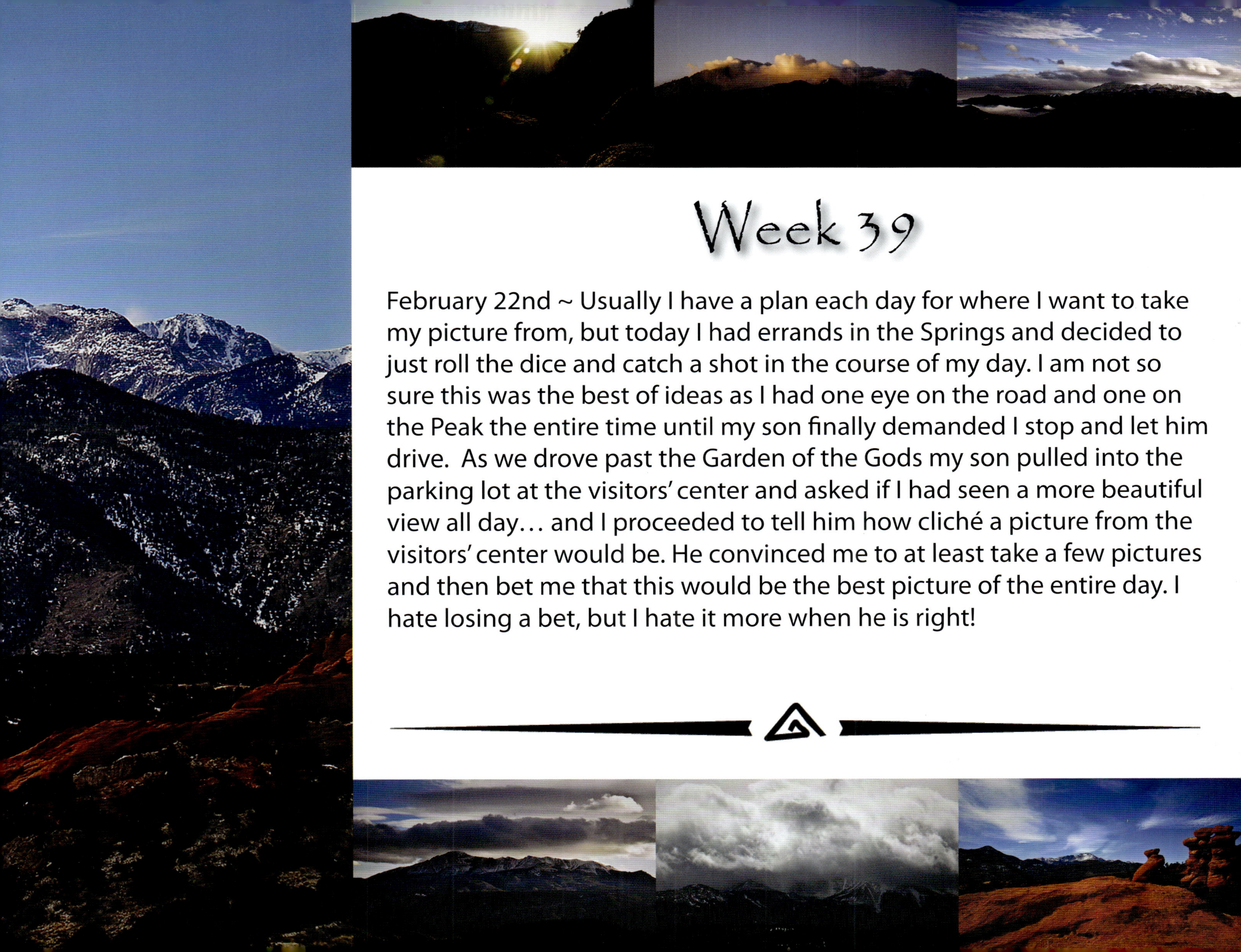

Week 39

February 22nd ~ Usually I have a plan each day for where I want to take my picture from, but today I had errands in the Springs and decided to just roll the dice and catch a shot in the course of my day. I am not so sure this was the best of ideas as I had one eye on the road and one on the Peak the entire time until my son finally demanded I stop and let him drive. As we drove past the Garden of the Gods my son pulled into the parking lot at the visitors' center and asked if I had seen a more beautiful view all day… and I proceeded to tell him how cliché a picture from the visitors' center would be. He convinced me to at least take a few pictures and then bet me that this would be the best picture of the entire day. I hate losing a bet, but I hate it more when he is right!

Chapter 4

Spring

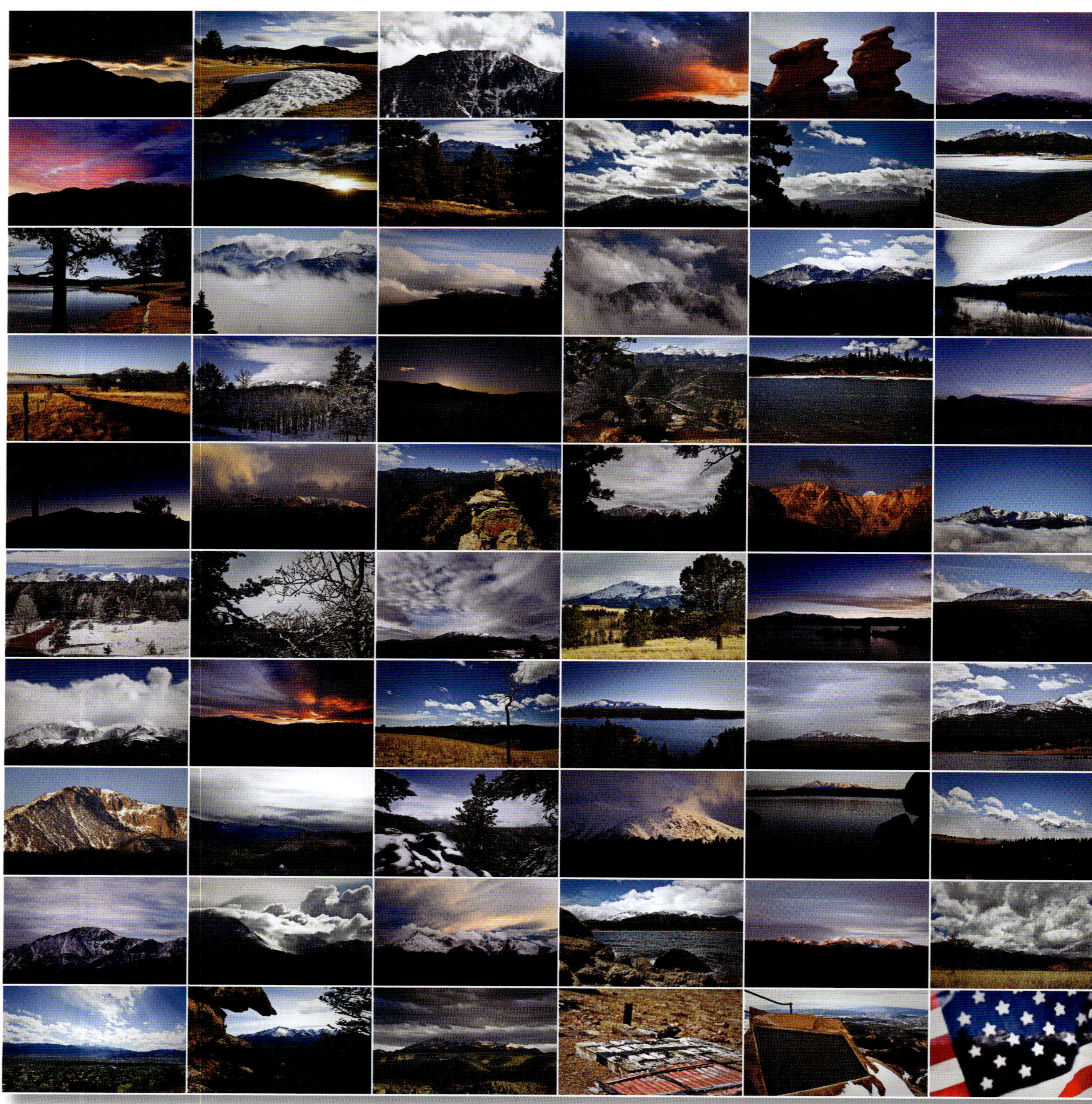

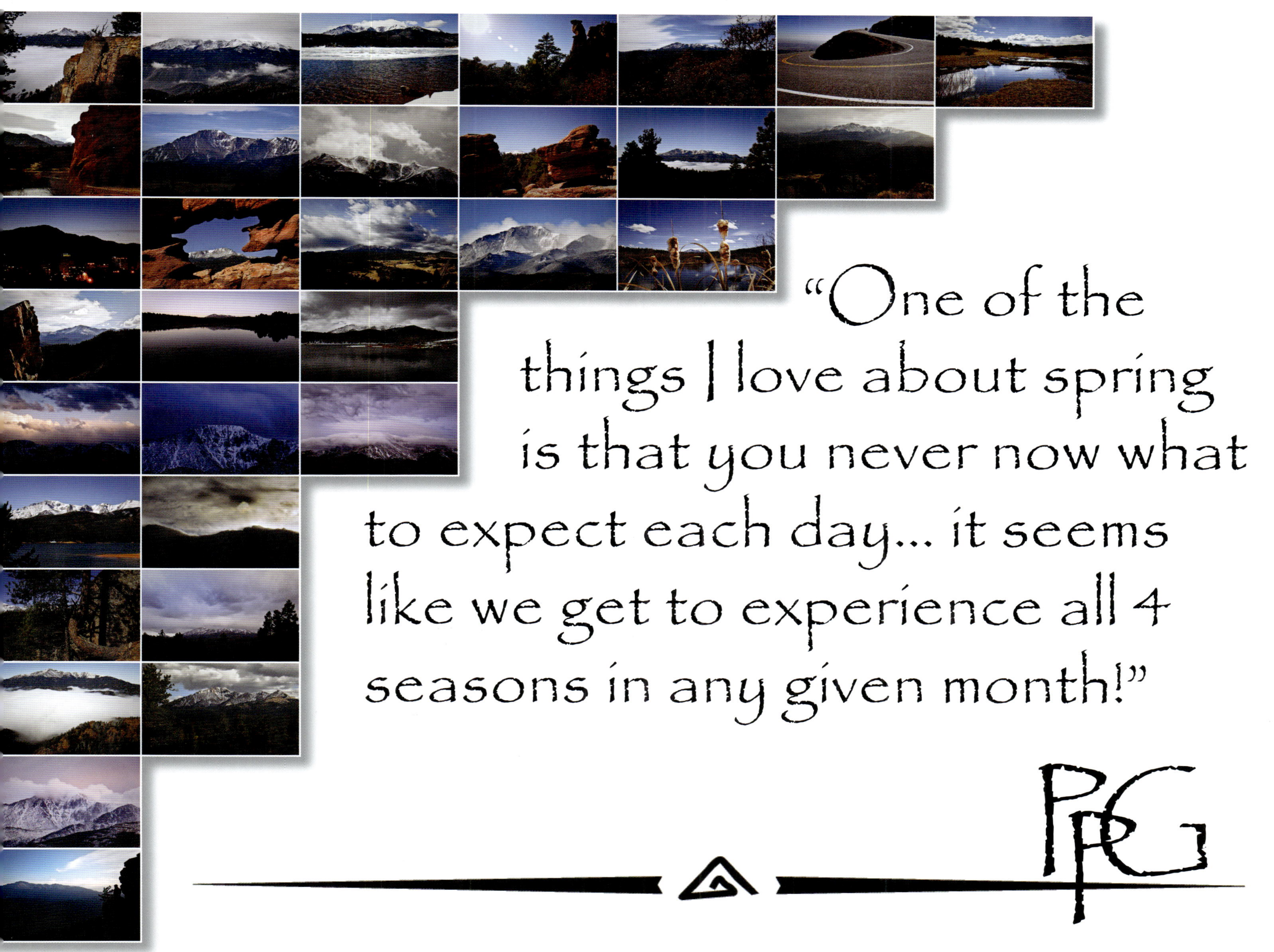
"One of the
things I love about spring
is that you never now what
to expect each day... it seems
like we get to experience all 4
seasons in any given month!"
PPG

Week 40

March 7th ~ Truth be told, I am a little frustrated with today's picture. I am not frustrated in the picture itself, I love this shot, but I am disappointed that this shot only shows the proverbial "tip of the iceberg". This project has hard restrictions that force me to shoot each picture in the same aspect ratio and the same orientation so that it all lays out properly in the book and on the web. Sticking to these guidelines is restricting as an artist, but I have embraced it as part of the challenge of the project. What is disappointing is, that as I stood on this ridge I could see all the way from Colorado Springs to Divide and beyond…the valley filled with clouds in both directions. It was spectacular! By sticking to my guidelines this was the best way I could try to capture the beauty of it, and beautiful it was.

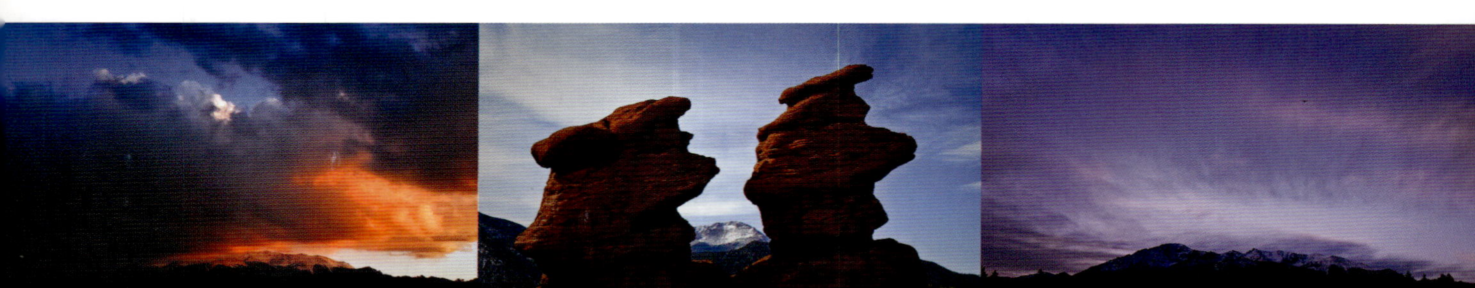

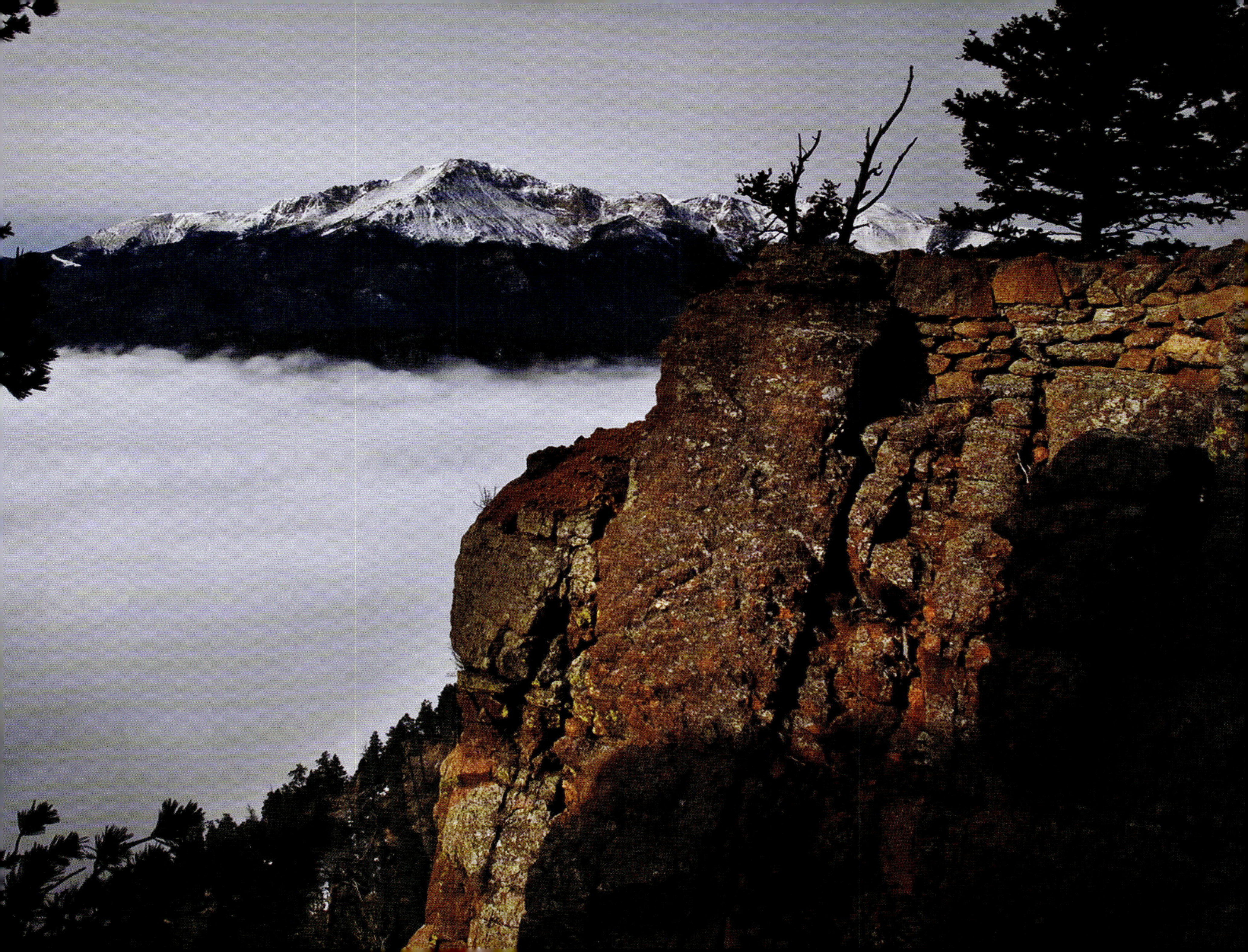

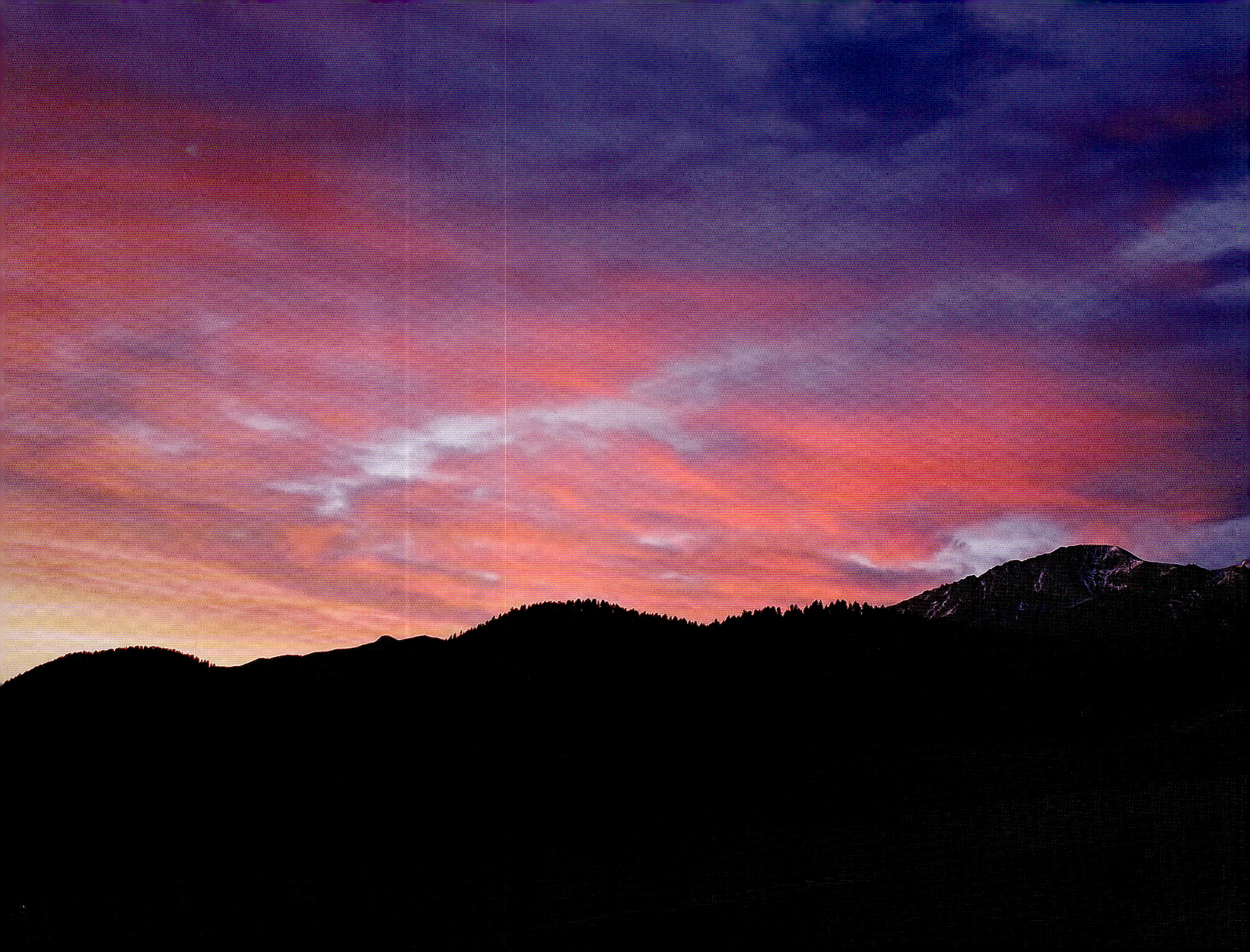

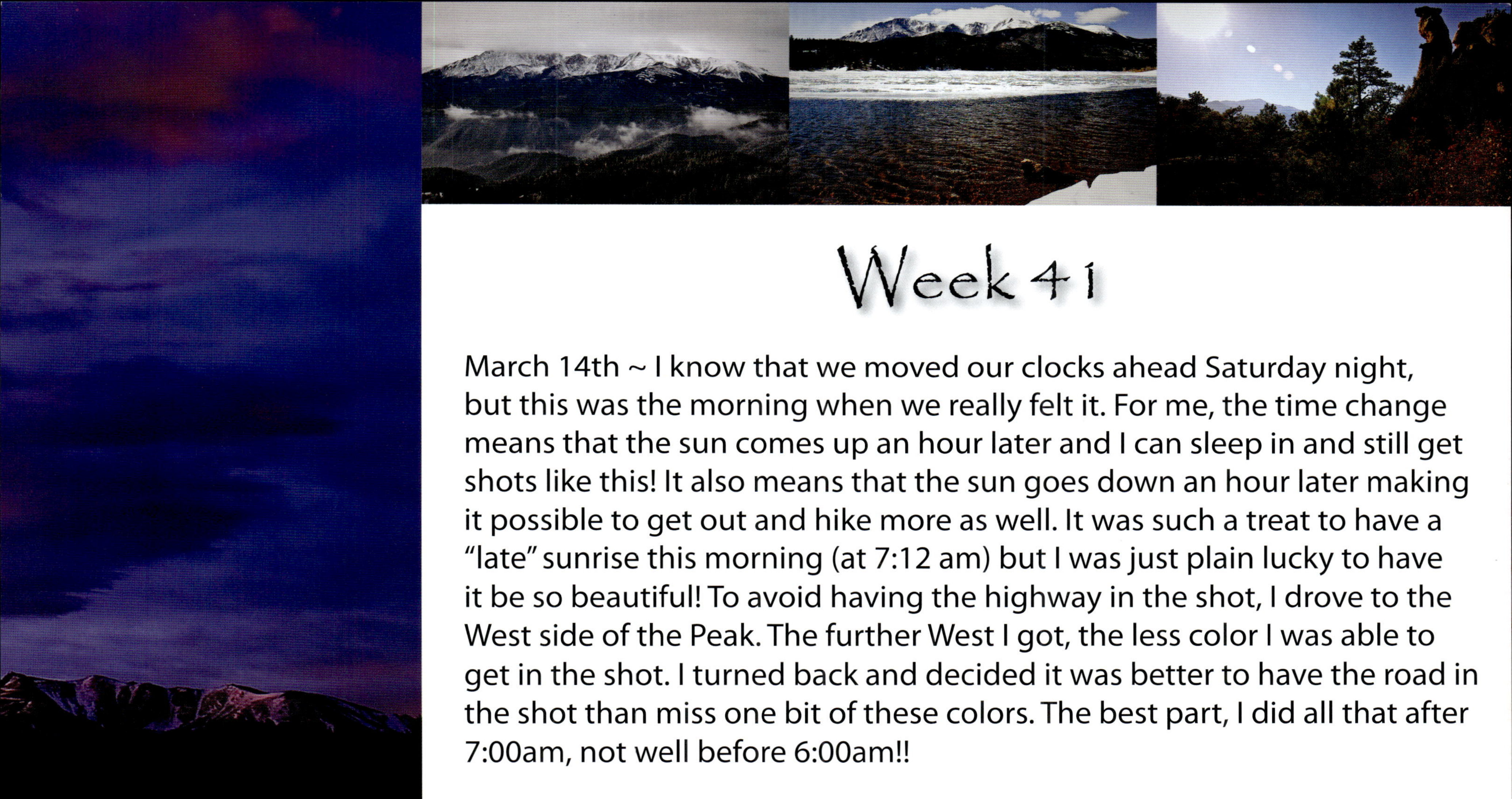

Week 41

March 14th ~ I know that we moved our clocks ahead Saturday night, but this was the morning when we really felt it. For me, the time change means that the sun comes up an hour later and I can sleep in and still get shots like this! It also means that the sun goes down an hour later making it possible to get out and hike more as well. It was such a treat to have a "late" sunrise this morning (at 7:12 am) but I was just plain lucky to have it be so beautiful! To avoid having the highway in the shot, I drove to the West side of the Peak. The further West I got, the less color I was able to get in the shot. I turned back and decided it was better to have the road in the shot than miss one bit of these colors. The best part, I did all that after 7:00am, not well before 6:00am!!

Week 42

March 19th ~ You would never know that today was the last official day of Winter. It was simply gorgeous. We joke about the long winters up here, but the honest truth is that Spring is the most wonderful gift of the entire year. Just hearing the word makes me smile. As I was going through all of my pictures from my morning hike up on the Peak I felt like this shot showed the Peak smiling back. The winds were blowing incredibly hard up there all morning (the top gust was 97 mph!) so I wasn't able to hike all the way around the reservoir like I wanted to, but I got exactly what I was after…a beautiful last day of Winter on my mountain! I am anxious to see what the first official day of Spring holds in store…

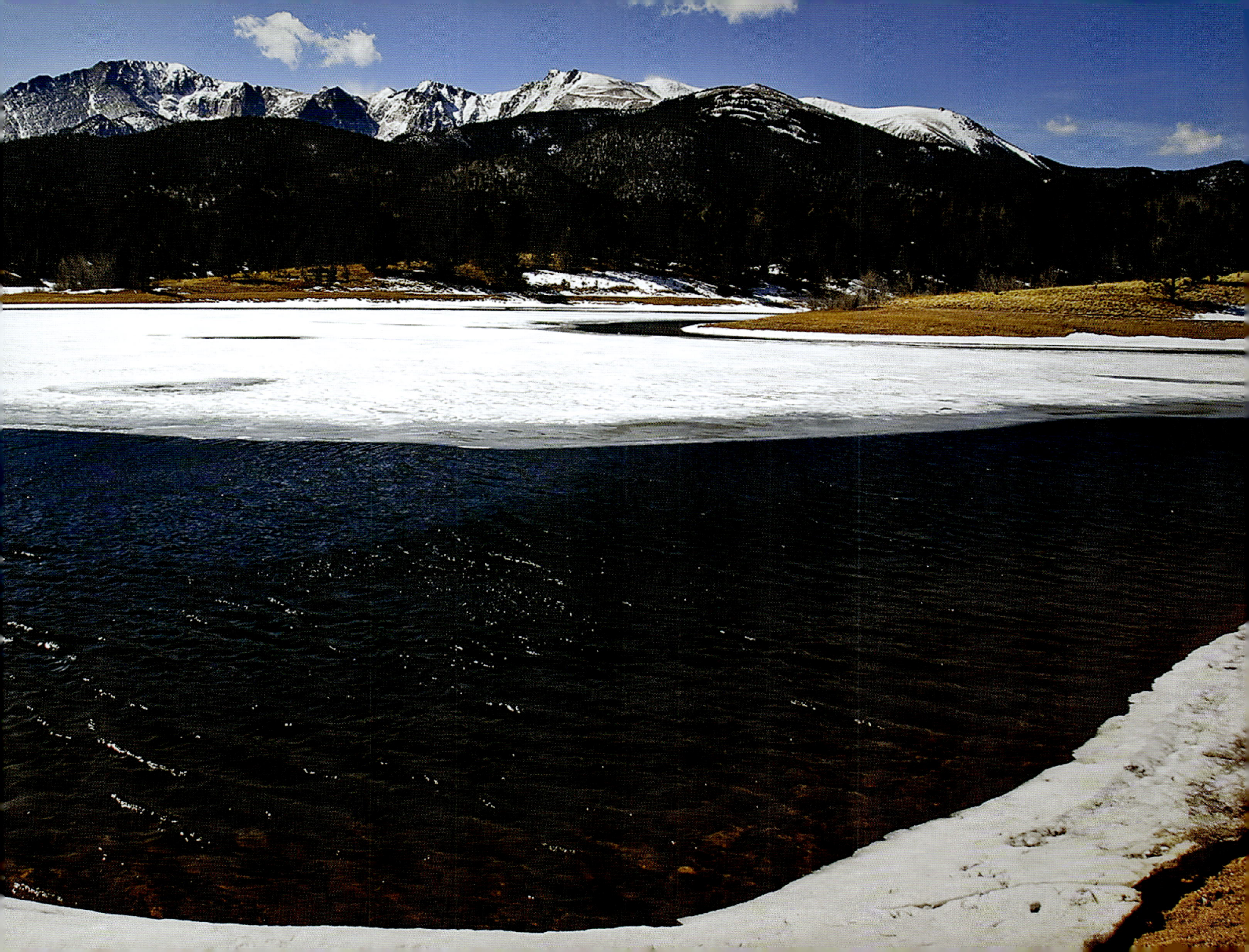

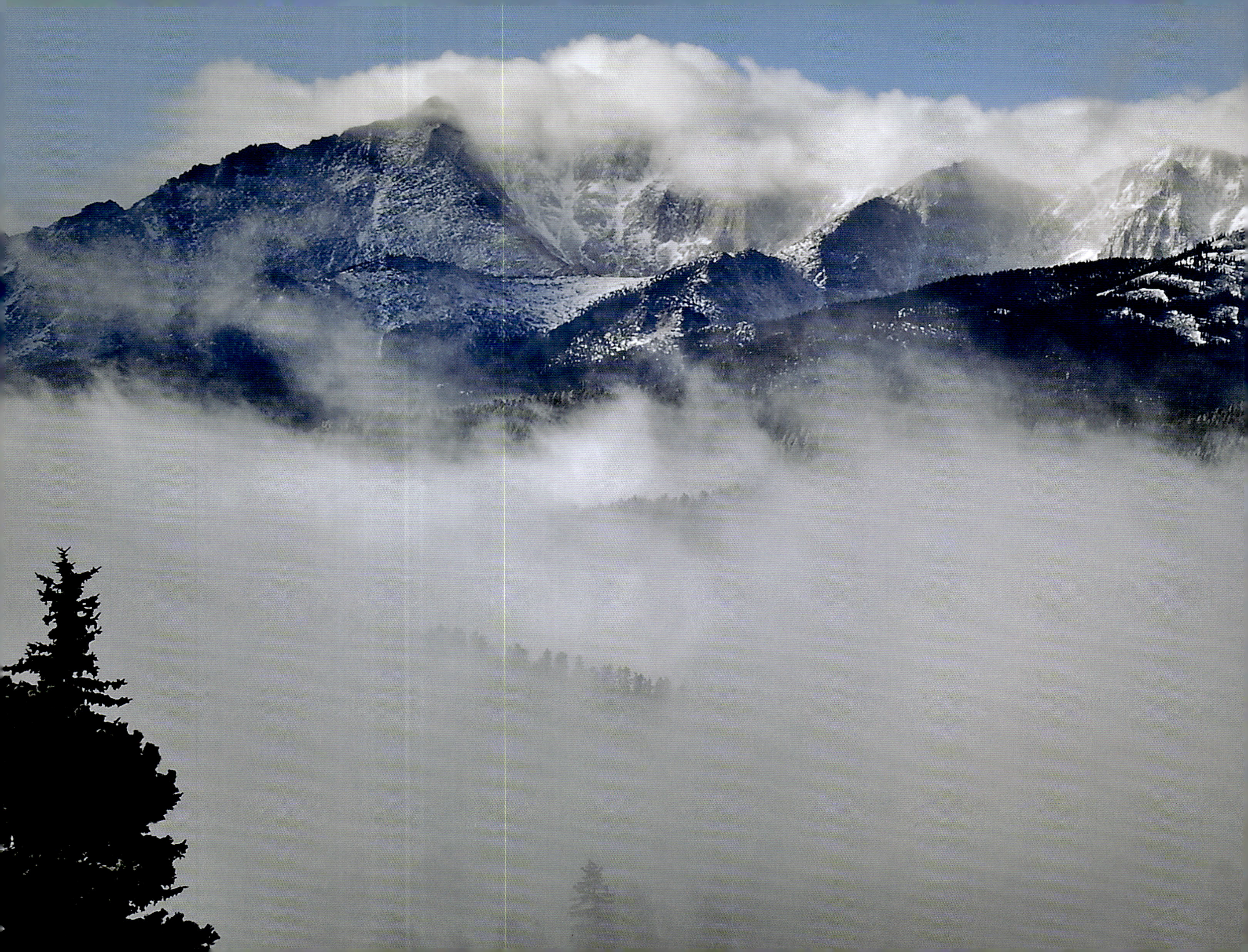

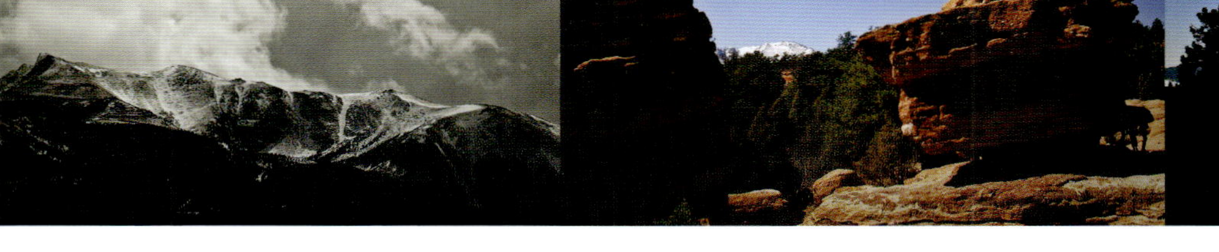

Week 43

March 27th ~ Today marks another milestone in the project, day 300. It really is hard to believe that I am this close to the end, and that I have made it this far! I wanted to have something interesting for my day 300 shot and since I didn't go up on the Peak yesterday, I decided that is where I would be today. Last night I tuned in to the tail end of the weather forecast and it simply said "unsettled weather for the next 3 days." My guess was that it just meant I would get some clouds for my shot and it would be a welcome addition. As you can see I didn't have to go all the way up the Peak to get a dramatic shot today. You just can't plan beauty in landscape photography, you have to just be there and ready when it happens!

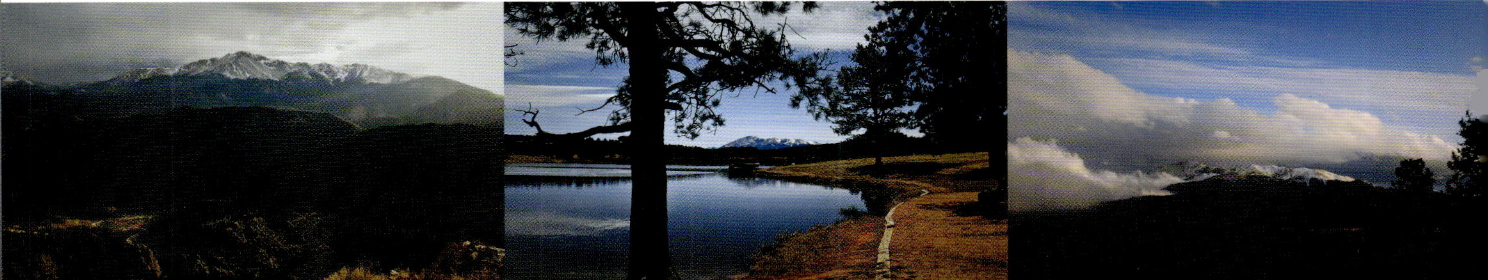

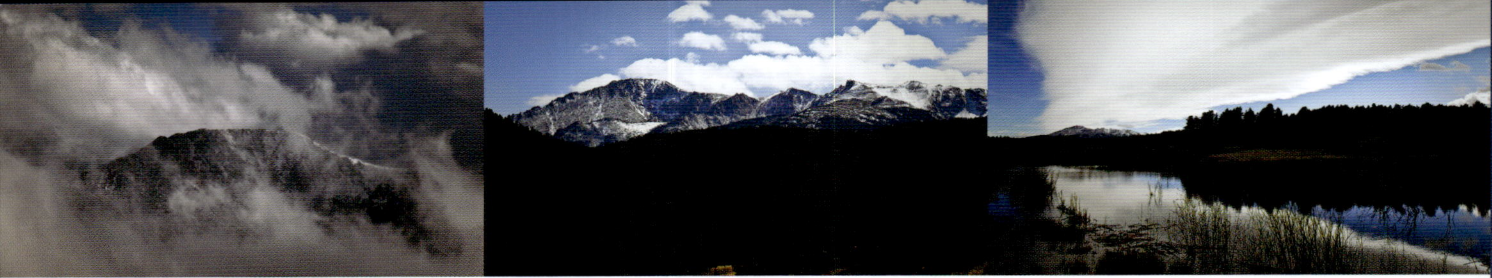

Week 44

April 1st ~ With only 2 months left in the project I started to really think about the pictures I have had on my list since the first day. A post-sunset shot of downtown Colorado Springs has been on that list for a very long time, but I really needed a warm clear night like tonight to pull it off. Normally I would be stomping around the forest on an evening like this, but tonight I was out doing some urban exploring to find just the right spot for this picture and it was really a fun departure from the norm. I didn't think it would be as hard to find a location for this shot as it ended up being, but in the process I "hiked" around downtown for hours and I really enjoyed myself. I usually work hard to keep buildings out of my shots, but tonight I ended up working harder than expected to get them all in ~ and it was well worth the effort!

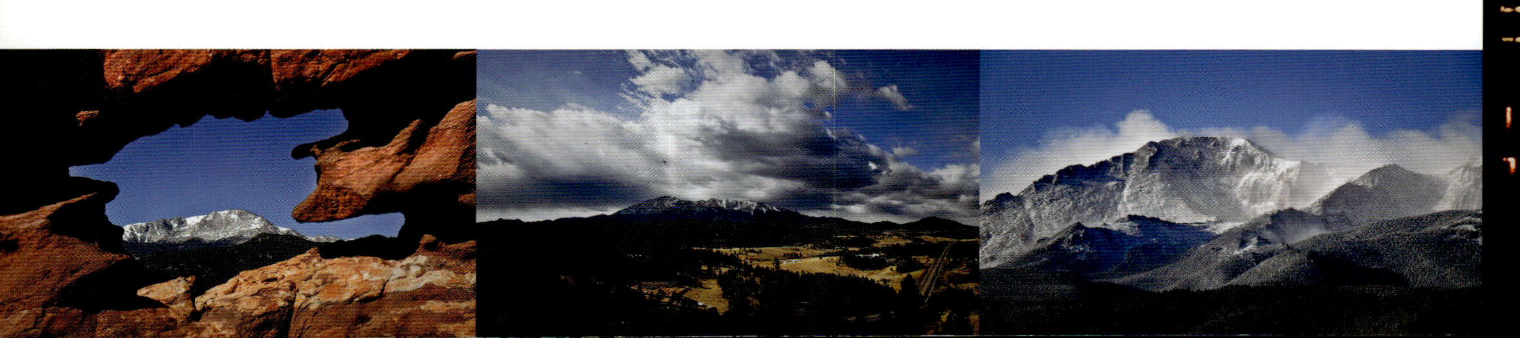

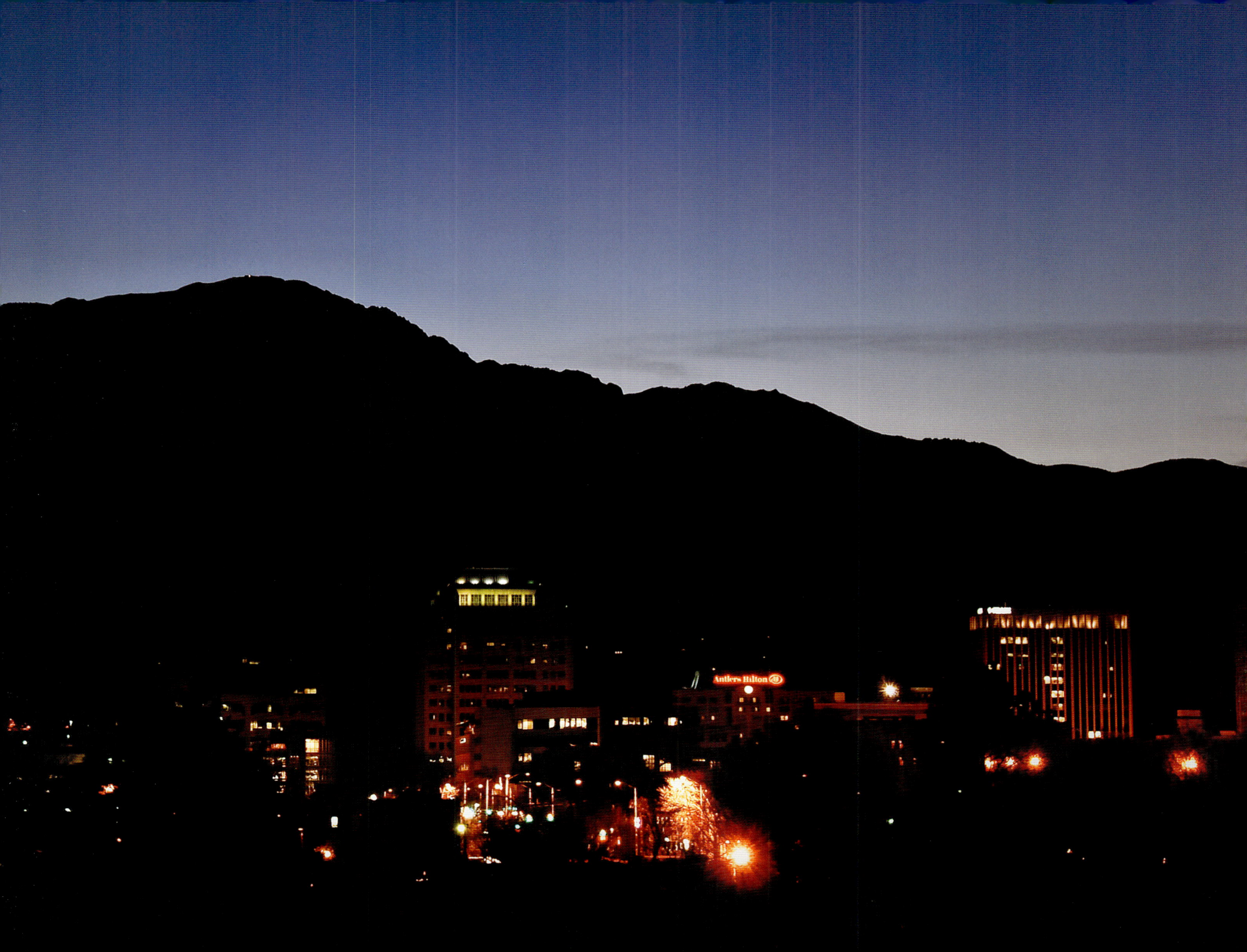
Antlers Hilton

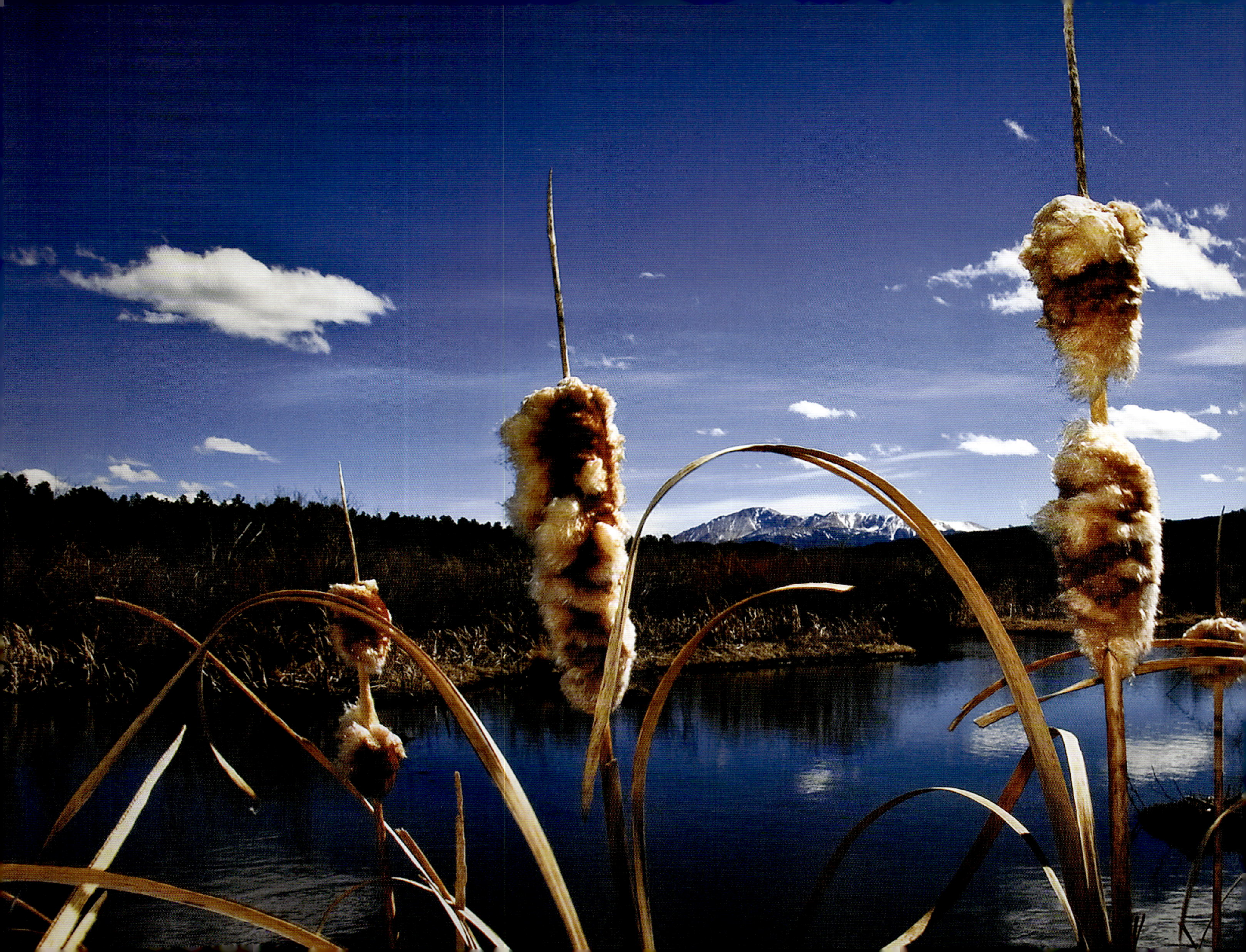

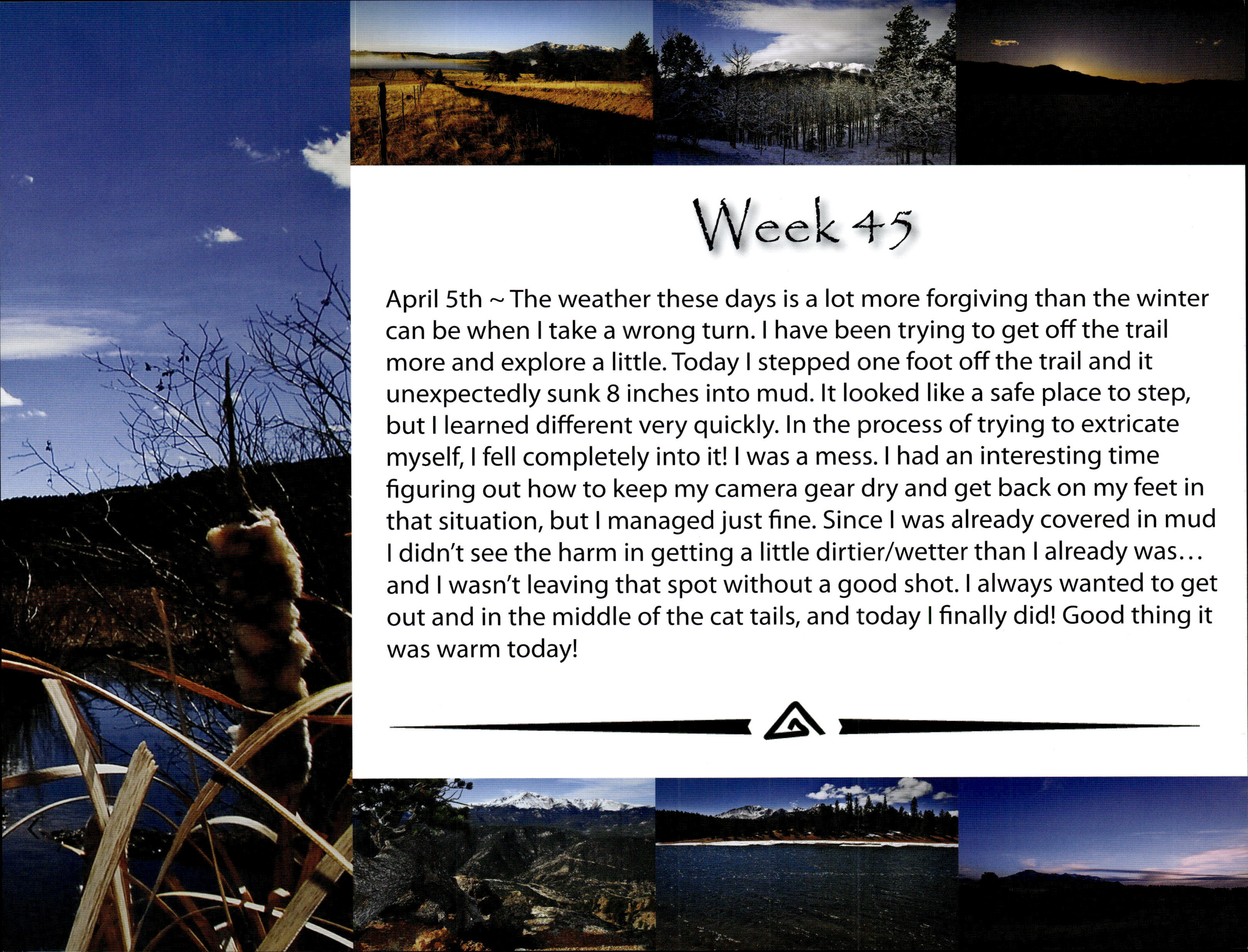

Week 45

April 5th ~ The weather these days is a lot more forgiving than the winter can be when I take a wrong turn. I have been trying to get off the trail more and explore a little. Today I stepped one foot off the trail and it unexpectedly sunk 8 inches into mud. It looked like a safe place to step, but I learned different very quickly. In the process of trying to extricate myself, I fell completely into it! I was a mess. I had an interesting time figuring out how to keep my camera gear dry and get back on my feet in that situation, but I managed just fine. Since I was already covered in mud I didn't see the harm in getting a little dirtier/wetter than I already was… and I wasn't leaving that spot without a good shot. I always wanted to get out and in the middle of the cat tails, and today I finally did! Good thing it was warm today!

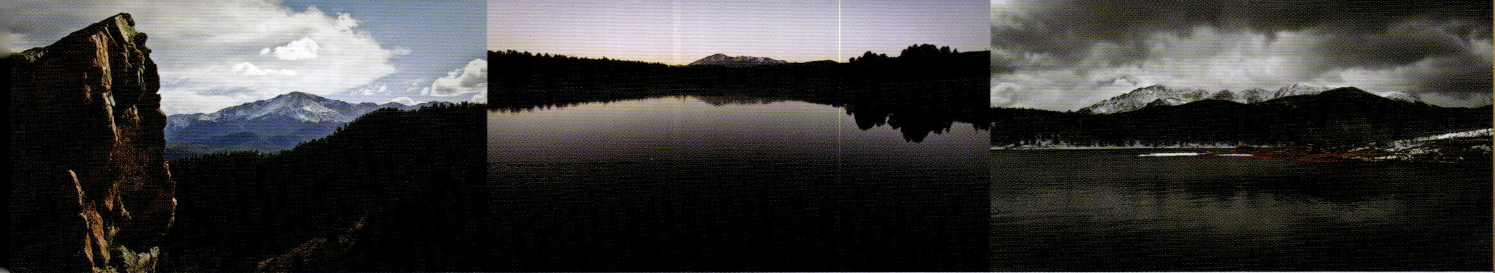

Week 46

April 16th ~ Today was one of those amazing days that starts out sunny with beautiful blue skies, but slowly gives way to storm clouds by the afternoon. By 4:00pm I actually thought those clouds may drop some rain, but we weren't so lucky. I caught pictures all throughout the day and actually had my final picture all picked out just before I sat down for some dinner, but I just knew there was more to come. Even though I had my shot picked out, I was restless about it and couldn't stay in the house… I kept getting up and going outside and looking at the sky wondering if those stormy clouds would turn orange. I finally just gave in and got in my truck and drove to a spot that was close by, but would give a great view if it really happened. As you can see, I got lucky and my hunch paid off and I'm glad I gave into that nagging feeling that I wasn't quite done for the day!

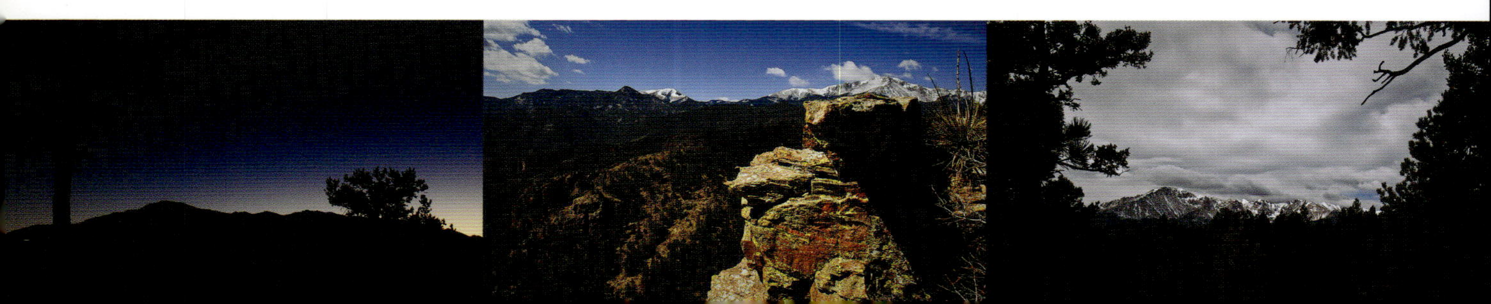

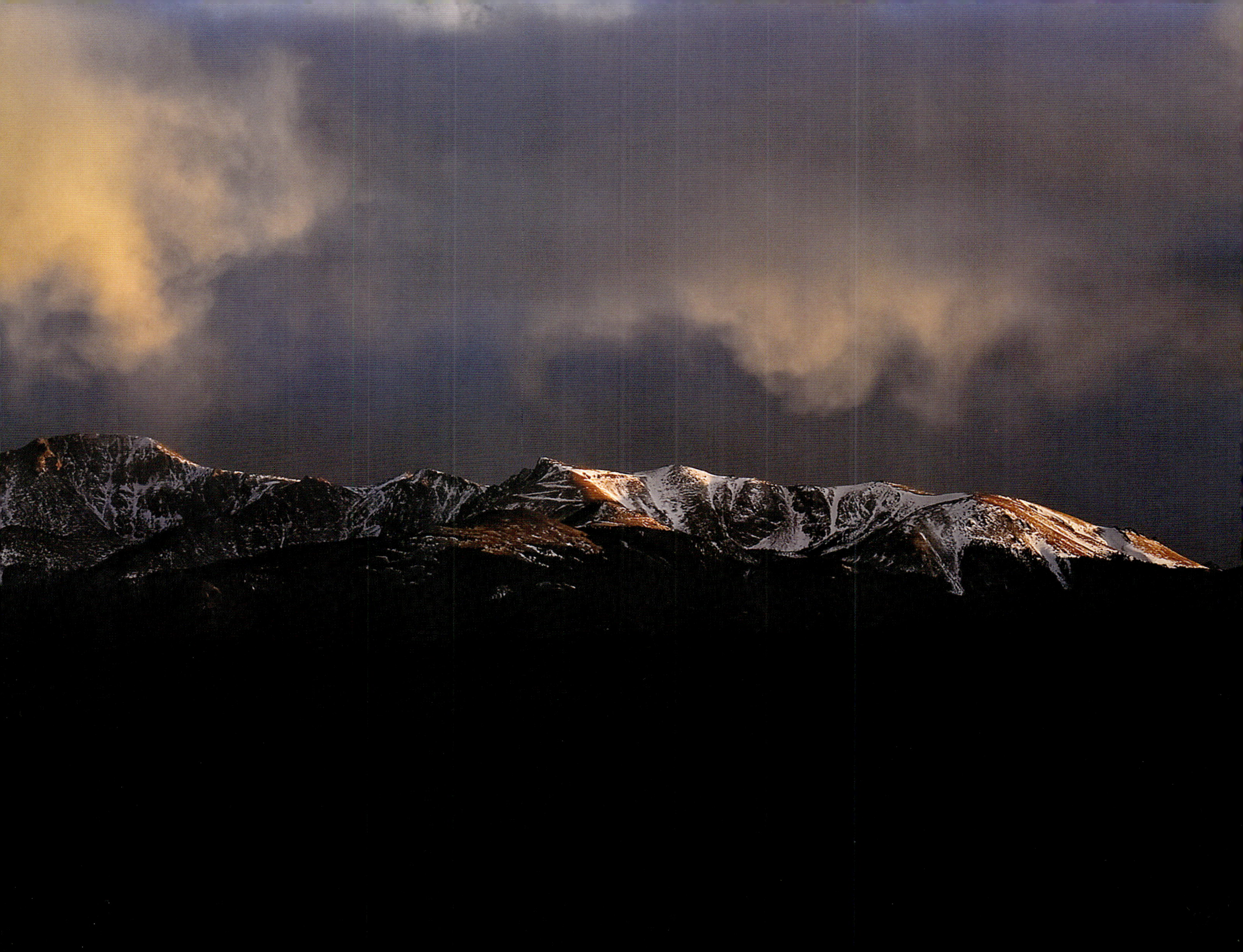

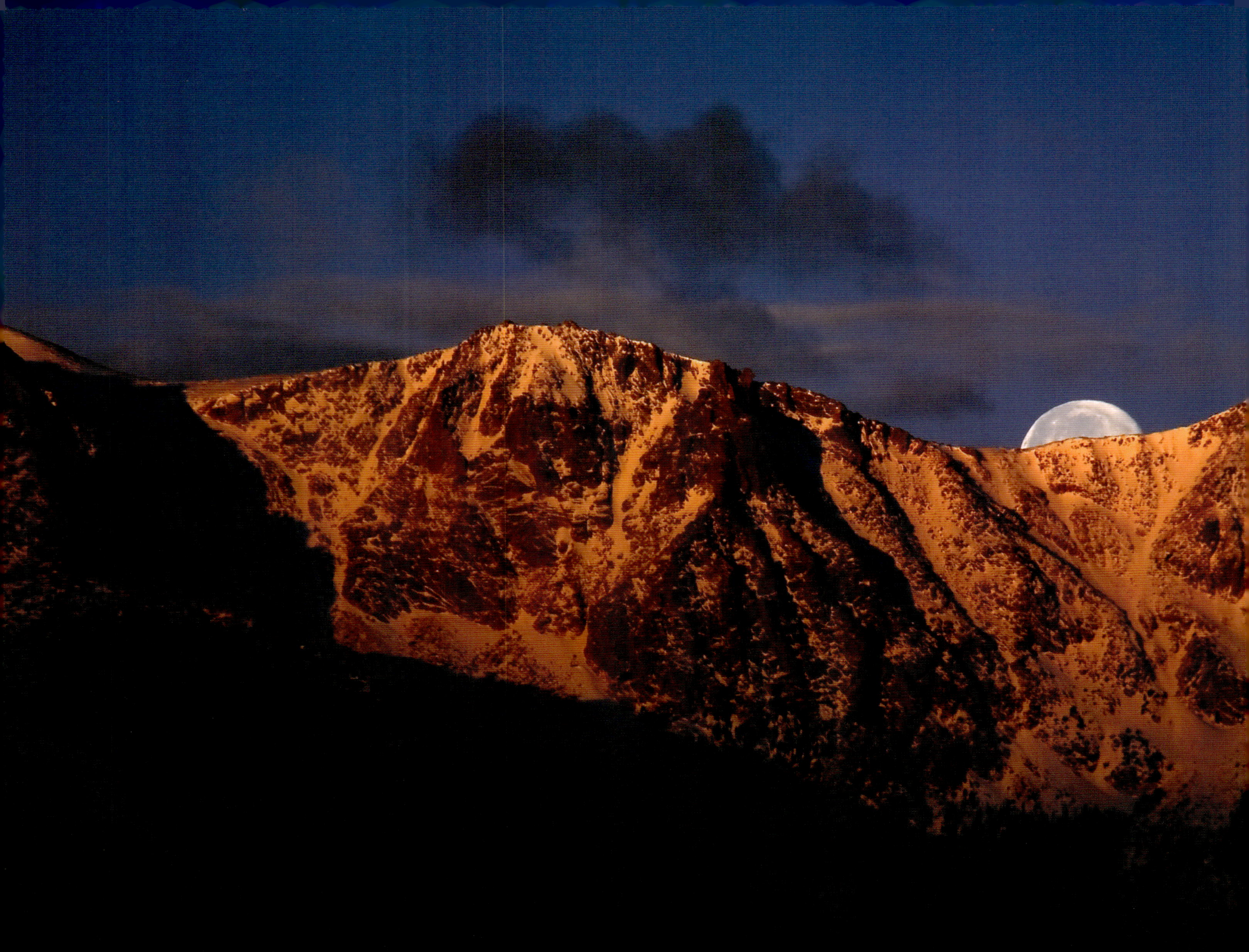

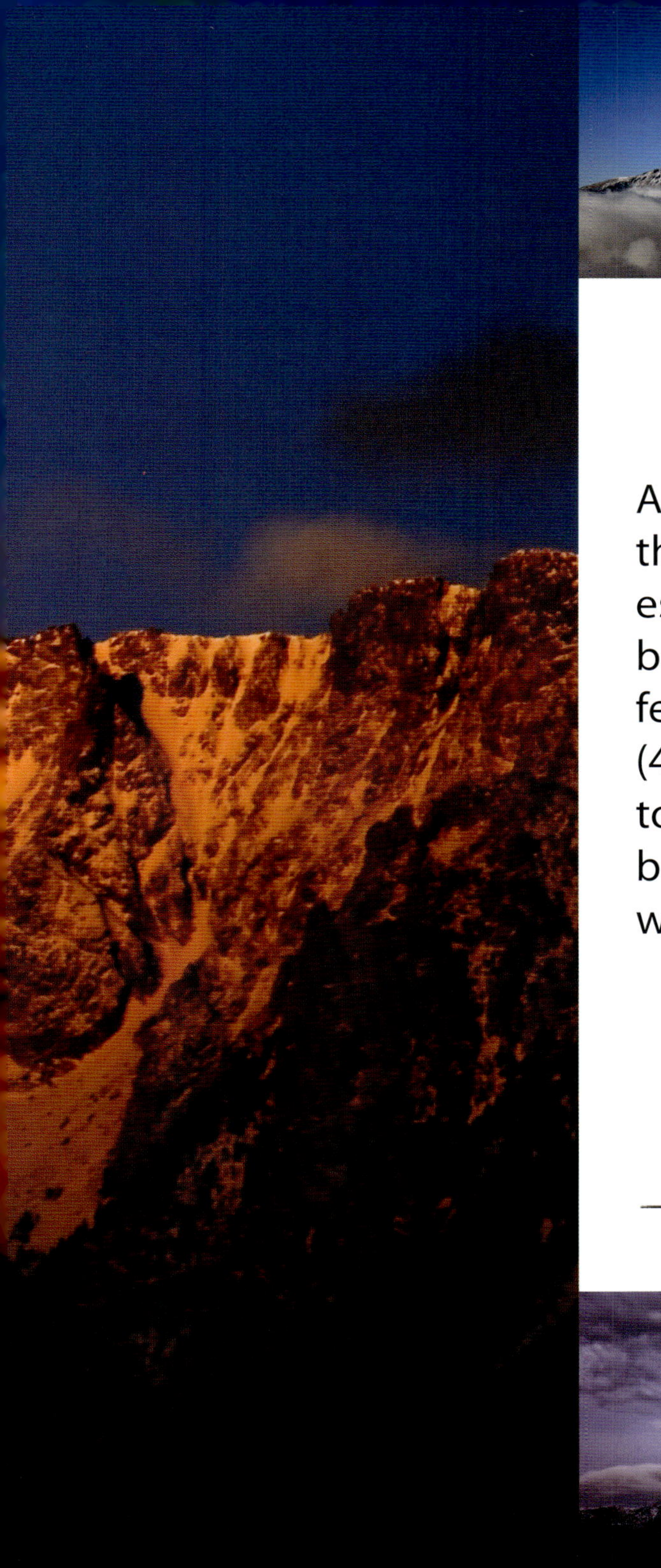

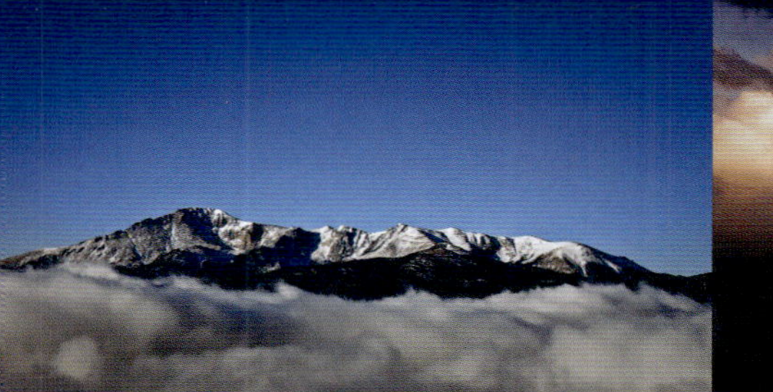

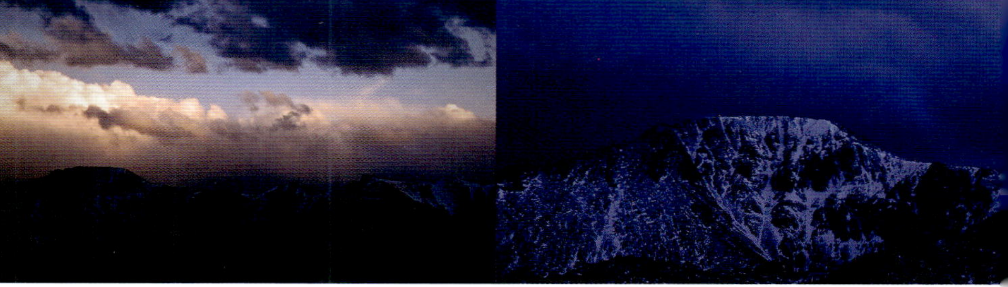

Week 47

April 19th ~ I have been trying to get a picture of the full moon and the Peak since I started this project, but it has been something that has escaped me until today. It seems like it would be a fairly easy thing to do, but it has been a huge challenge. When you consider that there are only a few lunar cycles each year where the moon actually sets behind the Peak (4 days in total), you start to realize how rare it is to even have the chance to get a shot like this. To capture a photograph of the full moon sinking behind the Peak just as the first light of sunrise painted the mountain pink was an amazing moment. My short list of shots is getting shorter!

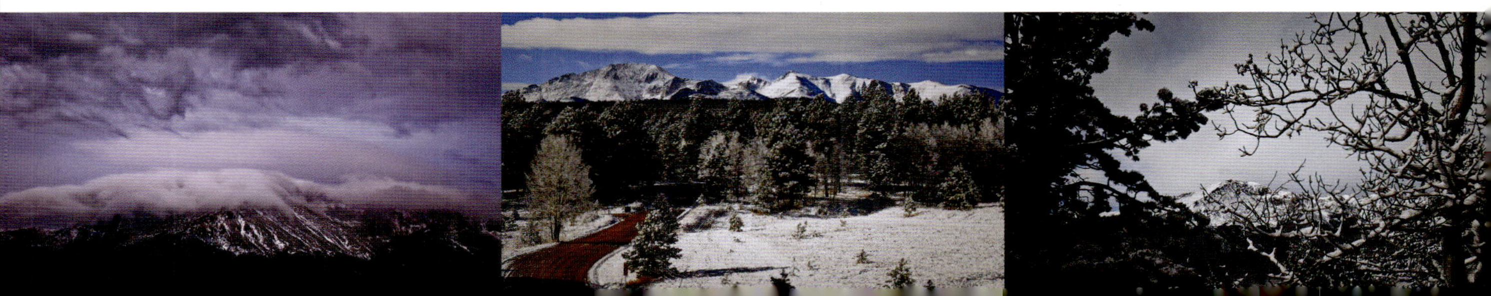

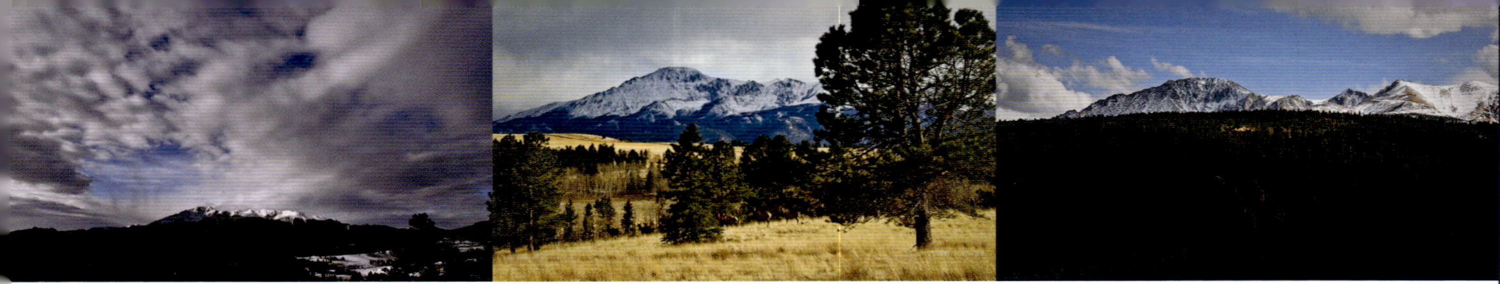

Week 48

April 28th ~ It may sound strange, but I have been waiting for this day for a very long time. Not the date specifically, but the chance to get back up to Rampart Reservoir and take a picture of the sunset. My last picture from this side of the reservoir was October 29th of the previous year, 1 day shy of exactly 6 months ago… but it was worth the wait. The reservoir is not fully open yet and you have to park on the North side of the dam and hike across to get this view. The hike was the best part of the night. I can't even begin to describe what it felt like to be the only person out there in the quietness and serenity of the evening, and when you add a beautiful sunset to the equation it all adds up to a perfect evening. If you have never hiked across the dam to watch the sunset with your significant other, get it on your Spring-to-do list because it is an amazing thing!

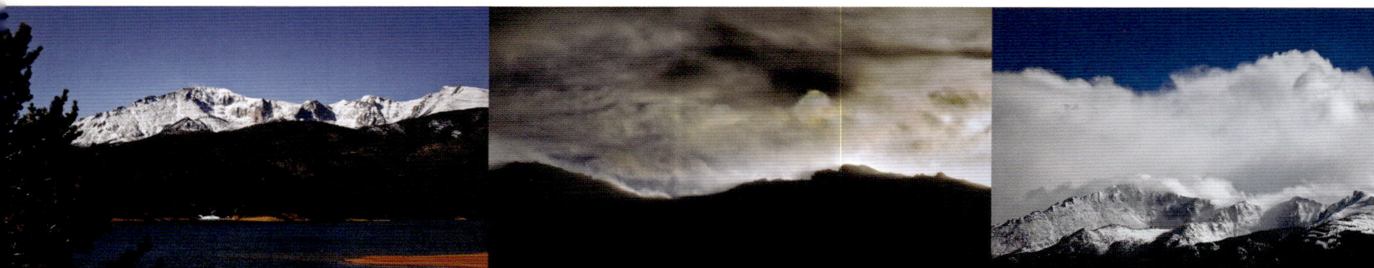

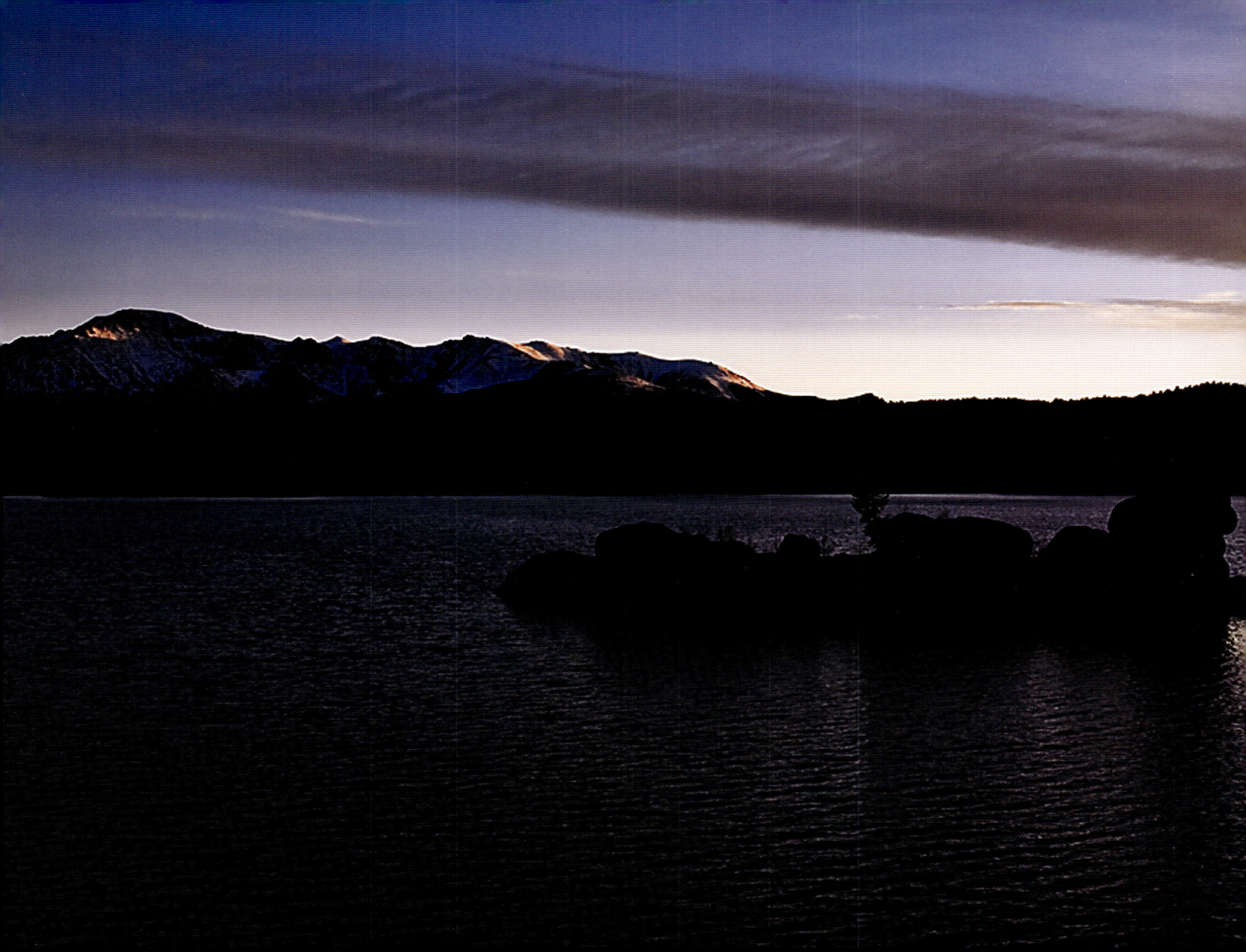

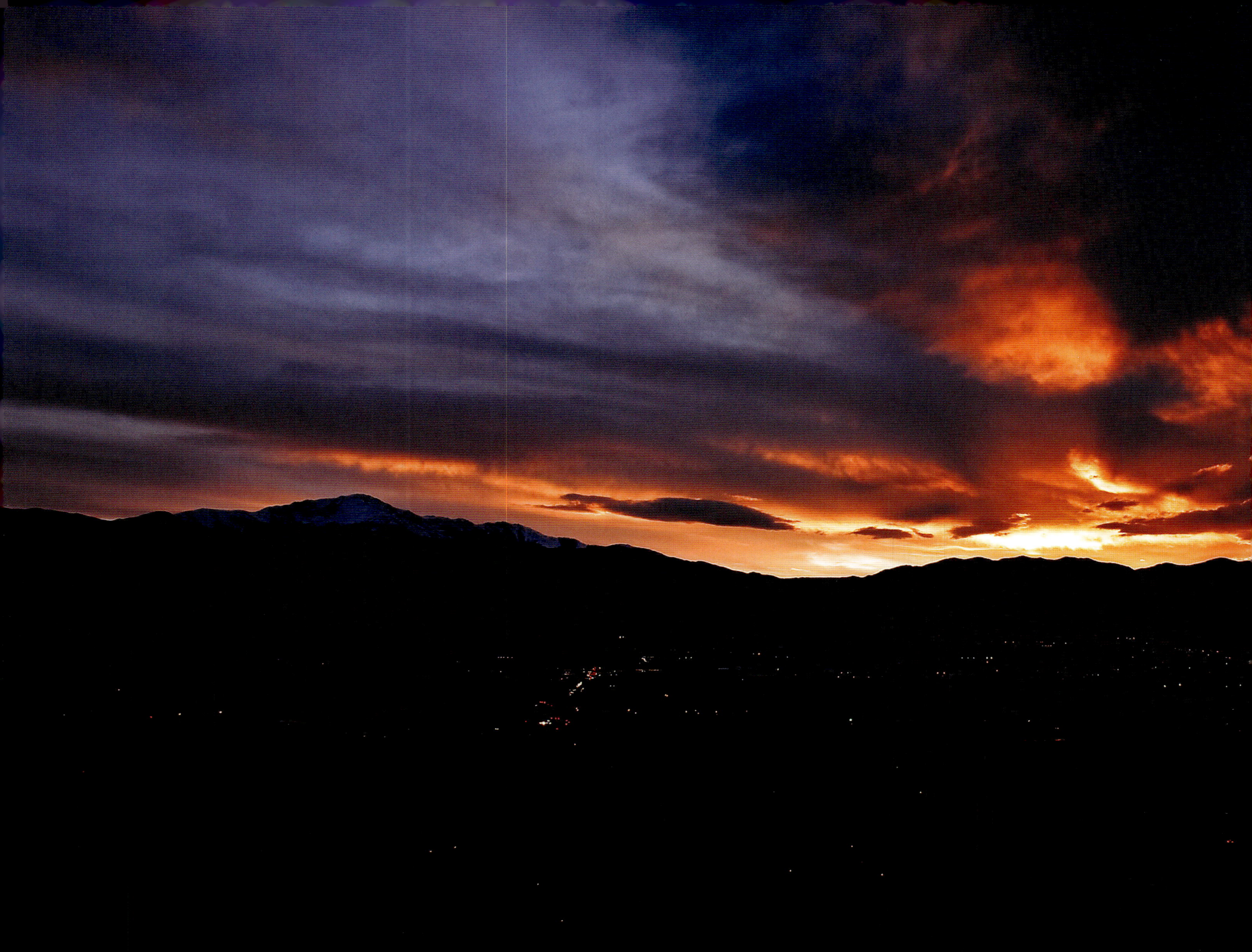

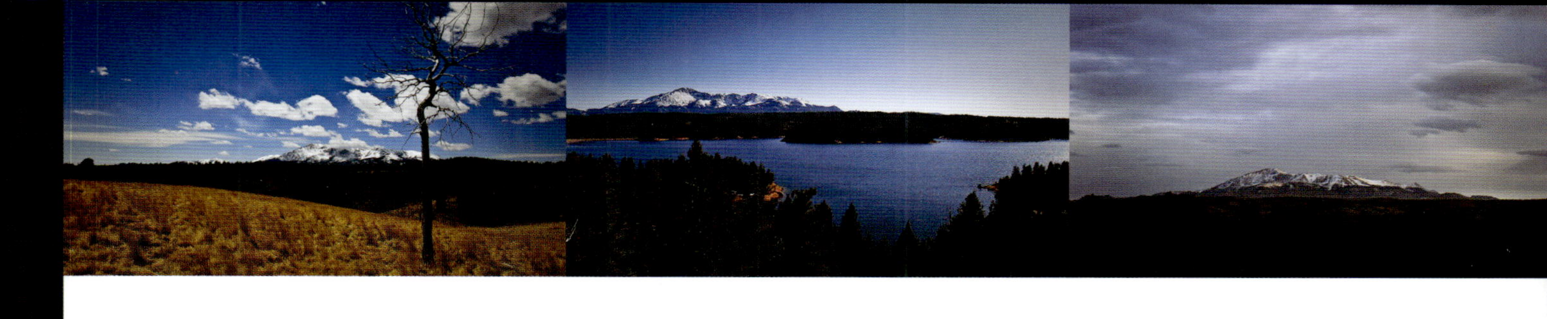

Week 49

May 3rd ~ I had my entire day all planned perfectly, but the Peak apparently had a completely different plan than I did. My plans were based on a bright sunny day and plenty of time to take a late afternoon hike while taking pictures along the way. There wasn't a single cloud in the sky this morning, but at some point that changed and a blanket of flat gray clouds moved in when I wasn't looking. All my plans went out the window and I had to figure out what I was going to do if it didn't clear up. Once I accepted that the clouds might stick around long enough for a sunset shot, I actually welcomed them and headed out to Palmer Park and just waited for the magic. Some days it is a love/hate relationship with the clouds, but tonight I had to say I love how they painted the sky!

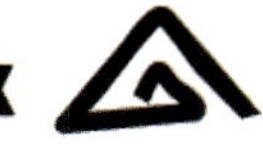

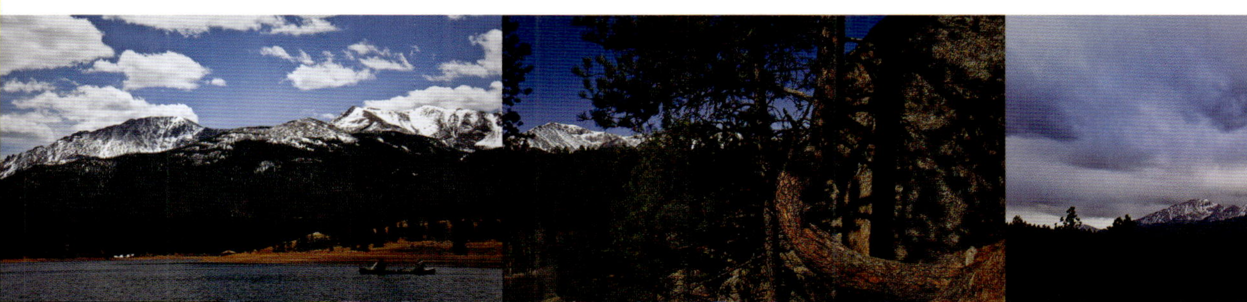

Week 50

May 16th ~ We've had fog every single day for five days straight around here, so when I woke up this morning and saw fog again I was a little surprised, but glad to see it! Crazy weather is like a gift for me. It creates a bit of a photographic playground that gives me choices and options that just aren't available on a clear, sunny day. Throughout the past year there have only been a few times when the weather has been like this and those times have taught me that somehow the Peak always seems to find its way out of the storms. I just needed to show up to catch the beauty of the moment when it happens. The fog seemed to slosh up and down the pass all morning and then around noon it all gave way to an absolutely beautiful sunny day. Days like this are what makes Spring the best time of the year!

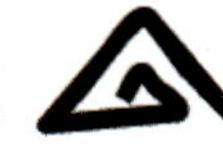

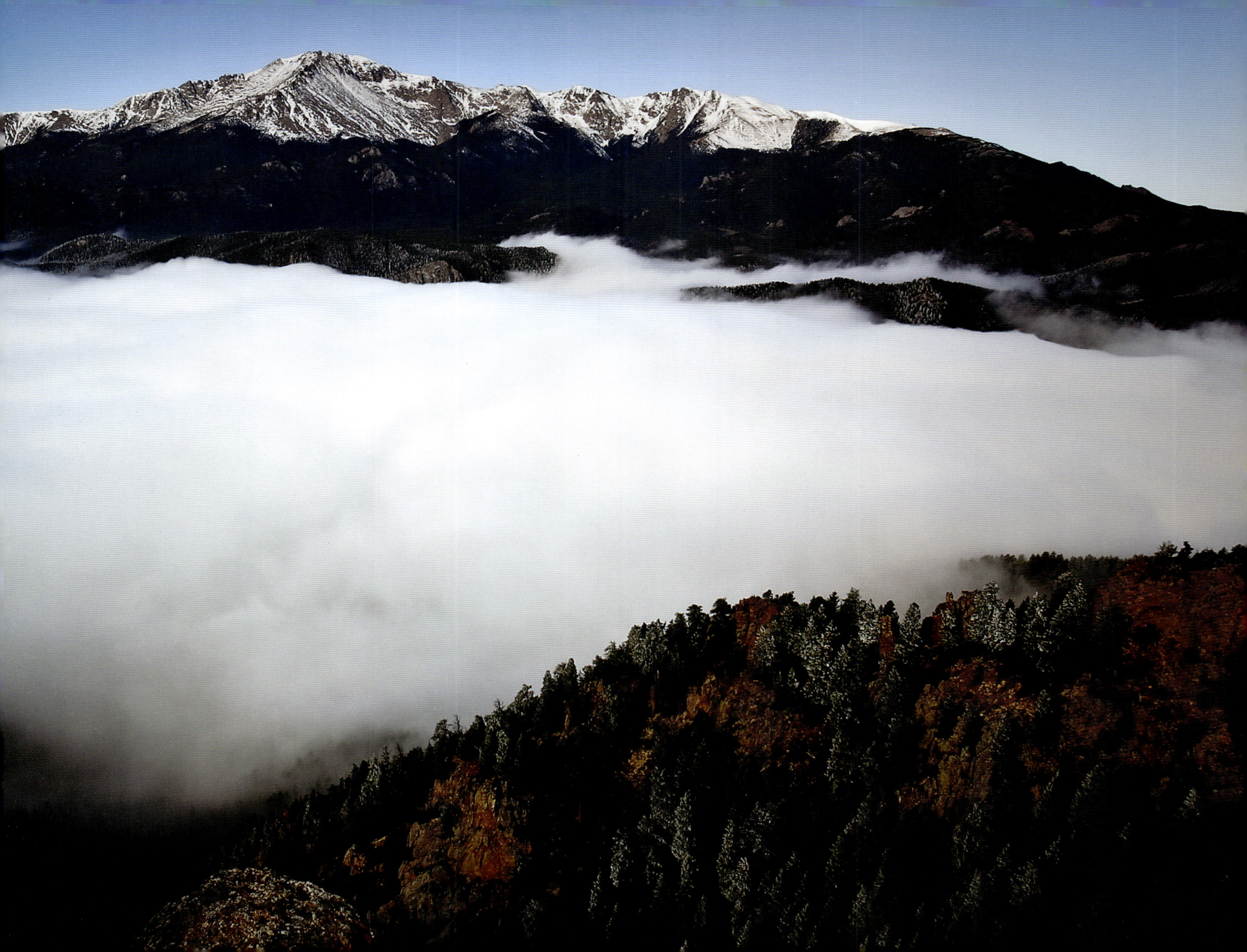

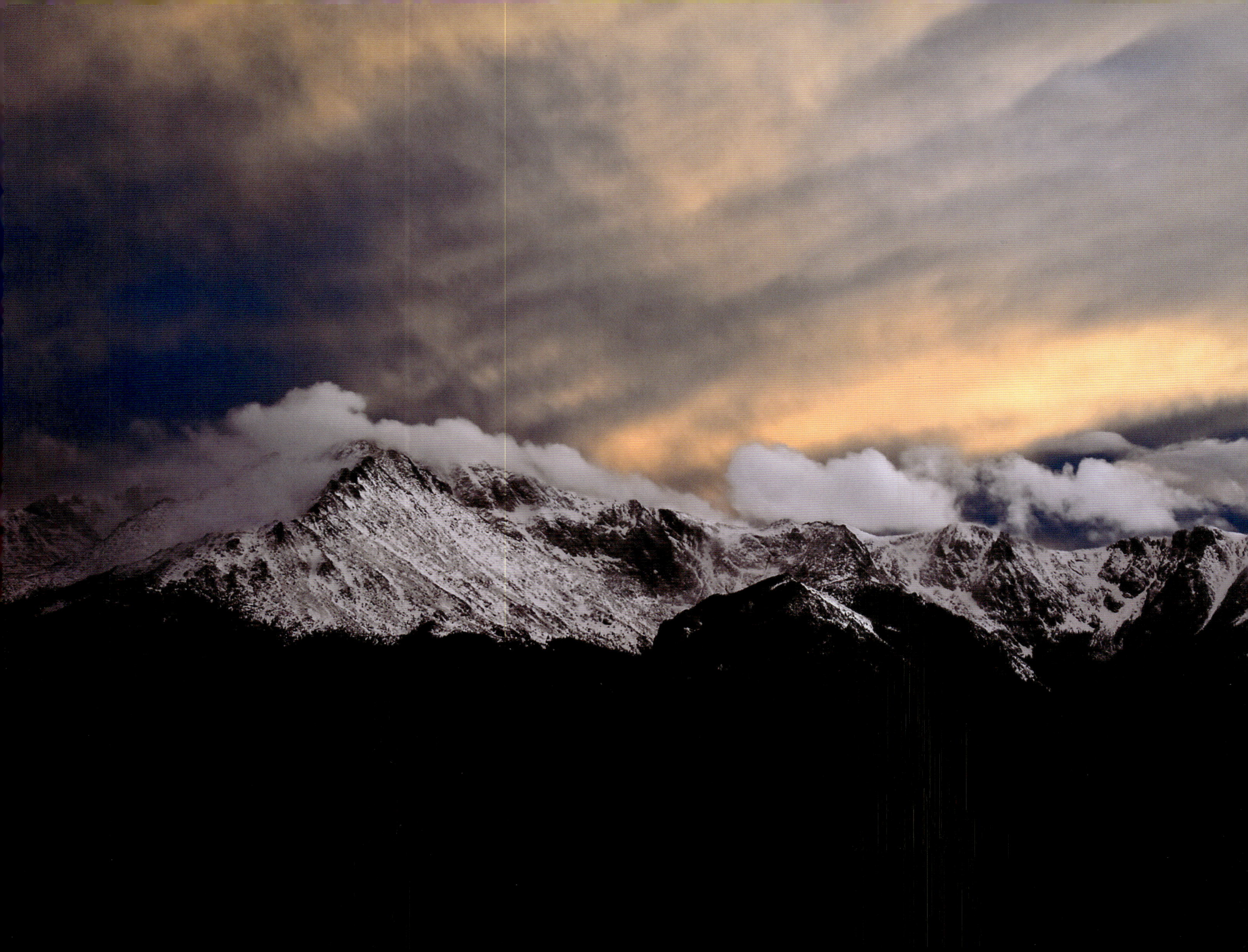

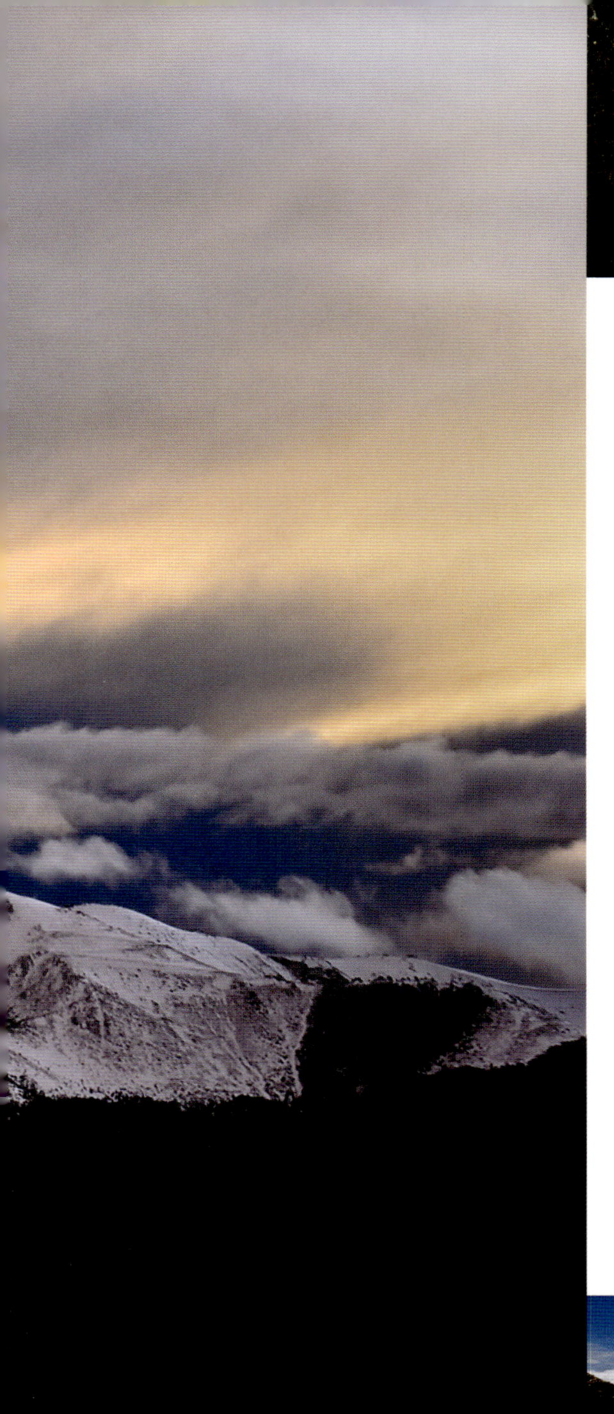

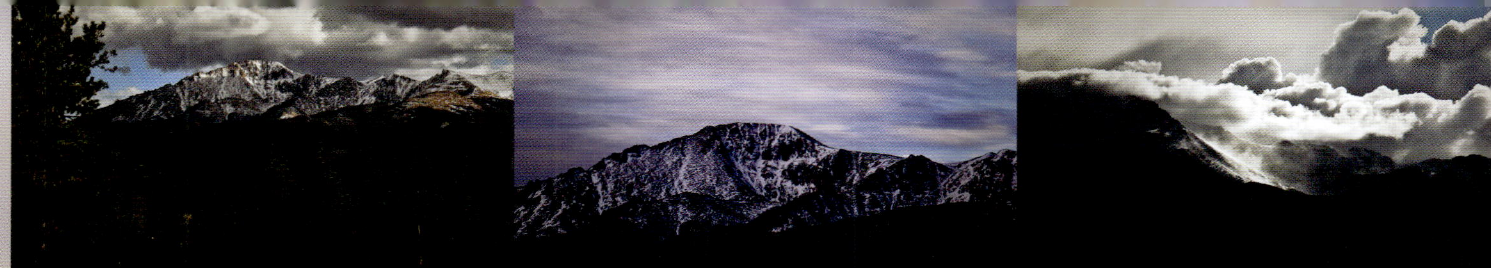

Week 51

May 20th ~ Tonight I found myself shirtless out in the forest during a blinding snowstorm and wondered if I had finally lost my mind! I had hiked about an hour out from my truck thinking the storms were over, but soon learned they had just paused for a little while. Out of nowhere a total white out snowstorm blew down the pass and my camera was getting coated in snow so I had to give up my hat to save my camera. I quickly realized that I needed the hat more than the camera and decided to strip off my 4 layers and use my undershirt to protect my camera, and get my hat back on my head so I didn't freeze out there. I don't think I have ever been so cold in my life! I would guarantee that tonight's sunset was beautiful no matter where you were, making me wonder if the things I do to get a shot are really necessary… or if I am just nuts!! Tonight was just a reminder how quickly the weather can turn, even in late May.

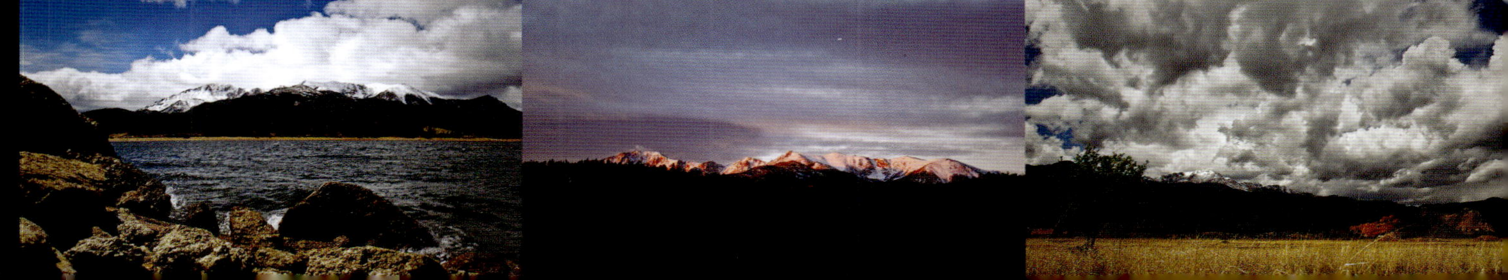

Week 52

May 27th ~ I had my entire day and picture all planned out, but about 7:00pm I realized that no matter what picture I had planned on getting (and actually got) earlier, the Peak had a completely different plan for me… again. They opened the Pikes Peak Highway all the way to the summit for the first time in a very long time, so I headed up there to get the shot I had in mind. When you are standing at 14,110 feet, you can see a lot of things, and I could see from the moment I got up there that at some point tonight the sun would actually dip below the clouds and make for something special. Just as I had anticipated, about an hour before sunset the entire Ute pass became a magnificent blend of shadows, highlights and colors. Most people think the magic happens after the sun goes down, but more often than not it's that balance between the colorful clouds above and beautiful light below, that turns out to be the best part of the sunset… and tonight, I was lucky enough to find that moment!

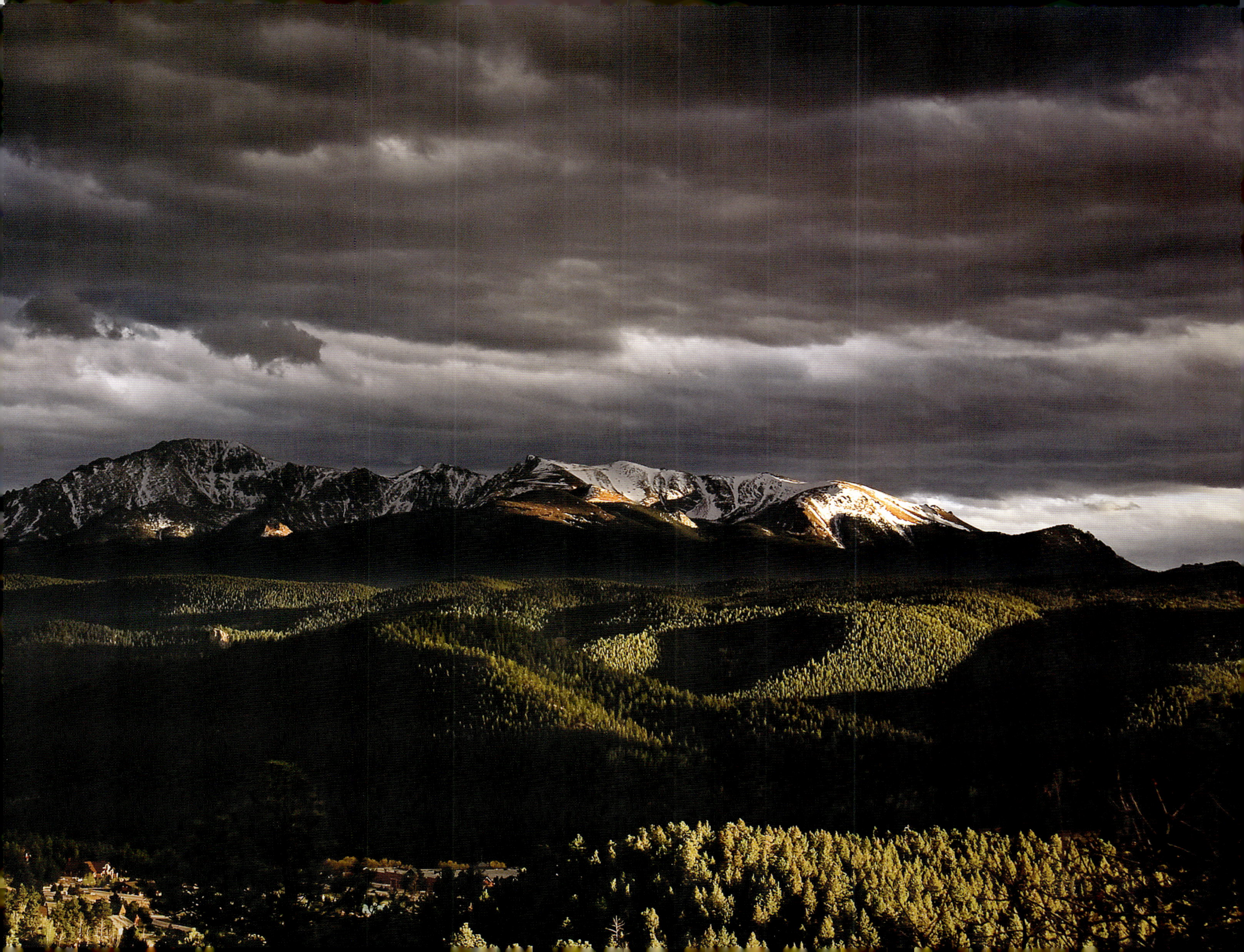

Acknowledgments

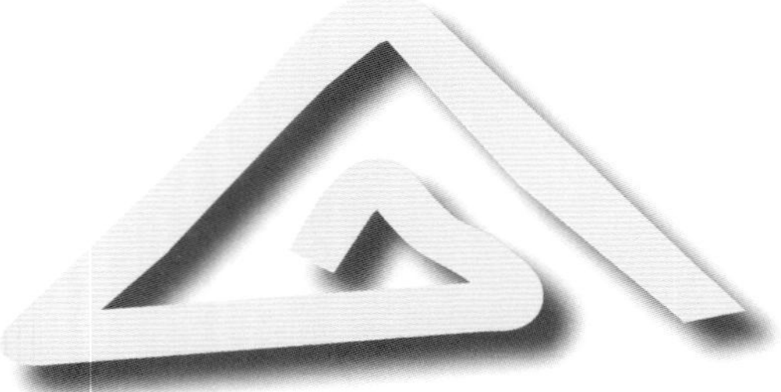

Even though this was mostly a solitary effort, it took an entire community of support to make this project happen. I need to take the time to thank those who have helped me along the way. Without all of their help and support this book would not exist.

The Editing team ~ I want to thank Andrea Furniss for her work editing this book. At the beginning of the project I had no intention of publishing my writings each day. This was mainly because I am not a writer, but also because I am not very good at it either. Andrea's work cleaning up my poorly structured sentences, horrible grammar and misspelled words was a huge help along the way. She didn't do this for a paycheck or for recognition; she did it because she, too, loves that mountain. Thank you Andrea! I also need to take the opportunity to thank my proofreader Karin Taylor. She, too, gave a tremendous amount of time to help polish things up and I am so grateful. Thank you Karin!

The Bovee's ~ I have to take the time to acknowledge the Bovee family. Without them and their encouragement to display and publish my photography, this book would not exist. They are true artists themselves and are an inspiration to me! Thank you Mark and Christi!!

Jon Dale ~ Well, no book is truly complete unless Jon Dale has shaped it in some way. Jon was the one who said, "Do it! Don't wait for it to be a finished product, get out there on the web and social media and let the world come along for the ride!" His advice, mentoring, and encouragement along the way shaped the success of this endeavor from inception. Thanks Jon, you truly are an agent of change!

Facebook and Twitter Fans ~ At the onset of this project I started a Facebook and Twitter page so that I could share my photos along the way. From the ever first person to join the Facebook page to the very last person to retweet my posts, I sincerely thank you all for coming along for the ride. Each of you fueled my desire and passion to get out there day after day and you make this project what it became. I had an idea at the beginning, but all of your comments and encouragement shaped what you are holding in your hand today. From the bottom of my heart, thank you!

The Pikes Peak Rangers ~ I want to thank all of the Rangers on Pikes Peak that put up with me over this year, but a special thanks to Ranger Supervisor Betty Kuhlman who greeting me with a smile and make me look forward to each trip up the mountain.

Property Owners ~ Thank you to those of you who let me share their view of Pikes Peak with the world!

My family ~ For every ounce of help, unwavering support and love, I thank each of you. Thank you for not having me committed or laughing at me and my crazy ideas. Only you truly know what an incredible effort this was and the multitude of sacrifices it took to pull this off. You were the ones who made most of the sacrifices and deserve a ton of credit.

I would like to extend a very special thank you to some of the people and businesses that had a huge impact throughout the is project and contributed in their own way to the success of this endeavor: The Taylor Family, the Woods Family, Krystal Coté, Rita Randolph, Phyllis Delaney, Karin Taylor, Troy Francis, Barry Patterson, Ben Caperton, Charlotte Poltenovage, Jeff Bivens, Melinda Truscelli, Tony Perry, Matthew Upton, Ralph Holloway, Ryan Boldrey, Cowbells and the Deersnake Gallery, Seven Arrows Gallery, Pikes Peak Paradise Bed and Breakfast, Park State Bank and Trust, Molly Wells of Design Savvy, Lowepro, The Pikes Peak Cog Railway, The Pikes Peak Courier View, The Peak Antler Company, and all the media who covered this project!

A final and special thanks to Justine, Jessica, Jared, Jenna and Krystal… words cannot describe my gratitude from all your love and support throughout this project.

WAIT!!

Did you wonder what happened to the Last day? Here it is~

Day 365… WOW, what a journey! I spent the entire day taking photos from each of my favorite locations…places I have come to know and love over the past year. I started out in my hometown, went to the top of the Peak and had a world famous "Pikes Peak Donut" and even set up a time lapse camera at the Taylor home in Woodland Park to capture an entire day in the life of the Peak. I was racing all over today to get the perfect last shot when I realized, what I really wanted to do was spend the last hour of the day watching the sun go down from a place I call "my perch". If there is one thing I have learned from this project it is that we all need to stop and take a moment to appreciate the beauty all around us each and every day, no matter how busy we are. I have also learned that this big rock we all call our mountain is also America's Mountain and something that binds us all as a community and a nation and that connection is powerful and amazing. I am so grateful to have had the chance to capture 1 short year on the life of our mountain, and I am incredibly grateful to each and every one of you for letting me share Pikes Peak with the world through this project.

With much love and gratitude ~The Pikes Peak Guy

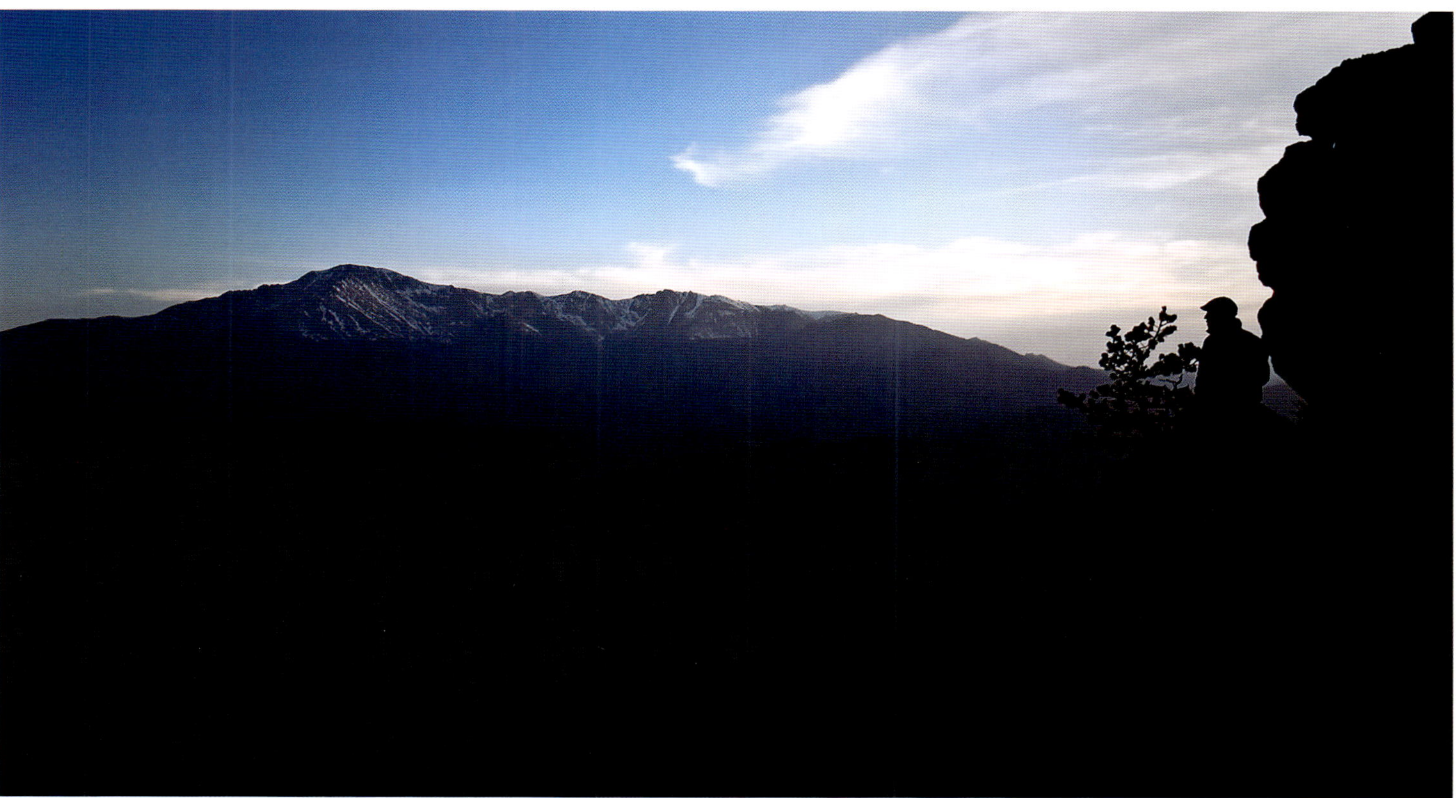